EVERYTHING®
INVESTING
BOOK
3RD EDITION

Dear Reader,

It's scary to even think about investing when the markets are in meltdown mode, like the recent severe financial downturn. We've become all too familiar with words like "recession," "crash," and "foreclosure." Giant financial corporations have simply disappeared. It's enough to make you want to stick all of your money under your mattress. I'm here to tell you: Don't be afraid to invest!

Here's why: You can't build wealth without investment, no matter what the markets are doing today. The key is to create a solid plan and follow it, and *carefully* search out investments that will keep your portfolio growing. Sounds impossible, but it isn't; in fact, it's pretty simple when you take time out to learn about the wild world of finance and investing.

That's what this book is all about. Inside, I'll tell you everything you need to know to build a profitable portfolio. From understanding the inner workings of Wall Street to figuring out how to ladder your bonds to choosing the best combination of mutual funds, this book will guide you toward wealth and prosperity.

Wishing you success,

Michele Cagan

Welcome to the EVERYTHING® Series!

These handy, accessible books give you all you need to tackle a difficult project, gain a new hobby, comprehend a fascinating topic, prepare for an exam, or even brush up on something you learned back in school but have since forgotten.

You can choose to read an *Everything*® book from cover to cover or just pick out the information you want from our four useful boxes: e-questions, e-facts, e-alerts, and e-ssentials.

We give you everything you need to know on the subject, but throw in a lot of fun stuff along the way, too.

We now have more than 400 *Everything*® books in print, spanning such wide-ranging categories as weddings, pregnancy, cooking, music instruction, foreign language, crafts, pets, New Age, and so much more. When you're done reading them all, you can finally say you know *Everything*®!

QUESTION

Answers to
common questions

FACT

Important snippets
of information

ALERT

Urgent
warnings

ESSENTIAL

Quick
handy tips

PUBLISHER Karen Cooper

DIRECTOR OF ACQUISITIONS AND INNOVATION Paula Munier

MANAGING EDITOR, EVERYTHING® SERIES Lisa Laing

COPY CHIEF Casey Ebert

ACQUISITIONS EDITOR Lisa Laing

SENIOR DEVELOPMENT EDITOR Brett Palana-Shanahan

ASSOCIATE DEVELOPMENT EDITOR Elizabeth Kassab

EDITORIAL ASSISTANT Hillary Thompson

EVERYTHING® SERIES COVER DESIGNER Erin Alexander

LAYOUT DESIGNERS Colleen Cunningham, Elisabeth Lariviere, Ashley Vierra, Denise Wallace

Visit the entire Everything® series at *www.everything.com*

THE
EVERYTHING®
INVESTING
BOOK

3RD EDITION

Smart strategies to secure your financial future!

Michele Cagan, CPA

Avon, Massachusetts

To Ethan,
the most important person in the world.

An Everything® Series Book.
Everything® and everything.com® are registered trademarks of F+W Media, Inc.

Published by Adams Media, a division of F+W Media, Inc.
57 Littlefield Street, Avon, MA 02322 U.S.A.
www.adamsmedia.com

ISBN 10: 1-59869-829-X
ISBN 13: 978-1-59869-829-9

Printed in the United States of America.

J   I   H   G   F   E   D   C   B   A

Library of Congress Cataloging-in-Publication Data
is available from the publisher.

This book is available at quantity discounts for bulk purchases.
For information, please call 1-800-289-0963.

Contents

Top Ten Things to Do Before You Invest $1 **x**

Introduction **xi**

1 Planning for Success 1

Laying the Foundation **2**

Taking Financial Inventory **2**

Building a Budget **4**

Do-It-Yourself Filing System **7**

Knock Out Your Debt **10**

Easy Ways to Cut Spending **11**

Set Your Investing Goals **11**

2 Designing Your Personal Portfolio / 14

Understand Your Investment Choices **15**

Every Choice Comes with Risk **15**

What's Your Tolerance for Risk? **18**

The Power of Time **21**

Diversification Tones Down Risk **22**

Understanding Asset Allocation **23**

A Lifelong Investing Strategy **26**

Your Investor Profile **26**

3 A Look at the Big Picture / 29

Why the Economy Matters **30**

How Interest Rates Affect Everything **30**

Understanding the Economic Indicators **31**

Know Your Sectors **35**

An Index for Everything **36**

The Whole World Impacts Investments **38**

4 Starting with Stocks / 39

It All Happens in the Exchanges **40**

The SEC Works for You **42**

Stocks Are Pieces of a Company **44**

Types of Stocks **45**

Blue-Chip, Income, Growth, and Preferred Stocks **46**

Size Matters: Small-, Mid-, and Large-Cap Stocks **48**

Cyclical, Defensive, and Value Stocks **48**

Penny Stocks **50**

5 Doing Your Homework / 52

Know What You're Buying, Buy What You Know **53**

Reading the Annual Report **55**

Two Proven Ways to Analyze Stocks **56**

Five Characteristics of Great Companies **57**

Investor Math Basics **59**

Avoid the Herd Mentality **63**

Know When to Sell **64**

Look Back at Your Profile **65**

6 **How to Buy and Track Stocks / 67**

Executing Stock Trades **68**

Dividend Reinvestment Plans (DRIPs) **71**

Seeking Out Bargain Stocks **72**

Know Your Stock Symbols **73**

Tracking Your Investments **74**

Working with a Stockbroker **75**

Working with an Investment Club **79**

7 **Bond Basics / 81**

What Are Bonds? **82**

Bonds Fit in Every Portfolio **84**

The Risks Unique to Bonds **85**

Credit Check: Know the Bond Ratings **87**

Bond Yields **89**

How Are Bonds Priced? **91**

How to Buy and Sell Bonds **92**

8 **Types of Bonds / 94**

Overview of Bond Categories **95**

U.S. Treasury Securities **96**

Municipal Bonds **96**

Zero-Coupon Bonds **99**

Corporate Bonds **99**

High-Yield Bonds **101**

Mortgage-Backed Securities **102**

How to Choose Bonds for Your Portfolio **103**

9 **The Basics of Mutual Funds / 104**

What Is a Mutual Fund? **105**

The Importance of Fund Managers **109**

Fund Families and Investment Styles **110**

Load or No-Load? **111**

Fees, Expenses and Operating Costs **112**

Decoding Fund Reports **114**

Trading Mutual Fund Shares **115**

Consider Dollar-Cost Averaging **116**

10 **Many Types of Mutual Funds / 118**

Benefits of Mutual Fund Stock Investing **119**

Index Funds **119**

Growth and Income Funds **120**

Value and Sector Funds **122**

International and Global Funds **122**

Balanced Funds and Asset Allocation **123**

Large-Cap, Mid-Cap, and Small-Cap Funds **124**

Bond Funds **125**

Socially Responsible Funds **129**

11 Maintaining the Right Fund Combination / 131

Risk Tolerance and Your Fund Portfolio **132**

Using Diversification to Minimize Risk **133**

Reading the Prospectus **134**

Look at (But Don't Rely on) Past Performance **136**

Six Fund Investment Strategies You Can Swear By **138**

Tracking Your Funds' Performance **140**

Know When to Sell **143**

12 All About Exchange-Traded Funds / 144

What Are ETFs? **145**

ETFs Versus Mutual Funds **146**

Covering Every Corner of the Market **147**

Spiders, Diamonds, Vipers, iShares, and Cubes **148**

Fitting ETFs into Your Portfolio **149**

Choosing the Right ETFs **150**

How to Buy and Sell ETFs **151**

Tracking Your ETFs **152**

13 Green Investing / 153

What Are Green Investments? **154**

Green Stocks **155**

Green Bonds **156**

Green Funds **157**

Avoid Scams: Look Beyond the Green **160**

Building a Profitable Green Portfolio **161**

14 Ground Rules: Investing in Real Estate / 163

Real Estate Investing Basics **164**

The Power of Leverage **164**

Fix-Up and Flip Properties **165**

Building Wealth with Rental Properties **168**

Managing Your Rental Properties **170**

Choosing the Most Profitable Real Estate **171**

Investing in Real Estate Investment Trusts **172**

15 Alternative Investments for Risk Lovers / 177

Risky Strategies: Enormous Returns or Devastating Losses **178**

Short Selling and Margin Buying **178**

Initial Public Offerings **180**

Commodities and Precious Metals **182**

Trading Currencies **185**

Deciphering Derivatives **187**

All About Options **188**

Trading Futures **190**

16 Teaming Up: Working with a Financial Advisor / 192

What Kind of Advice Do You Need? **193**

What Can You Expect from a Financial Advisor? **194**

Shopping for a Financial Advisor **196**

How Much Will You Pay? **199**

Where to Find an Advisor **201**

17 DIY Investing / 202

How Much Will You Do Yourself? **203**

DIY Investors Hit the Internet **203**

The Advantages of Online Investing **205**

Is There a Downside? **206**

Beware of Internet Scams **208**

What to Look for in an Investment Website **210**

The Ten Best Investment Websites **211**

18 You, Your Portfolio, and Uncle Sam: Investing and Taxes / 213

How Taxes Impact Your Portfolio **214**

Types of Investment Taxes **214**

Creating an Investment Tax Strategy **216**

Tips for Reducing Your Investment Tax Liability **218**

Understanding (Legal) Tax Shelters **222**

19 Investing for Education / 224

Start Planning for College Tuition Now **225**

Tax-Sheltered Education Savings Save the Day **226**

All About 529 Plans **227**

Coverdell Education Savings Accounts **228**

Should You Invest in a Prepaid Tuition Plan? **229**

Education Bonds and CDs **231**

20 Retirement Planning / 234

The Beauty of Tax-Deferred Investing **235**

Advantages of Investing Early and Often **236**

The 401(k) Plan **237**

Individual Retirement Accounts (IRAs) **239**

Stay Focused **243**

Appendix A: Online and Discount Brokers **245**

Appendix B: Investment Publications **249**

Appendix C: Investment Websites **255**

Appendix D: Glossary of Terms **263**

Index **283**

Acknowledgments

Special thanks to Meira Cagan (my mom), whose help got me over the final hurdles. I also want to thank my editor, Lisa Laing, who made every obstacle disappear and helped me make this a much better book.

Top Ten Things to Do Before You Invest $1

1. **Pay off every penny of credit card debt.** You'll earn sky-high (18 to 22 percent!) returns just by paying your credit card balance in full rather than making the minimum monthly interest-laden payments.

2. **Build yourself an emergency fund.** Start a separate bank account for this purpose alone. It should have enough money to cover at least three to six months of living expenses.

3. **Set up and follow a household budget.** Keep track of where your money comes from and (even more important) where it's going.

4. **Set clear financial goals.** Whether you want to save for a new car this year or retirement twenty years from now, you need to know why you're investing.

5. **Determine your time frame.** How long your money will be working for you plays a key role in designing the best portfolio.

6. **Know your risk tolerance.** Investing can bring about as many downs as ups, and you have to know just how much uncertainty you can comfortably stand.

7. **Figure out your asset allocation mix.** Before you start investing, know what proportion of your portfolio will be dedicated to each asset class (like stocks, bonds, and cash, for example).

8. **Improve your understanding of the markets.** That includes learning about the big picture, such as the global political and economic forces that drive the markets and affect asset prices.

9. **Set up your brokerage account.** Whether you decide to start out with a financial advisor or take a more do-it-yourself approach, you'll need to have an open brokerage account before you can make your first trade.

10. **Analyze every investment before you buy it.** Buy only investments that you have researched and fully understand; never risk your money on an unknown.

Introduction

INVESTING IS EASY; SUCCESSFUL or profitable investing isn't. It takes knowledge and understanding to build and maintain wealth, as many investors find out when the markets go south. Successful investors, though, sustain substantially smaller losses during downturns. Often, they even reap profits while less savvy investors lose their shirts.

When the markets are strong, even "unworthy" securities can take off, carried by market momentum. Investors who are normally risk-averse may find themselves buying risky securities when it seems like every choice is a winner. But as soon as the markets enter their inevitable down phases, as is the nature of cyclical markets, weak securities are the first to fail and risk-averse investors begin to lose sleep.

That doesn't have to happen. By designing a solid plan and sticking with it, investors can enjoy profitable portfolios in almost any financial environment regardless of market cycles. Having a sufficiently diversified portfolio with a well-designed asset mix makes all the difference. And this can be accomplished only when you know exactly what you're doing and why.

Too many investors buy or sell securities (especially stocks) on a whim. They've gotten a tip from someone in the office or read about a hot new stock on the Internet. Maybe a less than scrupulous broker or financial advisor has steered them toward something that sounds great—and it is, for the broker, who profits when clients place their buy orders. But smart, successful investors look past the "great deal," delving deeper into the potential of any investment before they buy even a single share. They gather the facts, and base decisions only on information, never on emotion.

That's the secret to a lifetime of wealth: knowledge. And that's what you'll find in this book. Whatever your financial goals, whether they're long-term or short-term, you need to know exactly how to reach them. From adequate college savings to a luxurious retirement to a down payment on your first house, you need to have a comprehensive financial plan in place to turn your dreams into reality.

Inside this book, you'll find a great deal of information on how to keep wealth creation simple and how to use what you know to secure your financial freedom. All the tools you need to develop a profitable portfolio are right here. You'll get straightforward information and guidance, presented in a way that makes even complex investing strategies easy to understand. You'll find out which investments to stockpile and which to avoid at all costs—no matter how good they look at first glance. And if you're not quite sure how to get started, there's a complete guide to financial professionals that can help you figure out which is the best one for your unique situation.

This book is designed to set you on the path to financial security. By following its basic principles and guidelines, you can become the master of your own wealth and build a substantial nest egg for your family. Use it to the best of your ability and take permanent control of your financial life.

CHAPTER 1

Planning for Success

Before you can conquer the markets and lie back to count your millions, you must have a clear picture of where your finances stand right now. Once you've taken that crucial first step toward your eventual wealth, you'll be ready to set your goals, analyze your style, and put together a real plan—one that will get you exactly where you want to go. The path to wealth comes with countless setbacks, many roadblocks, and dozens of disappointments. A solid plan will help you get through those impediments.

Laying the Foundation

Taking control of your personal financial situation is the first step toward building wealth. To set foot on the ladder of financial freedom, you have to know where you stand and how much further you'll need to climb to reach your destination. A daily glance at your investment portfolio isn't enough, though it certainly plays a part. Investment tracking is fun, but there's a lot more involved in taking a true snapshot of your current financial situation.

According to the most recently published Federal Reserve survey of consumer finances, the median net worth of Americans aged forty-five to fifty-four is $144,700. That's compared to a median net worth of $141,600 just three years earlier.

To eventually succeed in the world of investing, you have to start with the basics. This includes things like creating and sticking to a budget, balancing your checkbook, and determining your net worth. Taking charge of your everyday household finances and understanding your real financial picture are the actions that make up the solid base from which you grow your nest egg. These simple starting points also give you the insights you'll need to make well-informed choices when you're ready to enter the more complex world of investing. You wouldn't enter a black-belt competition knowing nothing about karate, and jumping into the intricate world of high finance is no different. You need to master the fundamentals before you can develop a winning game plan.

Taking Financial Inventory

Creating a personal financial inventory worksheet is the first step toward creating a unique guide on which you'll base all of your financial decisions. Although this initial inventory will be frozen in time, you'll revisit and reconstruct it regularly to chart the changes. At first, you'll probably need to revise it every three to six months; later, an annual revision will usually suffice. Even more important than looking at your personal balance sheet, it is vital that you understand what goes into it. This knowledge will carry you toward setting (and meeting) achievable financial goals.

Your net worth equals the difference between what you have (assets) and what you owe (liabilities). Your assets include things like bank accounts, investment portfolios, retirement accounts, the value of whole life insurance policies, the market value of real estate and vehicles, and any other property, such as jewelry. Liabilities encompass everything you owe, typically separated into short-term debt and long-term obligations. Short-term debt includes your regular monthly bills, credit card balances, income taxes, and anything else you might have to pay within the next twelve months. Long-term debts include mortgages and any other installment loans, such as those for your car. In taking stock of your assets, use current market value for things like real estate and vehicles.

ESSENTIAL

Good news! In addition to your savings and other accounts, you can also count money that is owed to you by other people as an asset. As long as this money is coming your way in the foreseeable future, it can be regarded as part of your financial inventory.

While getting a formal appraisal may give you the most accurate assessment, it's not necessarily the most efficient way to proceed. To get approximate market values for your house, you can check out your state's property tax assessment website. For your car, try the *Kelley Blue Book* (online at *www.kbb.com*). For smaller items, you can determine which may have significant resale value. Again, you can get a professional appraiser, or you can try looking up similar items on a website like eBay to get approximate market values. Once you've ascertained reasonable values for your belongings, add them to your cash and investment accounts for a total asset figure.

Once you've figured out your assets, it's time to take an honest look at your liabilities. For now, we'll just add in your true debt and leave out your regular monthly bills. In this section of your worksheet, include the outstanding balance of your mortgage and other installment loans, everything you owe on credit cards, and any unpaid personal loans. Total these and you have an accurate picture of your current debt load.

To calculate your net worth, subtract your total liabilities from your total assets. The result shows what you'd have left if you sold or cashed in all your assets and paid off all your liabilities. Here are some steps you can follow to calculate your net worth:

1. List all of your liquid (cash-like) assets: bank accounts, CDs, stocks, bonds, mutual funds, etc.
2. List your retirement accounts: every IRA, 401(k) plan, ESOP, etc.
3. List all of your physical assets at current market value, starting with your home, other real estate you own, vehicles, and any valuable smaller items (like jewelry) that you choose.
4. Add the value of all these items to get your total assets.
5. List all of your outstanding debts, and add those to get your total liabilities.
6. Subtract your total liabilities (step 5) from your total assets (step 4) to get your personal net worth.
7. Revisit your worksheet every three to six months at first, then at least once a year going forward, to adjust for any changes.

If the number you came up with as your net worth is greater than zero, you have a positive net worth, meaning you'd still have assets left if you settled all outstanding debts. If your bottom line is less than zero, you have a negative net worth, meaning you would still owe money even if you liquidated all your assets and put that cash toward your debts. Regardless of your personal bottom line, you now have a solid base to work from and will be able to make your financial plan accordingly.

Building a Budget

Once you've calculated your personal net worth, your next step will be looking at cash flow. When you're ready to start building your nest egg, you're going to need some cash to do it. However, there are things standing in the way of this cash stream, from your monthly bills to that nagging weekly urge to treat yourself to a dinner out. New technologies and new products crop up with amazing frequency, making it harder and harder to curb excess spending. The solution is to outline your total expenses, knock off the unnecessary ones, create a budget, and stick to it.

ALERT

It's remarkably easy to lose track of where your money is going. Many people indulge in small luxuries like buying coffee in the morning and ordering pizza for dinner more often than they realize. All these little extras add up to some big daily spending. Keep track of these expenditures for a week and see for yourself!

Resist the temptation to use your credit card for all your purchases as a simple way of tracking them. That strategy is great for the credit card companies, but it's not so good for your net worth. Instead, invest a little time in keeping an expense notebook; a mere two-week listing will do. You'll be glad that you don't have a whopping credit card bill at the end of the month, and you won't be making a year's worth of interest payments on a cup of coffee.

Budget Components

Before you get started building your budget, you should take a brief look at what makes up a budget. You may already know that budgets have both income and expense sections, but you may not recognize all the things that qualify for those categories. And since your budget will be used to help you create a nest egg, you should also add a section for savings.

Most budgets start with income. For these purposes, income includes all the cash you have flowing into your household. So, in addition to your regular take-home pay, you'll include items like interest and dividends you receive, any pension payments, and tax refunds. The second section, for expenses, will probably be a lot longer. This category includes things like mortgage or rent payments, utility and phone bills, groceries, cable, child care costs, and entertainment. Don't forget to add in periodic expenditures, like auto insurance premiums or vet bills. The savings section includes all the cash you put away at the end of the day. For planning purposes, a good savings number to shoot for is 4 to 10 percent of your expenses, at least until you have enough to cover about three months of regular expenses.

To make your budget the best it can be—and not so annoying to work on that you just throw up your hands and walk away—here are a few simple guidelines to follow:

- Be realistic when forming goals. If your target budget is too hard to live with, you won't follow it.
- Use real numbers, not estimates. Estimates may help you fill in the blanks, but they won't help further your goals. You can find true figures by backtracking through your checkbook.
- Use your computer to help track your budget. Create a spreadsheet in Microsoft Excel or pick up some prepackaged budget software, like Quicken or Microsoft Money.
- Make your budget easier to read by categorizing some of your expenses. For example, electricity, gas, water, and heating oil could all go under the heading "Utilities."
- Include absolutely everything you spend money on. Don't leave out even occasional expenses, like theater tickets, haircuts, and charitable donations.
- Initially, track your budget at least once a month. Even better, update the numbers every time you get a paycheck.
- Take an in-depth look at your budget each quarter to make sure it's accurate and to see how well you're managing your cash.

Completing Your Budget

Once you've listed all of your income and expenditures, add the components of each section to come up with totals. Then subtract your total expenses and savings from your total income. The result is your net cash flow. If that number is greater than zero, you have positive cash flow. If it's less than zero, you have negative cash flow. If your bottom line comes out to exactly zero, your cash flow is considered neutral. When your result is positive cash flow, you have options. You can spend the money, hide it away as extra savings, or consider investing the surplus, perhaps in stocks or mutual funds. With a negative cash flow result, you'll first have to concentrate on either increasing your income or cutting back your expenses wherever possible. You might have to sacrifice some favorites, but it'll be worth it if you can save some cash every month.

Throughout this entire process, you may find that sticking to your budget is very difficult to do. You're not alone. Many people struggle to stay inside the boundaries of their personal budgets. You're also not alone if you already have debt to deal with. Try not to let debt discourage you—it's never too late to improve your situation. Luckily, there are ways to get debt under control and start fresh.

FACT

> According to CardTrak.com, the average credit card debt for American households in 2007 was $9,659. On top of that, 13 percent of households surveyed owed more than $25,000 in credit card debt alone. Do everything you can to get out and stay out of debt. It's far easier to get in than it is to get out.

The first step to dealing with debt is to use your credit cards only when absolutely necessary. The second is to reduce the balance you're carrying. If you have equity in your home, you may want to consider a home equity loan while interest rates remain low. In addition to reducing your interest burden, you may be able to deduct some of the expense on your tax return (check with your accountant). Another approach is a debt consolidation loan. While the rates typically aren't as low as home equity loans, they are usually considerably lower than the interest credit card companies charge.

Do-It-Yourself Filing System

One major key to a good budget is organization. A basic filing system is an easy way to keep all your documents and records handy and in order. Of course, there are a few things you need to do to make this system work. First, you'll have to free up some space for this endeavor. It doesn't have to be very big or very fancy—a simple filing cabinet will do. You'll need to designate enough room to hold your monthly bills and other financial paperwork. Starting with a well-organized space can keep your budgeting tasks flowing more smoothly, saving you lots of time and aggravation.

As soon as you have the proper tools to work with, go through all your financial records. Get rid of everything you no longer need, like old phone bills, gas receipts, even pay stubs. Toss out the instruction manuals for appliances you don't have anymore; trash the payment books from old loans that you've paid off. Remember to shred anything with personal information on it to protect yourself from identity theft. Consider this list of documents you'll need to hold on to for a while; keep them where you can find them easily in case you need them:

- **Tax returns.** Keep these for six years. Include the full return, plus all related receipts for itemized deductions, in your file. Although the IRS usually only has three years from the date you file to audit your return, they occasionally get more time. For example, if they claim you've understated your income by at least 25 percent, they can hold your file open for up to six years.
- **Investment information.** Any time you buy or sell an investment, hold on to the written record of that transaction. In addition, keep the annual summary your broker or fund company sends you at the end of the year. When tax time comes around, you'll need all that information to properly report your income. Also, save all the paperwork for any nondeductible IRAs you contribute to. That way, if the IRS tries to tax you twice, you'll have the proof to show the taxes were already paid.
- **Credit card and bank statements.** Credit card statements are crucial for recreating expenses, and bank statements can include expenses as well as income outside your regular paycheck. When you come across tax-related items, highlight them and make a note in your tax file. Keep credit card statements and bank statements, including cancelled checks, for six years, filed along with your tax returns.
- **Medical bills.** Hold on to receipts for all your co-pays anytime you visit a medical professional or fill a prescription. Keep the receipts any time you buy tax-deductible items, like eyeglasses or hearing aids. It's also a good idea to keep benefit statements from your insurance company, in case there's any dispute with the service provider. If you pay for your health insurance out of pocket, hold on to those statements as well.

- **Real estate records.** For every property you own, you should have a file with following documents: the deed, property tax bills and assessments, receipts for major repairs and improvements, and any home warranties.
- **Personal documents.** In this folder you'll place the records of your life, starting with your birth certificate. Also include your current passport, marriage license, divorce papers, paperwork pertaining to your children, military service records, and any other important personal information.

When you're done going through all that paper and have figured out what you'll be keeping, start setting up your files. Create a folder for each category. Clearly label your folders so you can easily find any documents you're looking for. Put all the folders in your file cabinet—and be glad the most cumbersome part of this process is finished.

ESSENTIAL

Once you have a filing system set up, you'll need financial software, like Quicken or Microsoft Money. These programs deal with all the calculations, instantly track all of your account balances, and flow into your tax-return software at the end of the year.

To make sure no bills fall through the cracks, set up a payment schedule. Add each bill to the schedule the day it arrives, noting the due date. The simplest place to jot the due dates is on a calendar you use regularly. If you don't pay your bills as soon as they come in, set aside time every week to write checks for those bills coming due. If you use online banking services, make sure you record transactions in your checkbook. Remember to balance your checkbook each time, and reconcile it to your bank statement every month. Banks usually allow sixty days for you to bring errors to their attention. While you're at it, double-check your credit card statements when they come in, just to make sure there aren't any erroneous charges listed.

Knock Out Your Debt

Before you invest a single dollar, get control of your debt, particularly your credit card debt. If you're like most Americans, you have a wallet full of credit cards, and you use them for virtually everything, including things you could easily pay for with cash. The best way to control your debt is to stop using credit cards for minor expenses like these, especially if you don't pay off your balances in full every month. A year's worth of interest on coffee and lunch can more than double the cost.

QUESTION

Is the value of my donated items deductible?
Yes. Almost all items that you donate to charitable organizations are deductible. Just remember to get a written, itemized receipt. With noncash contributions, the rule is simple: No receipt means no deduction if you get audited.

Replace your credit cards with a debit card and a reasonable amount of cash for the week. If you find yourself running out of cash every week, analyze your purchases before you increase your allowance. Keep one credit card in your wallet, but use it only for emergencies.

When your credit card spending is under control, you can finally attack the debt monster. There's no magic way to vanquish the debt, but you can systematically pay off all of your credit cards—and sooner than you might think. Allocate a fixed monthly amount in your budget for paying down credit cards, calculated by adding all the minimum monthly payments and adding on some extra (between 2 percent and 10 percent more is a good place to start). With the extra portion, begin paying down the credit card with the highest interest rate; lowering that balance will go a long way toward knocking out your debt. The lower the balance, the less interest will be charged, which will help you pay it down even faster. As soon as the card with the highest rate has been paid off, start tackling the next in line, and so on until all of your credit card balances have been zeroed.

Easy Ways to Cut Spending

In order to cut down on your spending, you have to ask yourself a few questions. Does your priority list match your spending habits? Are you spending money only on the important things in your life? Money may be dribbling out of your pockets without your even realizing it.

ESSENTIAL

Not all debt is bad. Debt you incur to purchase an asset (like a house or a car) makes sense; at the end of the day, you actually own something of value. On top of that, this kind of debt usually comes with much lower interest rates than credit card debt.

Consider your workday lunch expenses, assuming you dine out. If you spend an average of $8 a day, you're spending $40 a week, or nearly $2,000 per year on lunch. Making your lunch can save you money, leaving more to cover other expenses. Little cutbacks can make a big difference in the long run. Make sacrifices like making lunch, trading in your daily soy latte for a regular cup of joe, or canceling magazine subscriptions. Consider how you could use the money you'll be saving to reduce or eliminate your debt, or how you could put it to work as the start of a great investment future. Tracking your spending and comparing it to your priorities will help you identify what spending habits you need to change.

It's not an easy thing to do, but most people can find areas of their budget they can cut. Some sacrifices such as reducing your cable service, eating at home more frequently, or forgoing the purchase of an SUV might be mildly painful, but keep in mind that they could make a real difference. While these are not fun choices, they may save you from financial troubles.

Set Your Investing Goals

Once you've compiled a current financial snapshot and gained a good understanding of how you handle your money, it's time to take the next step along the path. Now that you know where you stand, you can figure where you want to go. It's time to set your investing goals.

First, make your goals specific and measurable. Don't say you want to save more; say you want to save $1,000 over the next twelve months. Instead of dreaming about some far off retirement on a tropical island, set a goal to retire with $6 million when you're sixty-five. With goals like these, you can mark your progress and make adjustments as necessary to help you hit your targets.

ALERT

When you set your financial goals, remember to take inflation into account. Historically, inflation has averaged about 3 percent annually, but over the past few years it's skated higher (and it doesn't look to be heading back down any time soon). Some items inflate much faster, like college tuition, which has gone up by 8 percent a year.

The second rule is to allow for the unexpected, a critical part of every investment plan. Your car may break down, your hot water heater may stop working (probably while you're in the shower), or you might need a trip to the ER. All of these events take you by surprise, and they all cost money—money you were expecting to use in different ways, and probably at different times. To deal with unexpected expenditures, you'll need to have some easily accessible cash—but that doesn't mean uninvested cash. By planning for the unexpected and keeping some of your investment assets highly liquid, you'll be able to deal with situations like these without veering too far off your goal path. Remember, the reverse can happen, too. Whenever you get your hands on extra cash—like a pay raise, a bonus, or a loan finally paid off—use it to pay down debt or add to savings and investments. Extra cash is money you weren't counting on. You won't miss it, so use it to move you closer to your goals.

Make sure to include your expected retirement needs. If your lifestyle will tone down, some advisors figure you'll need about 60 to 70 percent of your current income. For more intricate calculations—like the potential effects of inflation and investment returns—check in with a financial planner, or try some retirement planning software.

Assess your current savings stage and plan your holdings accordingly. The further you are from your goal's timeline, the more risks you can afford to take with your investments. The key to all *of this: Start saving money now.*

Finally, design a preliminary investment plan that will move you toward meeting your financial goals. It can take time to refine and perfect your plan, but a basic model (such as the age method, where you convert your age to a percentage and invest that portion of your holdings in bonds and cash and the rest in stocks) is a good place to start. While your first instinct may be to take a chunk of cash and buy a hot stock, that probably isn't the best way to get where you want to go. Impulse investing, like impulse buying, can drain your money without giving you anything in return. So start with a basic plan until you gain some more knowledge and experience, or hire a professional to help you. Then, while your money is already beginning to work for you, you can take the time to plan an appropriate portfolio specific to your goals and timeline. That is the way to build your fortune and keep it intact.

CHAPTER 2

Designing Your Personal Portfolio

Whether you're working with a financial advisor or a brokerage firm, you're at the wheel of your own investment vehicle. You decide the pace at which you head into the investment world, and you determine how much risk you're willing to take in order to win. Some independent research will also be necessary. This includes due diligence on companies where you're considering parking some of your investment dollars, as well as portfolio tracking and performance monitoring to keep your investment portfolio chugging along in the right direction.

Understand Your Investment Choices

Having all the ingredients for success is a good start, but you won't get too far without the recipe. If you take all the ingredients for a delicious pastry and throw them together in equal parts, you'll end up with an inedible brick. Developing the art of measuring and mixing your ingredients so they work together to create investment perfection requires patience and diligence on your part. You need to figure out the delicate balance that will provide the most effective and productive investment portfolio for your needs.

FACT

Most investment portfolios consist of several components. Usually, they include some combination of the following: liquid assets (cash and equivalents), fixed income securities (bonds and annuities), equities (stocks), real estate, commodities (precious metals), and other investments.

Figuring out which securities will comprise your portfolio isn't a difficult process, as long as you apply the tried-and-true investment tenets: knowing your risk levels, having a fixed time horizon, employing investment diversification (through your asset allocation), and having set investment goals. Two of the more important factors in your portfolio decision-making process are risk and diversification.

Every Choice Comes with Risk

In the investment world, you'll have to walk a delicate (and very personal) balance between risk and reward. The more uncertain the investment, the greater the risk that your investment won't perform as expected, or even that you'll lose your entire investment. Along with greater investment risk, though, comes an opportunity to earn greater investment returns. If you're uncomfortable with too much risk and seek to minimize it, your trade-off will be lower investment returns (which can be a form of risk in itself). Truthfully, you can't completely eliminate risk. If you don't take any risk at all, you won't be able to earn money through investing.

Investment risk is directly tied to market volatility—the fluctuations in the financial markets that happen constantly over time. The sources of this volatility are many: interest-rate changes, inflation, political consequences, and economic trends can all create combustible market conditions with the power to change a portfolio's performance results in a hurry. Ironically, this volatility, by its very nature, creates the opportunities for economic benefit in our own portfolios, and that is how risk impacts your investments and your investment strategy.

There are many different types of risk, and some are more complicated than others. The risk classifications you'll learn about here are those you'll likely take into consideration as you begin to design your portfolio.

Stock Specific Risk

Any single stock carries a specific amount of risk for the investor. You can minimize this risk by making sure your portfolio is diversified. An investor dabbling in one or two stocks can see his investment wiped out; although it is still possible, the chances of that happening in a well-diversified portfolio are much more slender. (One example would be the event of an overall bear market, as was seen in the early 1990s.) By adding a component of trend analysis to your decision-making process and by keeping an eye on the big picture (global economics and politics, for example), you are better equipped to prevent the kinds of devastating losses that come with an unexpected sharp turn in the markets.

Risk of Passivity and Inflation Rate Risk

People who don't trust the financial markets and who feel more comfortable sticking their money in a bank savings account could end up with less than they expect; that's the heart of passivity risk, losing out on substantial earnings because you did nothing with your money. Since the interest rates on savings accounts cannot keep up with the rate of inflation, they decrease the purchasing power of your investment over time—even if they meet your core investing principle of avoiding risk. For this somewhat paradoxical reason, savings accounts may not always be your safest choice. You may want to consider investments with at least slightly higher returns (like inflation-indexed U.S. Treasury bonds) to help you combat inflation without giving up your sense of security.

A close relative of passivity risk, inflation risk is based upon the expectation of lower purchasing power of each dollar down the road. Typically, stocks are the best investment when you're interested in outpacing inflation, and money-market funds are the least effective in combating inflation.

Market Risk

Market risk is pretty much what it sounds like. Every time you invest money in the financial markets, even via a conservative money-market mutual fund, you're subjecting your money to the risk that the markets will decline or even crash. With market risk, uncertainty due to changes in the overall stock market is caused by global, political, social, or economic events and even by the mood of the investing public. Perhaps the biggest investment risk of all, though, is not subjecting your money to market risk. If you don't put your money to work in the stock market, you won't be able to benefit from the stock market's growth over the years.

Credit Risk

Usually associated with bond investments, credit risk is the possibility that a company, agency, or municipality might not be able to make interest or principal payments on its notes or bonds. The greatest risk of default usually lies with corporate debt: Companies go out of business all the time. On the flip side, there's virtually no credit risk associated with U.S. Treasury-related securities, because they're backed by the full faith and credit of the U.S. government. To measure the financial health of bonds, credit rating agencies like Moody's and Standard & Poor's assign them investment grades. Bonds with an A rating are considered solid, while C-rated bonds are considered unstable.

Currency Risk

Although most commonly considered in international or emerging-market investing, currency risk can occur in any market at any time. This risk comes about due to currency fluctuations affecting the value of foreign investments or profits, or the holdings of U.S. companies with interests overseas. Currency risk necessarily increases in times of geopolitical instability, like those caused by the global threat of terrorism or war.

Interest Rate Risk

When bond interest rates rise, the price of the bonds falls (and vice versa). Fluctuating interest rates have a significant impact on stocks and bonds. Typically, the longer the maturity of the bond, the larger the impact of interest rate risk. But long-term bonds normally pay out higher yields to compensate for the greater risk.

Economic Risk

When the economy slows, corporate profits—and thus stocks—could be hurt. For example, political instability in the Middle East makes investing there a dicey deal at best. This is true even though much of the region is flush with oil, arguably the commodity in greatest demand all over the planet.

What's Your Tolerance for Risk?

Your risk level as an investor depends on many factors, including your age, financial needs, number of dependents, and level of debt. If you're twenty-five years old, single, childless, and debt-free, you have far more tolerance for risk than a fifty-five-year-old nearing retirement with two kids in college. In addition to your current financial situation, you need to consider your ulcer factor, or how losing investments will impact your physical and mental health. For example, if seeing one of your stocks drop by 10 percent in one day will make your ulcer flare up, factor that in to your risk tolerance level.

Trying to pin down your tolerance for risk is an uncertain process that's forever susceptible to second-guessing. You can never be quite sure what your tolerance for risk will be from year to year. But the following test, developed by Lincoln Benefit Life, a subsidiary of Allstate Life Group, can help clear things up. Simply choose an answer from the choices given for each question and assess your results at the end.

1. If someone made you an offer to invest 15 percent of your net worth in a deal she said had an 80 percent chance of being profitable, you'd say:

A. No level of profit would be worth that kind of risk.

B. The level of profit would have to be seven times the amount I invested.

C. The level of profit would have to be three times the amount I invested.

D. The level of profit would have to be at least as much as my original investment.

2. How comfortable would you be assuming a $10,000 debt in the hope of achieving a $20,000 gain over the next few months?

A. Totally uncomfortable. I'd never do it.

B. Somewhat uncomfortable. I'd probably never do it.

C. Somewhat uncomfortable. But I might do it.

D. Very comfortable. I'd definitely do it.

3. You are holding a lottery ticket that's gotten you to the finals, where you have a 25 percent chance of winning the $100,000 jackpot. You'd be willing to sell your ticket before the drawing, but for nothing less than:

A. $15,000

B. $20,000

C. $35,000

D. $60,000

4. How often do you bet more than $150 on one or more of these activities: professional sports gambling, casino gambling, or lottery tickets?

A. Never.

B. Only a few times in my life.

C. Just in one of these activities in the past year.

D. In two or more of these activities in the past year.

5. If a stock you bought doubled in the year after you bought it, what would you do?

A. Sell all my shares.

B. Sell half my shares.

C. Not sell any shares.

D. Buy more shares.

6. You have a high-yielding certificate of deposit that is about to mature, and interest rates have dropped so much that you feel compelled to invest in something with a higher yield. The most likely place you'd invest the money is:

A. U.S. savings bonds.

B. A short-term bond fund.

C. A long-term bond fund.

D. A stock fund.

7. What do you do when you have to decide where to invest a large amount of money?

A. Delay the decision.

B. Get someone else, like my broker, to decide for me.

C. Share the decision with my advisors.

D. Decide on my own.

8. Which of the following describes how you make your investment decisions?

A. Never on my own.

B. Sometimes on my own.

C. Often on my own.

D. Totally on my own.

9. How is your luck in investing?

A. Terrible.

B. Average.

C. Better than average.

D. Fantastic.

10. Finish the following sentence: My investments are successful mainly because:

A. Fate is always on my side.

B. I was in the right place at the right time.

C. When opportunities arose, I took advantage of them.

D. I carefully planned them to work out that way.

Give yourself one point for each A answer, two points for each B answer, three points for each C answer, and four points for each D answer.

If you scored nineteen points or fewer, you're a conservative investor who feels uncomfortable taking risks. You probably realize you will have to take some calculated risks to attain your financial goals, but this doesn't mean you will be comfortable doing so.

If you scored between twenty and twenty-nine points, you're a moderate investor who feels comfortable taking moderate risks. You are probably willing to take reasonable risks without a great deal of discomfort.

If you scored thirty or more points, you're an aggressive investor who is willing to take high risks in search of high returns. You are not greatly stressed by taking significant risks.

Typical behavior indicates that most investors either don't understand risk or choose to ignore it. When the market is rising, money floods into stocks and mutual funds, even as each upward move in price increases risk and reduces potential returns. In a bear market, many investors engage in near-panic selling, even though each drop in price decreases risk and increases potential returns. For most investors, the two most effective ways to manage risk are to limit your aggressive exposure to a small part of the whole portfolio and to stick with your program once you have embarked on it.

The Power of Time

Time is one of the most important factors when it comes to growing your nest egg: The sooner you start, the more time your money has to work for you. In the business of finances, it's called the time value of money, and successful investors take full advantage of it. Part of the time value comes from your saving and investing; with more time, you'll be able to put away more money. A bigger part, though, comes from the magic of compounding.

Compounding sounds confusing, but it's really quite straightforward. Compounding refers to the money generated by your investments earning money. For example, you deposit $1,000 into your bank account and earn $100 in interest on that deposit the first year. The second year, you earn interest on the entire amount in your account—$1,100—not just your initial investment. By reinvesting your earnings, you can fully capture the power of compounding and watch your wealth grow more quickly.

So even if two people put away the exact same amount of money, the one who does it first will end up with more in the long run—and that's why it's critical to start right away. For example, if you invest $10,000 with an average annual earnings rate of 5 percent, in just ten years your initial investment will have grown to $16,290. But if you let that $10,000 work for thirty years, you'd walk away with $43,220. The difference is due solely to time. Still not convinced time can be your most powerful investing asset? Consider this: If you invest $25,000—more than double that $10,000 investment—at 5 percent for ten years, you end up with $40,720, about $2,500 less than if you put away $10,000 much earlier on.

Diversification Tones Down Risk

Diversification simply means dividing your investments among a variety of types. It's one of the best ways to protect your portfolio from the pendulum swings of the economy and the financial markets. Since your portfolio will hold many different securities, a decline in the value of one security may be offset by the rise in value of another. For example, bonds often perform well when stocks are performing poorly.

ALERT

No matter how diversified your portfolio, you can never completely eliminate risk. You can reduce the risk associated with individual stocks, but general market risks affect nearly every stock, so it is important to also diversify among different assets. The key is to find a medium between risk and return.

Diversification takes different forms. For example, you can diversify your common stock holdings by purchasing stocks representing many different industries. That would be safer than concentrating in a single sector, such as holding only technology stocks. You can diversify your bond holdings by buying a mixture of high-quality bonds and some lower-rated bonds. The high-quality bonds tend to reduce the overall risk associated with the bond portfolio, while the lower-rated bonds may increase your overall returns (as they typically pay more interest).

You can also diversify with time. For example, your portfolio could include thirty-year corporate bonds and five-year Treasury notes. Long-term bonds typically offer higher interest rates than short-term ones, but short-term investments give you more flexibility to take advantage of fluctuating interest rates.

FACT

Preferred stock (which you'll learn more about in Chapter 4) is often considered a fixed-income investment, even though it's technically an equity investment. That's because preferred stock shares typically come with fixed, guaranteed dividend payments, a form of steady income. In fact, preferred stock is sometimes referred to as "the stock that acts like a bond."

Another important form of diversification is obtained when you invest in different types of securities—stocks, bonds, real estate, and money market instruments, to name the major investment types or asset classes. Diversifying your holdings over several asset classes, particularly among those that tend to perform differently under the same economic circumstances, adds an extra layer of protection to your portfolio.

Understanding Asset Allocation

Investors often find the concept of asset allocation confusing or intimidating—at least initially. But it's actually quite simple. Asset allocation is nothing more than determining in which types of assets your investment capital should be placed. This determination is based on variables like net worth, time frame, risk acceptance, and other assets the investor owns. Generally, properly allocating your investment dollars means assembling a portfolio primarily from the three major asset categories: cash, fixed income, and equities. Cash includes money in the bank, short-term investments such as U.S. Treasury bills and money market mutual funds, both of which are considered "cash equivalents," meaning they can be very quickly converted to cash. Fixed-income investments include bonds, guaranteed investment certificates, and other interest-generating securities. Equities are stock market investments. Equities can be further subdivided into more specific categories, such as value and growth.

ESSENTIAL

When establishing an asset allocation strategy, first determine how long you'll be investing. Decide how much risk you can take. Next, pick a target mix that's right for you, and select investments that will help you achieve that mix. Adjust your investments gradually. Start with your future deferrals to match your asset mix and redirect existing balances to fit into your overall plan.

It is a tricky business to achieve the right mix of stock types (small, mid, and large caps, as well as internationals, just to name a few) and bonds (short, medium, and long-term, corporate and government) for maximum return. To complicate matters, you must take into account your volatility tolerance and the diversity of your investments. For that reason, considering whether to consult a qualified financial planner or advisor to help you during this critical planning stage should be at the top of your investment to-do list.

Time and Asset Allocation

Many financial advisors say, quite sensibly, that your asset allocation plan depends on where you are in life. If you're just starting out, a long-term strategy that emphasizes stocks is advised. This strategy tends to emphasize growth of assets by investing in more aggressive stocks. In order to moderate risk, it may also include a commitment to income investments, such as bonds. An example of a portfolio that employs a long-term strategy may include 70 percent equities, 25 percent bonds, and 5 percent short-term instruments or cash.

If you're nearing or are in retirement, advisors often advocate a short-term strategy that relies more heavily on bonds to place more emphasis on capital preservation. This strategy is designed to emphasize current income, capital preservation, and liquidity, while maintaining a smaller portion of the portfolio in stocks for growth potential. An example of a portfolio that employs a short-term strategy may include 50 percent bonds, 20 percent equities, and 30 percent short-term instruments or cash.

Two Ways to Allocate Assets

There are two primary ways of allocating assets. The first method is to use a stable policy over time. Based on your income needs and risk tolerance, you might pursue a balanced strategy. This might require putting 25 percent of your dollars in each class of assets, such as stocks, bonds, cash, and real estate. Each quarter or year, rebalance those dollars to maintain your original allocation of 25 percent in each class. This forces you to sell off some of the best-performing assets while buying more of the weakest performers. This allocation system eliminates the need to make decisions on the expected return for each class and instead allows for more stable returns over long periods of time.

The alternative is an active strategy. Use your tolerance for risk and your long-term goals as the basis for your allocations to each class. Thus, if you need a good mix of growth and income, you might allow your investment in stocks to range from 35 percent to 65 percent of your portfolio, based on the market. You would develop these ranges for each asset class.

Obviously, an active strategy requires a lot of homework and a good knowledge of the financial markets and what impacts them. You'll have to track your investments at least weekly and adjust your holdings based on your revised expectations—as well as on their actual performance. You'll also have to take into account greater market forces and trends, changes in the global political and economic scene, even seasonal differences in sector performance. If you consistently make the right calls (an outcome that becomes more frequent as you gain experience and insight), you can make substantially higher returns.

Organizing your asset allocation campaign is a fairly straightforward process once you get the hang of it. Keep in mind, though, that your asset allocation plan is subject to change over time; what's right for you today may not be five years from now. Your asset allocation strategy can be changed to accommodate your life changes.

A Lifelong Investing Strategy

Your investing needs and strategies will change over time, depending on both your age and the stage of life you're in. The portfolio of a thirty-year-old with very young children will be vastly different than that of a thirty-year-old with no children or a forty-year-old with very young children.

QUESTION

Where does asset allocation start?
The simplest way to get started is through the old rule of thumb: 100 minus your age, where the result is your stock allocation percentage, with the rest of your portfolio allocated to fixed-income investments and cash. This oversimplified method won't deliver the perfect allocation ratio, but it makes a good starting point.

With that in mind, there are several lifestyle factors to take into account as you design your portfolio. Along with your age, you will want to consider factors like your current and future family situation, your current and future employment prospects (especially if you plan to open your own business), and your current and expected debt levels. As these factors change, so will your investing strategies and asset allocation choices. For example, as your life progresses or as your time horizons shorten, your asset allocation strategy may shift away from growth and toward wealth preservation.

Another thing to keep in mind as you're mapping out your investment strategy: You can make adjustments when necessary. Life throws up challenges (like finding out you're having twins) and delivers surprises (like inheriting $500,000 from a long-lost relative). Though your overall strategy will not (and should not) change frequently, there is enough flexibility to make changes when the need arises.

Your Investor Profile

Managing your own expectations is a big part of your investment planning process, and it starts with figuring out exactly what kind of investor you are. Once you know that, the rest of your investment planning will fall into place much more easily. Though there are many subtle variations in investor profiles, the two main types are buy-and-hold and market timing. Where you are along the time horizon, your risk tolerance, and your personal style all factor into the type of investor you will be.

Here are some good questions to ask yourself to determine your investor profile:

1. Do market fluctuations keep me awake at night?
2. Am I unfamiliar with investing?
3. Do I consider myself more a saver than an investor?
4. Am I fearful of losing 25 percent of my assets in a few days or weeks?
5. Am I comfortable with the ups and downs of the securities markets?
6. Am I knowledgeable about investing and the securities markets?
7. Am I investing for a long-term goal?
8. Can I withstand considerable short-term losses?

ALERT

Market timing in funds used to be viewed as a nuisance, an arcane practice by a handful of cunning investors. But timing is now under the microscope of regulators in Massachusetts and New York, who say the practice is unfair to individual investors—and illegal, in some cases.

If you answered yes to the first four questions, you are most likely a conservative investor. If you answered yes to the last four questions, you are more likely an aggressive investor. If you fall somewhere in between, you could call yourself a moderate investor. Conservative investors typically follow the buy-and hold strategy, where aggressive investors are often market timers. As you might expect, moderate investors tend to mix the two types into one blended profile.

Buy-and-Hold Investing

When it comes to buy-and-hold investing, you may have heard that it doesn't really matter what the market is doing when you get in, as long as you stay in. There's a great deal of truth in that line of thinking. Studies show that stocks can grow on average up to 10 to 12 percent annually, and long-term U.S. Treasury instruments can grow at a rate of up to 6 to 8 percent per year. Combined with the miracle of compounding, a long-term outlook coupled with a solid, disciplined investment strategy can yield big bucks over twenty, thirty, and especially forty-plus years.

The trick is in staying in the markets and not missing its sharp upturns. People who engage in market timing—market timers, those Wall Street daredevils who try to get in and out of the stock market at the most optimal moments—risk missing those market spikes. And that money is hard to make back.

The Downside of Market Timing

Market timers also generally experience higher transaction costs compared to those of a buy-and-hold strategy. Every time an investor sells or buys securities, a transaction fee is incurred. Even if the market timer achieves above-average returns, the transaction costs could negate the superior performance. Plus, trying to time the market can create additional risk. Consider the time period from 1962 to 1991. An investor who bought common stocks in 1962 would have realized a return of 10.3 percent with a buy-and-hold strategy. If that same investor tried to time the market and missed just twelve of the best-performing months (out of a total of 348 months), the return would have been only 5.4 percent. It must be admitted that there's a flip side to this theory. If the investor had jumped out of the market during its worst periods (like the 1987 crash and several subsequent bear markets), returns would have been even higher than if he'd stayed invested during the downturns.

One additional negative aspect of using market-timing techniques is tax reporting complications. Going in and out of the market several times in one tax year (sometimes several times in a month) generates numerous taxable gain and loss transactions, all of which must be accounted for on your income tax return.

CHAPTER 3

A Look at the Big Picture

In fall 2008, we learned again just how important the big picture is to the investment world. Problems in the housing market effectively crippled Wall Street, wiping out corporations and pensions alike. The government stepped in, and the markets began to limp back to normal. And we're all left with piles of public debt, which won't be paid down any time soon. The experience generated a lot of market fear and distrust. But markets—like old-growth forests—go through periodic meltdowns and rebirths. And there's money to be made in every part of the cycle.

Why the Economy Matters

Investing is about making your money grow. That can't happen unless the securities you invest in grow and pay out earnings. And that is directly tied into the health of the economy.

The most basic premise of the economy is this: If consumers spend money, the economy can grow; if they don't, it can't. When the economy is sluggish, consumer spending lags, overall corporate growth stagnates, and investors see poor returns. When the economy is booming, people spend money, corporations prosper, and investments grow. In fact, consumer spending makes up most of our gross domestic product (GDP), and that keeps the economy flowing.

Understanding how the economy works, the cycles it goes through, and the impact changes have on the markets can help make you a more successful investor. In fact, investors who pay attention to the economy can be more successful because they can take advantage of impending changes. While everyone else is focused on what's happening right now, economically savvy investors can focus on what's coming—and profitable investing is all about future growth.

How Interest Rates Affect Everything

From stocks to bonds to real estate, every investment is somehow affected by interest rates, albeit to a different extent. To understand that impact, you first have to understand how interest rates work. For most of us, interest is just something we earn on our savings accounts, or (more often) more money we have to pay to credit card companies. For some, it's the mysterious number connected with mortgage payments. And that's where it ends for us; that's the direct impact of interest rates on our lives.

It begins, though, with the Federal Reserve. The Federal Reserve has the power to manipulate the federal funds rate, which is the interest rate that Federal Reserve banks charge other banks like yours to borrow money. That rate sets the tone for all other interest rates, like the ones on your car loan, mortgage, and credit cards. The Federal Reserve uses this rate to control inflation. To keep inflation from spiraling out of control, the Fed raises its rate, which has the effect of limiting the amount of money available for consumer spending. Higher interest rates mean that more money goes to interest payments and less to shopping.

When people and businesses have to pay more in interest, which leaves them less to spend, investors can take a hit. So while a change in the federal funds rate doesn't immediately impact the markets, it does affect them indirectly, through both consumer spending and corporate bottom lines. When corporations have to pay more to borrow money, that's less money for the dividend pool and less money to put toward future growth. Plus, corporations with diminishing profits usually see their share prices drop right alongside the disappearing earnings. So even if nothing else changes, an interest rate increase can push stock prices down.

ESSENTIAL

When the Fed lowers interest rates, the money supply increases. That often signals investors to buy stocks, as lower interest rates make stocks appear more attractive on the risk-return scale. Lower rates also aid economic expansion, which leads to corporate growth, which increases the value of corporate shares.

There's a flipside to this, though. A higher federal funds rate also means higher interest rates paid out on newly issued Treasury securities. These risk-free investments guarantee you steady returns, and when rates go up, you're guaranteed bigger interest payments on these government securities. This also has the effect of higher interest rates on newly issued municipal and corporate bonds.

Understanding the Economic Indicators

Whether the economy is poised to take a turn or remains on course, there are special economic statistics that give us clues to what's about to happen. These clues are called leading indicators, and, as their name suggests, they take the lead in predicting which way the economy is headed. Then their cousins, coincident and lagging indicators, are used to confirm economic trends, illustrating where the economy stands now and where it's been.

Economic indicators are often tied with inflation. One reason for this is that inflation strongly influences the level of interest rates, which impact the stability of the economy. Some are also linked with production or foreign trade, both of which eventually impact consumer goods prices.

While you don't need a degree in economics to be a good investor, you need to understand how and when the economy can impact your portfolio. It makes sense for investors to have a thorough understanding of how the economy works and how economic activity is measured.

FACT

Though economists also look at coincident and lagging indicators, investors typically focus on leading indicators. For an investor, profits often come from future events and expectations. Knowing where the economy is headed can help investors (especially traders) make more profitable investment choices at the most opportune times.

Eight of the most important economic indicators are discussed here. You've probably heard of some of them, like the GDP, the consumer price index (CPI), the unemployment index, job growth, and housing starts. Others, such as the producer price index, consumer confidence index, and business inventories, are less widely known but are important all the same.

Gross Domestic Product

The GDP is the most important economic indicator published. Providing the broadest measure of economic activity, the GDP is considered the nation's report card. The four major components of the GDP are consumption, investment, government purchases, and net exports. This lagging index takes months to compute and even longer to finalize. The GDP lets us know if the economy is growing or shrinking.

Consumer Price Index

The CPI, released by the Bureau of Labor Statistics (BLS), is directly linked with the inflation rate. This index tracks retail-level price changes by comparing prices for a specific basket of goods and services to base-period prices. Unlike some other inflation measures, the CPI covers both domestically produced and imported goods. Some critics say the CPI, and therefore the measured inflation rate, is purposely understated, as the CPI is the factor used to increase Social Security payments.

Consumer Confidence

The consumer confidence index monitors consumer sentiment based on monthly interviews with thousands of households. The consumer confidence index dropped drastically after the terrorist attacks of September 11, 2001. Then, for several years, the index remained fairly steady; consumers were maintaining buying patterns despite rising gasoline prices and interest rates. In fall 2008, the index dropped again, as news of home foreclosures, the credit crisis, struggling markets, and government bailouts frightened consumers into saving their money. In bad times or good, consumer confidence serves as a reflection of the nation's financial health. This index is particularly important to the financial markets during times of national crisis or panic. If consumers aren't confident, they aren't spending money, and the markets may slump further.

Job Growth

Second only to the GDP, the government's employment report is one of the most important economic indicators. Job growth statistics include employment information such as the length of the average workweek, hourly earnings, and the current unemployment rate. As such, this indicator sets the tone for the upcoming investing month. When job growth is up, consumers feel more at ease and tend to spend more. But when job growth shrinks, people get nervous—a strong indicator that the economy could be entering a downturn.

Unemployment Index

The unemployment index is a subset of the government's employment report. Unlike the total jobs data, which is considered a coincident indicator, the unemployment index is a lagging indicator; it changes following a change in the economy as a whole. Essentially, this makes the unemployment index less significant to investors, who are looking toward the economic future. However, several months of low unemployment rates can signal that higher inflation is right around the corner.

Housing Starts

The housing starts indicator measures the new construction of single-family homes or buildings each month. For the purposes of this survey, each individual house and every single apartment count as one housing start; a building with 150 apartments counts as 150 housing starts.

FACT

There's an index for everything, including one that measures the leading economic indicators (called the LEI), which purports to predict future economic activity. Basically, when the LEI moves in the same direction for three consecutive months, that suggests an economic turning point. For example, three positive readings in a row would indicate an impending recovery.

Why are housing starts important? The housing industry represents more than 25 percent of total investment dollars and about 5 percent of the total economy, as per the U.S. Census Bureau. Declining housing starts indicate a slumping economy, and increases in housing activity can help turn the tide and put the economy on the road to recovery.

Business Inventories

As a monthly running total of how well companies are selling their products, business inventories are like a big neon sign to economists and investors alike. The business inventory data are collected from three sources: the manufacturing, merchant wholesalers, and retail reports. Retail inventories are the most volatile component of inventories and can cause major swings. A sudden fall in inventories may show the onset of expansion, and a sudden accumulation of inventories may signify falling demand and hence the onset of recession.

Producer Price Index

The producer price index (PPI), also put out by the BLS, tracks wholesale price changes. It includes breakdowns on raw materials (a.k.a. commodities), intermediate goods (items that are in production), and finished goods (ready to hit the shelves). Every month, nearly 100,000 prices are collected from approximately 30,000 manufacturing and production companies and manufacturing businesses. This coincident indicator is often a good predictor of the direction of the CPI.

Know Your Sectors

Anyone beginning to learn about investing will soon hear the phrase "sector rotation." Different types of industries perform better during specific stages in the economic cycle. For example, some industries take off when the economy is expanding, while others actually profit more when the economy is in a slump. That means that investors can always find a way to profit in the markets, as long as they know where to look.

To capitalize on sector rotation, you first need to get a handle on the sectors themselves. Essentially, a sector is a unique industry group. A lot of people—including financial professionals—use the terms *sector* and *industry* interchangeably, but they aren't really the same. Industry describes a specific set of businesses, while sector is a broader term. In fact, a sector is technically a broad section of the overall economy and can include more than one industry. For example, the financial sector includes banking, investment banking, mortgages, accounting, insurance, and asset management—six distinct industries.

Next you'll need to know at which point in the cycle the economy currently stands: downturn, recession, upturn, or recovery. You can find current economic analysis in most of the big financial newspapers, such as the *Wall Street Journal*. You can also find detailed information on the state of the U.S. economy from the Bureau of Economic Analysis at *www.bea.gov*. Once you know where the economy is, you can better predict where it's going to go from there, even if you can't predict the timing. That's because the economic cycle follows a very definite pattern. For example, when the economy is in a deep recession, the next phase of the cycle will be an upturn, a very good time to begin investing more actively. That knowledge, combined with a grasp of sector rotation, can help you profit regardless of the prevailing economic state.

ESSENTIAL

You can diversify your portfolio and take advantage of sector rotation by investing in sector funds. These mutual funds invest in single economic sectors (like technology or healthcare), and sometimes even more focused sector subsets (like electronics or pharmaceuticals). While sector funds expose investors to more risk than more broad-based mutual funds, they can also bring higher returns.

Sector rotation describes the movement of profitability through different sectors as the economy goes through its cycles. Different sectors thrive in different portions of the cycle. The basic sectors are highly predictable, following the economic cycle like clockwork. For example, the utilities and services sectors tend to perform well during an economic downturn; and as that downturn segues into a full recession, the technology, cyclicals, and industrial sectors will start to flourish. As the economy begins to turn toward recovery, basic materials and energy perform best. In a full thriving economy, the consumer staples sector will really take off. So if you know what stage the economy is in now, you know where in the cycle it will be going next, and you can reasonably predict which sectors will prosper.

An Index for Everything

Financial professionals look to benchmarks to measure just how well (or how poorly) their investments are doing. These benchmarks are known as indexes, and they cover every sector of the financial markets, from small-cap stocks to emerging nation bonds. Most of these indexes consist of a group or sample of representative investments that indicate how the overall market or a segment of the market is performing. Some widely used indexes track thousands of individual securities, while others look at fewer than fifty.

The Dow Jones Industrial Average (DJIA, also called the Dow) is the most prominent stock index in the world. It was named after Charles H. Dow, first editor of the *Wall Street Journal,* and his one-time partner Edward

Jones, although Jones was not instrumental in creating the index. Dow's creation revolutionized investing, as it was the first publicly published gauge of the market. The thirty stocks on the Dow, which are all part of the New York Stock Exchange (NYSE), are all those of established blue-chip companies like McDonald's, Coca-Cola, DuPont, and Eastman Kodak. The Dow was created to mimic the U.S. stock market as a whole, and its companies represent a variety of market segments such as entertainment, automotive, health care products, and financial services.

FACT

General Electric is the only company that was included in the original Dow Jones Industrial Average, created in 1896, that is still part of its makeup today. However, it hasn't been there the entire time. General Electric was dropped in 1898, restored in 1899, taken out again in 1901, and then put back on the list in 1907.

The thirty stocks of the Dow Jones Industrial Average companies are weighted by stock price, rather than market capitalization, which is how most indexes are weighted. Basically, the Dow number is calculated by adding up the prices of all the stocks, then dividing by the number of stocks included in the index, adjusted for stock splits. The important point to remember is that each company carries equal weight.

Some indexes are capitalization weighted, giving greater weight to stocks with greater market value. For example, consider Standard & Poor's (S&P) Composite Index of 500 Stocks. The Standard & Poor's 500 Index, commonly known as the S&P 500, is a benchmark that is widely used by professional stock investors. The S&P 500 represents 500 stocks—400 industrial stocks, twenty transportation stocks, forty utility stocks, and forty financial stocks. This index consists primarily of stocks listed on the NYSE, although it also features some over-the-counter (OTC) stocks.

The Russell 2000 index covers the small-cap equities market, so it tracks corporations that fall into the small-cap segment of the market, those with market capitalization falling between $300 million and $2 billion. The Russell 2000 is a subset of the Russell 3000 index, following the performance of only the 2,000 smallest companies in the Russell 3000.

Other indexes treat each stock equally. The Value Line Index tracks 1,700 equally weighted stocks from the NYSE, the National Association of Securities Dealers Automated Quotations (NASDAQ), and OTC markets. It acts as a market barometer, widely held to be the best measure of the overall market and a crucial monitoring tool for any investor.

The Whole World Impacts Investments

Investments don't exist in a vacuum. What happens on the U.S. stock markets has global consequences. Changes in the interest rates on U.S. Treasury securities can impact bond markets across the ocean. A downturn in the U.S. economy hits the rest of the world almost immediately. And the reverse is also true. Major shakeups around the world affect stock prices, bond prices, commodities, and currencies.

At the same time, the breadth of the world markets practically ensures that there's always a profit to be made somewhere. When major economies are tanking, emerging economies may begin to thrive. A natural disaster in one part of the world can cause the economies in other parts of the world to go into overdrive—or it can cause shortages and slowdowns, depending on the type and extent of damage.

In addition, the Internet has made the world a much smaller place. We now know instantly when something happens in the farthest corners of the earth. We know the second a stock exchange in Asia or Europe goes up or down a few points. Extensive international trade means the dollar can be affected when another country's currency strengthens or weakens.

And all of this affects investors. Whether you invest in individual stocks, fixed income securities, mutual funds, real estate, or more exotic financial instruments, your investments will feel the impact of world events—sometimes immediately, other times slowly. It used to be that only investors in foreign securities had to pay close attention to foreign and global economies. Now every investor needs to know and understand what's going on around the world, because every investor is impacted by what goes on in the rest of the world.

CHAPTER 4

Starting with Stocks

It's time to learn all about stocks, from what they are to all the different types available to what they can mean for your portfolio. Buy-and-hold investors invest in companies that have stood the test of time. Traders take a more active approach to investing, placing more emphasis on stock price movement than on the real value of the company. Regardless of which strategy you apply to your holdings, the same underlying rule applies: Know what and why you're buying (or selling) before you make any trade.

It All Happens in the Exchanges

Back in the 1990s, it became clear that individual investors were becoming serious players in the world of Wall Street. With the advent of online investing and an aggressive play for smaller investors by the two leading stock markets in the United States (the NYSE and the NASDAQ), buying and selling investments has gotten easier and less expensive.

FACT

The markets that make up what is known in general as the stock market are the New York Stock Exchange (NYSE) and the National Association of Securities Dealers Automated Quotations (NASDAQ). Other cities like Boston, Chicago, Philadelphia, Denver, San Francisco, and Los Angeles have exchanges, as do major international centers like London and Tokyo.

Competition, both domestic and global, continues to make stock transactions more transparent and more accessible to all investors. By understanding how the different stock markets work and compete for your business, you'll be better equipped to succeed in the investing world.

The NYSE

The NYSE (known to insiders as the Big Board"), now formally known as NYSE Euronext, is home to prominent industry players like Wal-Mart, General Electric, and McDonald's. The Big Board is not for little-league players. Among other requirements for inclusion on the NYSE, a company must have at least 1.1 million publicly traded shares of stock outstanding, with a market value of at least $100 million. It must show pre-tax income of at least $10 million over the three most recent fiscal years, and have had earnings of at least $2 million in the two most recent years. And seats on the exchange don't come cheap, either. The lowest amount paid for a seat, way back in 1871, was $2,750; the highest price paid for a single seat was $4 million paid in December 2005.

The NYSE, with the distinction of being the oldest stock exchange in the United States, is housed in a 36,000-square-foot facility in New York City's financial district. In 2007, the NYSE combined with the European stock exchange Euronext, to form NYSE Euronext, a global milestone for the trading community. This market broke a new record, trading more than 5 billion shares in a single day: on August 15, 2007, trading volume hit an unprecedented 5,799,792,281 shares.

ESSENTIAL

More than 200 years ago, a group of twenty-four Wall Street merchants signed a document called the Buttonwood Agreement. The agreement laid out all the rules for buying and selling shares of public stock, including the price for a trading seat. Their rules eventually transformed into today's rules of trading and the foundation of the New York Stock Exchange.

Not content to rest on its laurels, NYSE Euronext acquired the American Stock Exchange (AMEX) in 2008, and fully integrated trading began in early 2009. Now this combined exchange offers expanded trading capabilities, including stock options, exchange-traded funds, and other specialized securities.

The NASDAQ

When it first launched in February 1971, the NASDAQ hosted only 250 companies. Its first claim to fame: the NASDAQ opened as the first electronic stock market in the world. The exchange hit a milestone in 1996, when its trading volume finally exceeded 500 million shares per day. Now it has become a full-fledged stock market, listing about 3,200 corporations, and it's destined to grow; out of all the U.S. stock markets, the NASDAQ (which is now officially known as the NASDAQ OMX Group) hosts the most initial public offerings (IPOs).

The NASDAQ is attractive to new and growing companies primarily because the listing requirements are less stringent than those of the NSYE, and the costs can be considerably lower. Not surprisingly, you'll find a lot of technology and biotech stocks listed on this exchange, as these types of companies typically fall squarely in the aggressive growth category. In fact, the NASDAQ boasts more than a $2 trillion total market value in the IT sector.

Unlike the auction style of the NYSE, the NASDAQ works with more than 600 securities dealers called market makers. These market makers compete against one another to offer the best bid/ask prices or quotes over the NASDAQ's complex network, joining buyers and sellers from all over the world. The NASDAQ dealers help make it easier to buy and sell stocks by helping to ensure their liquidity (making sure there's a ready market).

FACT

The NASDAQ is an OTC market, which means its securities are traded through telephone and computer networks as opposed to an exchange floor. NASDAQ is also the world's largest stock market and, on average, trades more shares in a day than any other exchange.

The SEC Works for You

During the Great Depression, Congress passed the Securities Exchange Act of 1934 creating the U.S. Securities and Exchange Commission (SEC). The 1934 Act was designed to restore confidence in capital markets, setting clear rules and giving the SEC power to regulate the securities industry. Basically, the SEC watches over the securities industry to make sure no illegal activity takes place. To help with that enormous task, the agency sets strict standards for brokers, investors, and publicly traded corporations. Every corporation whose stock trades on a U.S. exchange must be registered with the SEC.

The agency's main goal is to protect investors by making sure the securities markets remain honest and fair. One way the SEC meets this goal is by making sure publicly traded companies disclose enough accurate information for investors to make informed decisions. There's a slew of ongoing paperwork required of all companies whose stocks trade on the public markets, including annual audited financial statements. In addition to keeping close tabs on publicly traded companies, the SEC also regulates any companies involved with trading and any professionals who offer investment advice.

Insider trading is one of the most widely known issues covered by the SEC. Insider trading, or insider information, refers to buying and selling publicly traded securities based on confidential information that has not been released to the general public. Because such information is not available to everyone, those insiders have an unfair advantage. And though it makes for splashy headlines—think Martha Stewart, Enron, and World-Com—a good story does nothing to help investors recoup their losses.

ESSENTIAL

More than 200 years ago, a group of twenty-four Wall Street merchants signed a document called the Buttonwood Agreement. The agreement laid out all the rules for buying and selling shares of public stock, including the price for a trading seat. Their rules eventually transformed into today's rules of trading and the foundation of the New York Stock Exchange.

The SEC's Division of Enforcement does just what the name suggests; it makes sure federal securities laws are followed to the letter. This division investigates possible legal violations, and when it finds that laws haven't been followed, it recommends ways to remedy the situation.

Most important, though, the SEC is all about you: protecting you from swindles, providing reliable information, and keeping your broker in line. On its website, you can visit a special section called EDGAR (Electronic Data Gathering, Analysis, and Retrieval), a complete database of all corporate reports (such as 10-Ks and 10-Qs) filed by public companies—all the way back to 1994! It's very easy to search EDGAR for information on any company you plan to invest in, so make this your first stop. In addition to complete financial reports, you'll also find out if any complaints have been filed against a company.

FACT

On its website (*www.sec.gov*), the SEC offers everyone the opportunity to investigate any questionable activities. They also make available a wide range of public services, including free investment information, up-to-date complaint tracking, and a toll-free information line at 1-800-SEC-0330.

Stocks Are Pieces of a Company

Purchasing shares of stock is like buying a business. That's the way Warren Buffett, one of the world's most successful investors, views it—and his philosophy is certainly worth noting. When you buy stock, you're actually buying a portion of a corporation. If you wouldn't want to own the entire company, you should think twice before you consider buying even a piece of it. If you think of investing in these terms, you'll probably be a lot more cautious when singling out a specific company.

It's important to become acquainted with all of the details of the company you're considering. What products and services does the company offer? Which part of the business accounts for the greatest revenue? Which part of the business accounts for the least revenue? Is the company too diversified? Who are its competitors? Is there a demand for the company's offerings? Is the company an industry leader? Are any mergers and acquisitions in the works? Until you understand exactly what the company does and how well it does it, it would be wise to postpone your investment decision.

FACT

The Altria Group, formerly known as Philip Morris, is primarily associated with tobacco products, but the company also profits from its popular beer subsidiary. It holds 28.5 percent of SABMiller Brewing, the home of Miller beers. In addition, the company holds Philip Morris Capital Corporation, which is involved with the financing and leasing of major assets.

Let's say you want to buy a convenience store in your hometown. You've reviewed such factors as inventory, the quality of the company's employees, and customer service programs. In addition to selling staple grocery items, the company also rents videos and operates a gas pump. The grocery side of the business may only account for a small percentage of the overall revenue. It would be in your best interest to value each part of the business separately in order to get a complete and accurate picture of the company's profit potential. Many companies have traditionally been associated with a specific business, yet may have expanded into totally new venues.

Disney, for example, has historically been associated with the Disneyland and Disney World theme parks. The reality is that Disney is also involved in a host of other ventures. Among other things, the multifaceted company has interests in television and movie production, including Touchstone Pictures and Miramax Films. Disney's ABC, Inc., division includes the ABC television network, as well as numerous television stations and shares in various cable channels like ESPN and SOAPnet.

It should be increasingly clear that making money through investing requires work. The more research and thought you put into your strategy, the more likely you are to reap rewards. Although there are no guarantees in the world of investing, the odds will be more in your favor if you make educated and well-informed investment decisions. When you make an investment, you are putting your money into a public company, which allows you—as part of the public—to become an owner or to have equity in the company. That's why stocks are often referred to as equities.

Types of Stocks

Common stocks are equity securities that are sold to the public, and each share constitutes ownership in a corporation; when people talk about trading shares, they're talking about common stock, and this type is the primary focus of this chapter. Preferred stocks are somewhat different; while they still denote ownership in a corporation, they also have some characteristics more in common with bonds than with common stocks.

Corporations come in all sizes. You can invest in a wildly successful mega-company or a micro-cap company that is just beginning to show signs of growth potential. Some people prefer to buy the common stock of well-established companies, while other investors would rather invest in smaller, growth-oriented companies.

No matter what type of company fits in with your overall strategy, it's important to research every potential stock you buy. Just because a company has been around for decades doesn't mean it's the best investment vehicle for you. Furthermore, companies are always changing, and it's important to make sure that the information you are reviewing is current. Mergers and acquisitions have become commonplace, and it's essential to know if a company you are considering buying is undergoing, or is planning to undergo, such a transaction.

Find out about a company's market capitalization, or the market value of all of the company's outstanding shares. To calculate the market capitalization, multiply the current market price of a stock by the number of outstanding shares. The number of outstanding shares refers to the number of shares that have been sold to the public.

The math is pretty straightforward: A publicly traded corporation that has 30 million shares outstanding that are currently trading for $20 each would have a market capitalization of $600 million. Although there are a few different groupings used to categorize stocks by their capitalization, here's a general rule of thumb you can follow:

- **Large cap:** $10 billion and over
- **Mid cap:** Between $2 billion and $10 billion
- **Small cap:** Between $300 million and $2 billion
- **Micro cap:** Under $300 million

In addition to market cap, there are also different categories of stocks, enough to round out any portfolio. The variety includes blue-chip, growth, cyclical, defensive, value, income, and speculative stocks, and socially responsible investments (SRI)—and don't forget preferred stock.

Blue-Chip, Income, Growth, and Preferred Stocks

Blue chips are considered to be the most prestigious, well-established companies that are publicly traded, many of which have practically become household names. Included in this mostly large-cap mix are General Electric (which trades on the NYSE under the symbol GE), McDonald's (NYSE: MCD), and Wal-Mart (NYSE: WMT). A good number of blue-chip companies have been in existence for more than twenty-five years and are still leading the pack in their respective industries. Since most of these organizations have a solid track record, they are good investment vehicles for individuals leaning to the conservative side in their stock picks.

Growth stocks, as you can probably guess from the name, include companies that have strong growth potential. Many companies in this category have sales, earnings, and market share that are growing faster than the overall economy. Such stocks usually represent companies that are big on research and development; for example, pioneers in new technologies are often growth-stock companies. Earnings in these companies are usually put right back into the business, rather than paid out to shareholders as dividends.

ESSENTIAL

If you had purchased 100 shares of Wal-Mart in January of 1990, you would have paid $533. By January 1995, your investment would have been worth $1,144—more than 100 percent profit. And by January 2008, your investment would have been worth $5,074, almost ten times more than your original purchase price.

Growth stocks may be riskier than their blue-chip counterparts, but in many cases you may also reap greater rewards. Generally speaking, growth stocks perform best during bull markets, while value stocks perform best during bear markets, but that's not guaranteed. A word of caution: Beware of stocks whose price seems to be growing faster than would make sense. Sometimes momentum traders will help run growth-stock prices to skyscraping levels, then sell them off causing the stock to plummet.

Income stocks do just what the name suggests, provide steady income streams for investors. These shares come with regular dividend payments, sometimes big enough that people can actually live off their dividend checks. Though many income stocks fall into the blue-chip category, other types of stocks (like value stocks) may offer consistent dividend payments as well. These stocks make a good addition to fixed-income portfolios, as they also provide the opportunity for share-price growth.

Preferred stocks have almost as much in common with bonds as they do with common stock. Essentially, this type of stock comes with a redemption date and a fixed dividend that gets paid regardless of the company's earnings. If the corporation has financial difficulties, holders of preferred stock have priority when it comes to dividend payments. In times of prosperity, some preferred shares (called participating preferred) may get a second dividend payout that is based on earnings. As the owner of preferred stock, you normally don't have the rights that come with common stock ownership (like voting). However, preferred stock can be a good portfolio addition for income-oriented investors.

Size Matters: Small-, Mid-, and Large-Cap Stocks

The small-cap stock category includes many of the small, emerging companies that have survived their initial growing pains and are now enjoying strong earning gains, along with expanding sales and profits. Today's small-cap stock may be tomorrow's leader—it can also be tomorrow's loser. Overall, such stocks tend to be very volatile and risky. A safe way of adding these to your portfolio can be through a professionally managed small-cap fund. That way, you'll have exposure to potentially explosive profits without the added risk of investing in a particular company.

Mid-cap stocks, as the name suggests, are bigger than small caps but smaller than large caps. Large-cap stocks are the biggest players in the stock market.

A large-cap corporation typically has a more solidly established presence and more reliable sales and profits than smaller corporations. Most of the time, larger companies make less risky investments than smaller companies; the trade-off, though, can be slower growth rates. Most investors hold large-cap stocks for the long-term, and for good reason: more than fifty years of historical market returns show that these corporate giants yield only slightly lower returns than short-term investments, with much less volatility.

Cyclical, Defensive, and Value Stocks

Companies with earnings that are strongly tied to the business cycle are considered to be cyclical. When the economy picks up momentum, these stocks follow this positive trend. When the economy slows down, these stocks slow down, too. Cyclical stocks would include companies like United Airlines (NASDAQ: UAUA).

Defensive stocks, on the other hand, are relatively stable under most economic conditions, no matter how the market is faring. Stocks that fall into this category include food companies, drug manufacturers, and utility companies. For the most part, these companies produce things people can't live without, no matter what the economic climate is at any given time. The list of defensive stocks includes General Mills (NYSE: GIS) and Johnson & Johnson (NYSE: JNJ).

FACT

Socially responsible investing has also been popular in recent years. This strategy has people investing only in companies that embody their personal values. Socially responsible investments are often chosen for their "don'ts" more than their "dos." These corporations don't produce tobacco products, liquor, weapons, or environmentally damaging products.

Value stocks appear inexpensive when compared to their corporate earnings, dividends, sales, or other fundamental factors. Basically, you're getting more than what you pay for: a good value. When investors are high on growth stocks, value stocks tend to be ignored, making them even better bargains for savvy investors. Value investors believe that these stocks make the best buys given their reasonable price in relation to many growth stocks. Of course, a good value is highly dependent on current stock prices, so a good value today might not be a good value next month. A good rule of thumb is to look for solid companies that are trading at less than twice their book value per share. An example of good value (at least as of May 2009) is NYSE Euronext (yes, that's the stock exchange itself), with a price to book value ratio of 0.94.

Income and Speculative Stocks and Green Investing

Income stocks may fit the bill if generating income is your primary goal. One example of an income stock is public utility companies; such stocks have traditionally paid higher dividends than other types of stock. In addition, preferred stocks make excellent income vehicles, typically providing steady dividends and high yields. As with any stock, it's wise to look for a solid company with a good track record.

Beware of speculative stocks. Any company that's boasting about its brilliant ideas but doesn't have the earnings and revenue to back them up would be classified as a speculative stock. Since these companies have yet to prove their true worth, they make risky investments.

Another investment strategy that is growing in popularity is green investing. Here, investors put capital into companies that mirror their personal ethics and values. These investors may be looking to avoid certain negative products (like tobacco and weapons) or companies whose products or services destroy the environment. In the same vein, socially responsible investors look for companies that leave a positive mark on society. Investors look for companies whose interests align with their own social agendas; for instance, they may support companies that promote fair trade or whose products are not made in sweatshops.

Penny Stocks

Penny stocks are stocks that sell for $5 or less, and in many cases you're lucky if they're worth even that much. Most penny stocks usually have no substantial income or revenue. You have a high potential for loss with penny stocks. If you have a strong urge to invest in this type of company, take time out to follow the stock to see if it has made any headway. Learn all you can about the company, and don't be tempted to act on a hot tip that may have been passed your way.

ESSENTIAL

Penny stocks trade in either the pink sheets, a forum operated by the National Quotations Bureau, or on the NASDAQ small-cap market. Pink sheets, in brief, are listings and price information literally printed on pink sheets of paper that go to select brokers.

The companies behind these stocks are thinly capitalized and are often not required to file reports with the SEC. They trade over the counter, and there is a limited amount of public information available. This in itself is reason for concern. How many astute investors want to put their money into an investment offering little or no information? Nonetheless, people do invest in these stocks.

One of the most interesting—and alarming—aspects of penny stock dealing is that brokers are not always acting as a third party but instead set prices and act as the principals in the transaction. Penny stocks most often do not have a single price but a number of different prices at which they can be purchased or sold.

Okay, so there's little information about the company, the price, or anything else to investigate. But the guy on the phone—making a cold call— says it will be the next Starbucks! This is where they get you. Thanks to the Internet and the selling of phone lists, penny stocks dealers can reach out far and wide. They use high-pressure sales tactics and armies of callers to tell you anything to make you buy the stocks. Beware!

ALERT

Unscrupulous brokers often hype and promote companies that have minimal assets. With these "pump and dump" schemes, hard-selling wheeler-dealers hype the stocks, making outrageous claims about the company that are wholly unsubstantiated by the facts. They drive up the share price so that they can cash in on artificial price inflation for a company that is worth nearly nothing!

All of this is not to say that there are no low-priced legitimate stocks on the market. There are. They are usually small grassroots companies that can grow over time—if you pick the right one and wait a while. You should invest cautiously and conservatively at first. Look for a new company with good leadership in an industry where you see growth potential. It's also advantageous to find a company that holds the patent on a new product. If the product takes off, so could your stock. You must seek out all of this information—it will not come to you via a cold caller.

CHAPTER 5

Doing Your Homework

Most educators will tell you that 75 percent of all learning is gained by doing homework; this is true of investing as well. When you are interested in investing, it's important that you do your homework, including research, analysis, and investigation. Look up the stock you own on the Internet and find any company news listings. Read the company newsletter, its annual or semiannual reports, and ask your broker for any updated news about the company. An educated investor is more likely to be a patient and relaxed investor.

Know What You're Buying, Buy What You Know

One of the benefits of being a consumer is that you are called on to evaluate products and services every day. You have learned that you can get the best results by thoroughly researching your options before you make a purchasing decision. Maybe you've recently purchased some new electronics that you just can't put down, switched cereal brands to cut some of the sugar out of your kids' diet, or started a new medication that actually made you feel better without any side effects. These are experiences you can put to work when you're making your investment decisions.

Your observations are another way to gain valuable insight. During your recent trip to Japan, did you notice people consuming huge quantities of a new Coca-Cola product? While waiting to pay for dinner at your favorite restaurant, did you notice that many of the patrons pulled out American Express cards? Part of doing your homework as an investor is noticing the companies whose products and services are prominently displayed and used by the people around you.

ALERT

Putting serious thought into your investments early on will most likely pay off in the long run. Unfortunately, many people are introduced to the world of investing through a hot stock tip from their barber, buddy, or bellman. There's really no way to make an easy buck, and by jumping into a stock because of a random tip, you'll probably end up losing money.

Another huge consideration when buying stocks is price. Would you pay any amount to buy a car or a house? Probably not. Most people like to feel that they've gotten a good deal. They're looking for a price that's proportionate to their buying budget and what they get from the purchase. It's the same with stock investing: The price of a particular stock is a critical part of the buying and selling equation. Taking a business attitude toward stock buying is important—it is wise to base your investment decisions on a variety of factors, including purchase price. That's the only way to ensure profitability in the long run. You want high quality at a fair (or better than fair) price.

Fortunately, good-quality companies in this country are plentiful. Finding these companies, however, is something of a challenge. Some investors are more inclined to look for the current hot stock, while others prefer to hunt out a great deal. The terms *growth investing* and *value investing* describe these differing approaches.

FACT

According to a special report put out by Wells Fargo, large company stocks have brought in average annual returns of 11.3 percent since 1926. Compare that with a 12.6 percent return on small company stocks and just 5.6 percent on long-term corporate bonds over the same period.

Growth Investing

Essentially, growth investors want to own a piece of the fastest-growing companies around, even if it means paying a hefty price for this privilege. Growth companies are organizations that have experienced rapid growth, such as Microsoft. They may have outstanding management teams, highly rated developments, or plans for aggressive expansion into foreign markets. Growth-company stocks rarely pay significant dividends, and growth investors don't expect them to. Instead, growth companies plow their earnings right back into the business to promote even more growth. Among other things, growth investors pay close attention to company earnings. If growth investing fits in with your overall investment strategy, look for companies that have demonstrated strong growth over the past several years.

Value Investing

Value investors are on the prowl for bargains, and they're more inclined than growth investors to analyze companies using such data as sales volume, earnings, and cash flow. The philosophy here is that value companies are actually undervalued, so their stock price doesn't really represent how much they're worth. Value investors are often willing to ride out stock price fluctuations because of the extensive research they have done prior to committing to a particular stock.

Get the Facts

Both styles of investing can be lucrative. The idea is to figure out which style of investment better fits your personality and investment strategy. Sometimes you may lean toward growth investing; other times, you may feel that taking a value-investing approach is the way to go. Still other times you may want growth and value all wrapped up in one neat package. In that case, you would be looking for growth at a reasonable price, known in industry lingo as GARP.

ESSENTIAL

Every investor should use a research checklist to evaluate stock under consideration. Look for annual reports, financial statements, industry comparisons, and current news items. Analyze your findings before making investment decisions. Once you become a shareholder, you will find that your main information needs are filled with press releases, ongoing financial statements, and judicious stock price monitoring.

Whichever style you choose, you need a place to get the information on which you can base your decision. These days, there's no better starting point than the Internet. On the web, you can easily find the best investment information in real time, mostly for free. More and more, investors both young and old are turning to websites to limit their reliance on expensive financial advisors. In addition to the prospect company's web page, there are dozens of sites that provide in-depth company data and even more that offer real-time stock quotes.

There is no shortage of good market research available to you as an investor. Part of your job is to determine which sources work best for your needs. You can find a listing of trusted investment sites in Chapter 17.

Reading the Annual Report

When it comes to reading financial documents, most people would rather walk over hot coals then peruse endless rows of numbers. Corporations count on that and fill their annual reports with glossy color photos and colorful commentary; a lot of people assume that a heavy, glossy report means a successful year. The numbers inside, though, may tell a completely different story. It's up to you to get comfortable with the numbers; when you do, you'll find a wealth of information about the company's current success.

If you're already a shareholder, you'll automatically get a copy of the annual report every year; if you're not yet invested in the company, you can simply call and ask for one or look at it online. Every company's report looks different, and they may be assembled in different orders. However, every publicly traded company's annual report contains the same basic items:

- Letter from the chairman of the board (expect a big pile of spin here)
- A description of the company's products and services (more spin)
- Financial statements (read the footnotes carefully; they contain some of the meat)
- Management discussion (sort of a big picture look at the company, with a little spin)
- CPA opinion letter (read this to make sure the company's financial position is accurately represented)
- Company information (locations, officer names, and contact information)
- Historical stock data (including dividend history and dividend reinvestment plan program information)

Two Proven Ways to Analyze Stocks

Investors generally favor one of two stock-picking techniques: technical analysis or fundamental analysis. Technical analysis is all about stock prices and how they move, and it relies on charts and graphs to determine patterns. Fundamental analysis, more common among beginning investors, involves studying the company itself, with a focus on financial statements and performance. For optimum results, many savvy investors combine both techniques when making trade decisions. For example, a stock with great fundamentals and sagging price trends could indicate trouble on the horizon.

Technical analysis focuses on charts and graphs showing past stock price and volume patterns. There are a number of patterns technical analysts recognize to be historically recurring. The trick is to identify the pattern before it is completed, then buy or sell according to where the pattern indicates the stock is headed. Those who use this technique believe you can forecast future stock prices by studying past price trends. They make trades based primarily on stock price movements. Technical analysts tend to do much more buying and selling than fundamental analysts.

QUESTION

What's a good first step in selecting stocks?
Learn about all the products and/or services offered by the company you're considering. A company may have one high-profile product and several other products and/or services that are not as visible. Even if a high-profile product is getting rave reviews and profits, the company's lesser-known products may be taking a toll on the total profits—or vice versa.

Fundamental analysis is a long-used, common way to review stocks. The technique involves an analysis of the company's ability to generate earnings and an examination of the value of the company's total assets. Value investing and growth investing are two subdivisions of fundamental analysis. Proponents of fundamental analysis believe that stock prices will rise as a result of growth. Earnings, dividends, and book values are all examined, and a buy-and-hold approach is usually followed. Fundamental analysis advocates maintain that stock in well-run, high-quality companies will become more valuable over time.

Five Characteristics of Great Companies

Once you've narrowed your focus to a handful of companies, you need to fine-tune your research even more. One of the primary reasons to buy a particular stock is because of its future outlook. It's wise to buy and hold onto a stock for the long term, so quality is an important part of your investment strategy. Among other factors, you want to purchase stock in a company that you believe has the following traits:

- **Sound business model.** You want to single out a company that has a solid business plan and a good grasp of where it wants to be in the years ahead, and a plan to get there. A company with a clear focus has a better chance of reaching its goals and succeeding than a company that just rolls along without a concrete plan.
- **Superior management.** An experienced, innovative, and progressive management team has the best chance of leading a company into the future. Star managers have had a major impact on their prospective companies, and a company will often witness dramatic changes when a new management team comes on board. When key management leaves an organization, you will often see major changes in the way a company operates.
- **Significant market share.** When a majority of individuals rely upon the products and/or services of a designated company, odds are the company has good insight into consumer preferences. Industry market leaders usually have a well-thought-out vision. However, the strongest company performance doesn't always indicate the best stock to buy. Be careful and look more closely at markets with a glut of competitors; sometimes the second-best company makes the best stock investment.
- **Competitive advantages.** A company that is ahead of the pack will often be on top of cutting-edge trends and industry changes in areas like marketing and technology. You want to single out those companies that are—and are likely to stay—one step ahead of the competition.
- **New developments.** If a company places a high priority on research and development, it's likely to roll out successful introductions. If the product or service takes off, the stock price may very well follow.

If the future outlook for a particular company appears promising—that is, as long as a company continues to exhibit these traits and act upon them—owning a portion of that company might make good business sense.

The Buffett Approach to Success

Many individuals want to emulate the successful investors. And why not? Warren Buffett, for example, has earned his fame by investing in quality companies instead of relying on technical analysis strategies. Buffett believes that if you buy stock in quality companies, you have no reason to sell your investments unless there is a serious underlying problem behind a price dip. Buffett believes that investors should understand a company and its industry before making any investment decisions.

ALERT

When evaluating an analyst's report, make sure you read the fine print. If the author is a representative of the company being profiled, the report is not objective. If it's based on research paid for by the company, view that information with some healthy skepticism and do a little more research.

Although Buffett prefers to buy companies at prices below their potential, price is not the sole consideration in his stock selection process. Buying quality companies for the long haul is key. If one of your star companies suffers a dip in its stock price, Buffett says, it might be a good chance to pick up some additional shares.

Investor Math Basics

After you've narrowed your focus to a handful of companies, continue your research efforts by reviewing a few factors for each company. Find out about each company's earnings per share, price/earnings ratio, book value, price volatility, dividends, number of shares outstanding, and total return. These factors will give you greater insight into the stocks.

While some of the numbers (like earnings per share) can be pulled straight from a corporation's annual report, others may require a little math on your part (like price/earnings ratio). Don't let the math stop you—it's all pretty straightforward and not terribly time-consuming. And the information you'll get from it is well worth the effort.

Earnings Per Share and Price/Earnings Ratio

Earnings per share (often abbreviated EPS) is the company's net income divided by the number of common shares outstanding. Simply, it is the portion of the company's profit (or net income) for each share of stock. A company's growth rate is often determined by how its earnings per share have changed over the years. Finding a company with a strong earning growth is advisable. You can find that by looking at a company's earnings per share over the past several years to see if it is growing on a consistent basis.

Reviewing a company's price-to-earnings (P/E) ratio is also an integral part of the stock selection process. P/E ratio is the stock price divided by the earnings per share, so the result tells you how much you'll be paying for one dollar of the company's earnings. Since stock prices reflect investor demand, this ratio tells you the price investors are currently willing to pay in proportion to the company's earnings. A P/E ratio of 20 means investors are willing to pay twenty times more for a stock than the stock's earnings per share. More important, though, is the relationship of one stock's P/E ratio to others in the same class. In most instances, you can find a company's P/E ratio, and those of its peers, in the newspaper or online.

FACT

To be entitled to dividends, you must actually own the shares on the record date, which is the day the Board of Directors declares a dividend. Compare the current dividend with the dividends paid over the past five years. Shrinking dividends may indicate plans for expansion; when a company's primary goal is growth, dividends may be small or nonexistent.

When investigating a particular stock, compare its P/E ratio with that of other companies in the same industry. Since every industry has its own unique qualities, you want to find out what the average P/E is for that sector. If a company has an exceptionally low P/E compared to others in its industry, find out why. For example, the company's growth could be stagnant or it could be burdened with excessive debt. Alternately, it could simply be undervalued—making it a great buy for value investors.

Book Value and Price Volatility

A company's book value per share is calculated by subtracting its liabilities from its assets, then dividing the result by the number of shares outstanding. Essentially, book value (which is also known as accounting value) shows the company's net worth. This can help you figure out whether the share price (the market value) makes sense compared with the company's actual intrinsic value. Many experts say that a good way to find value stocks is to look for companies whose stock price is less than double their book value.

Price volatility refers to how much the share price varies, usually calculated by looking at the difference between a stock's high and low prices over a set time period. This factor is important in determining the risk of an investment. You might not be as willing to pay a lot for a stock if you knew that its price had jumped up and down dramatically over the past few months. In stocks, the term that describes price volatility is *beta,* a quantitative measure of the variability when compared with the market as a whole. In most analysis, beta compares the changes in a stock's price against the S&P 500 stock index. For example, a stock with a beta of 2 moves twice as much as the S&P 500. That stock can be expected to rise in price by 40 percent if the S&P 500 rises by 20 percent or drop by 40 percent if the S&P 500 falls by 20 percent.

Dividends and Shares Outstanding

Dividends are payments to shareholders that are not based on the stock price but are made simply because the company has reaped healthy profits and chooses to reward shareholders. Depending on the company's profits, the board of directors will decide whether and how often to pay a dividend to shareholders. Dividends are usually most important to investors looking for income, and stocks that pay dividends are thus known as income stocks. Many companies pay dividends on a quarterly basis, and special one-time dividends may also be paid under certain circumstances.

The term *shares outstanding* refers to the number of shares a company has issued to the general public, including its employees. It's a good idea to start your investing career by looking at companies with at least 5 million shares outstanding. This indicates that the stock is heavily traded, which means there will be a ready market for it should you decide to sell your shares. At the same time, more shares outstanding can mean smaller dividends per shareholder (there's only so much money to go around, after all), so keep that in mind when you're looking for steady income.

Total Return

Most investors in stocks tend to think about their gains and losses in terms of price changes, not dividends, whereas those who own bonds pay attention to interest yields and seldom focus on price changes. Both approaches are incomplete. Although dividend yields may be more important if you are seeking income, and price changes take center stage for growth stocks, the total return on any stock investment is extremely important. Knowing a stock's total return makes it possible for you to compare your stock investments with other types of investments, such as corporate or municipal bonds, treasuries, mutual funds, and unit investment trusts.

To calculate total returns, add the stock's price change (or subtract it if the price has gone down) and dividends for the past twelve months and then divide by the price at the beginning of the twelve-month period. For example, suppose you buy a stock at $45 per share and receive $1.50 in dividends for the next twelve-month period. At the end of the period, the stock is selling for $48 per share. Your calculations would look like this:

Dividend: $1.50
Price change: up $3.00 per share
$1.50 + $3.00 per share = $4.50
$4.50 divided by $45.00 = .10

Your total return is a 10 percent increase.

But suppose, instead, that the price had dropped to $44 per share by the end of the period. Then your calculation would look like this:

Dividend: $1.50
Price change: down $1.00 per share
$1.50 – $1.00 per share = $0.50
$0.50 divided by $45.00 = .011

Your total return is only a 1.1 percent increase.

Avoid the Herd Mentality

When people first start investing, they often believe they'll make their investment decisions based purely on facts and research, but they end up letting their emotions run the show. This can lead to investments that don't fit into the investor's plans and portfolios. For example, it's very tempting to follow the herd and buy what everyone else is buying. But when a bubble bursts, like the tech bubble did at the end of the 1990s, investors learn the hard way not to invest just because everyone else is doing it.

ALERT

You can't outperform the market if you buy the market. Bernard Baruch, an economic advisor to Woodrow Wilson and Franklin Roosevelt, was a firm believer in this principal of market investing, saying repeatedly, "Never follow the crowd." If you buy with the crowd, you will achieve the same results as everyone else, good or bad.

Following the crowd is a major part of behavioral finance, a relatively new analysis approach that many investment professionals now use as part of their overall strategies. Traditional market analysis is founded on the idea that investors behave rationally and make their decisions only after carefully considering all available information. Behavioral finance adds a more human component by combining basic psychology with investing.

It turns out that many individual investors often act irrationally when it comes to making their buy and sell decisions—for example, they might trade based on the popularity of a stock rather than its value or growth potential. This emotional trading usually leads to losses, yet these investors continue to make the same types of investment decisions. In the relatively new field of behavioral finance, these poor decision-making strategies are examined and linked to market irregularities like crashes and bubbles.

Here's how behavioral finance tends to work. People jump to buy a stock because it's hot. That drives up the price, and more investors snap up shares. It makes no difference that the company has an unproven track record or is loaded with debt—all that matters in the heat of the trading moment is the excitement of owning this very popular stock. The number of investors who jump on that bandwagon alters the patterns and directions of the stock market—and not necessarily for the better.

Corporate websites are an invaluable source of information in helping you make your investment decisions. In a study of individual investors, 74 percent said they visit a company's website before investing in a company and 53.6 percent visit often before making a final decision to invest.

The irony is that while many investors have no problem plowing their hard-earned money into portfolios stuffed with complicated creatures like biotech or nanotechnology stocks, these very same investors pause when given the opportunity to invest in a classic alternative investment like a hedge fund or a real estate trust.

Know When to Sell

Knowing when to hold and when to sell a particular stock is an art in itself. You may have every intention of sticking with your investments for the long haul, but the first sign of turbulence sends you into a panic to sell. History has revealed that holding onto solid stocks for a minimum of five to ten years has produced the best results. Therefore, buying good companies and holding them for the long term is a sound strategy for most investors.

When you decided to buy your stock, you thoroughly researched its balance sheet, income statement, and ratio analyses. The same holds true when you're thinking of selling a stock. Before you jump on a sell bandwagon because of something you see on the news or hear at the water cooler, reevaluate your holdings carefully. If the share value is still growing, selling too soon can mean you will miss out on additional profits. At the same time, though, you don't want to hold on to a losing stock. Selling at the wrong time can easily destroy your investing plan, so don't do it on impulse. And don't worry about losing your shirt; there's a simple way to make sure that doesn't happen.

QUESTION

Whose advice should I avoid when it comes to choosing investments?
No one's! Always get as many opinions as you can about which companies to invest in. There is something to be learned even from bad advice. Consult coworkers, friends, family, and any other resources available. Once you can discern between good and bad guidance, you'll be better equipped to make an informed decision and the choice that's best for you.

The primary way to lock in your profits and limit your losses is with a standing stop-loss order. A stop-loss order is a specialized instruction to your broker that tells him to sell a stock when its price has declined by a certain percentage. A stop-loss can be placed based on the original buy price, or it can move with the stock price (called a trailing stop). Here's how it works: Suppose you buy a stock for $10 per share. You want to limit your losses to 10 percent. You would place a stop order for $9 per share, which means that if the share price fell to $9, your broker would automatically sell the stock.

With a trailing stop, the sell price increases proportionally when the stock price goes up, helping you both limit losses and lock in already earned profits. Suppose you bought that same $10 stock, and you want a 10 percent loss limit. When the stock goes up to $15.00, your trailing stop increases to $13.50, 10 percent less than the new share price.

Look Back at Your Profile

Understanding yourself is an integral component to mapping out an investment plan. What's right for you might be disastrous for another investor. Knowing your long-term goals and determining how much risk you can tolerate is critical when dealing with stocks because of their inherent volatility. Look back at your investor profile and let it guide you.

If you find at any point after you've invested that you simply cannot handle the market's mood swings, you may want to re-evaluate your strategy. Your investment plan is not set in stone, but you should be fully aware of your reasons for changing your original strategy. Maintaining realistic expectations will keep beginning investors from growing frustrated, disappointed, and disillusioned. It's unrealistic to expect a 15 percent return on your investment if you aren't willing to take any risks. Understanding market volatility and your reactions to it can help you create the best portfolio.

ESSENTIAL

A good way to gradually enter the world of investing is through paper trading. Before you commit actual cash to an investment, test out your skills by buying and selling stocks on paper only. This gives you a feel for what it's like to invest and allows you to gauge your tolerance for risk and market fluctuations.

Once you have developed a strategy you're comfortable with, don't second-guess yourself. Stick with the plan until it makes sense to reassess; don't let herd movements derail your strategy. No matter what your investing style, you have a good shot at success if you invest in high-quality companies you believe will—among other things—continue a track record of good financial execution and financial management.

CHAPTER 6

How to Buy and Track Stocks

Now that you've learned the basics, studied the different types of stocks out there, and done your homework on companies you might want to invest in, it's time to take the next step and put some of your hard-earned dollars to work. You've got the fundamentals down, and you're prepared to enter the world of stock trading. Whether you make your entrance on your own or with the help of a broker, this chapter provides you with the necessary information to elevate you from student to player.

Executing Stock Trades

As an individual investor in the stock market, your first concern is how to go about executing a stock trade; fortunately, it's usually as simple as picking up the phone or clicking the mouse. For example, if you trade through a broker, you can simply call and place an order for 100 shares of IBM. Almost immediately, you'll get confirmation that your order has been filled and that you now own stock in IBM. When you make your own online trades, you simply follow the point-and-click instructions on the brokerage website to execute your trade, and a confirmation should follow almost immediately.

ALERT

Get an idea of the fifty-two-week highs and lows of the stocks you're looking to purchase and use this to set target prices for when to sell. As the stock approaches the target price you can start selling off shares, and then gauge to what degree you believe it might pass the target. Don't use the target as an absolute figure but as a barometer.

Of course, things can get a little more complicated, as there are several different types of stock orders. Your options include: a market order (like the IBM example), a limit order, a stop/limit order, or a stop/loss order. You can also determine the length of time your order is in effect, so that it is good for the specific day it is placed, another specific time period (like a week or a month), or good til canceled (GTC).

Market Order

When you want to buy or sell a stock at the current market price, you place a market order. This means you want to buy or sell a stock at whatever price the stock is trading for when your order reaches the floor. In other words, you're buying or selling a given stock at the going rate. Depending on whether you're buying or selling, the market price may differ. The broker's terms for these prices are the bid (buy) or ask (sell), and the difference between these two prices is known as the spread.

For example, IBM's bid price may be $114.25 (usually notated as 65¼), while its asking price is $114.50 (or 65½). In this case, the spread is one quarter.

Unlike IBM, securities that are thinly (infrequently) traded often have bigger spreads. Dealers in a security generally keep a large part of the spread in exchange for playing the role of middleman. Like all middle-men, dealers are in the business of selling goods at a higher price than what they initially paid. Stock prices, especially in heavily traded stock, can change in just seconds. By the time your order is filled with a market order, you might find a slight difference in the price that you were quoted.

Limit Order

Limit orders are placed if you don't want to purchase stock for more or sell a stock for less than a predetermined price. A limit order, like other types of orders, can be placed as a day order or as a GTC order. Your limit order may not fill with either one of these two options; however, you have a greater chance of your order being filled with a GTC order since it can remain open for a longer period of time.

Limit Order Buy

If you want to buy a stock for a specified price, you can place a limit order. Let's say Amazon.com is currently trading at $75. You want to buy 100 shares of Amazon, but only if it dips to $70. In this case, you place a limit order for 100 shares of Amazon at $70 per share. The order may fill for $70 per share if the price dips to that level. If it does not, your order will remain unfilled. Your order to buy stock may also be filled for less than $70 per share if the stock hits $70 and continues to fall. In that case, your order would fill at the first available price under $70 (since price movement can move more quickly than trades can be settled). However, your order will not fill for more than $70.

Limit Order Sell

If you own Amazon.com, you might want to sell the stock if it dips to $65 per share. If so, you would place a limit order to sell. In this case, your order will fill for at least $65 per share. Your order to sell the stock may be filled for more than $65 per share if the stock hits $65 and continues to rise. In this circumstance, your stock would be sold at the first opportunity at $65 or higher; again, stock prices move faster than sell orders. However, your order will not fill for less than $65 per share.

Stop Order

Stop orders (also called stop loss orders) are crucial for investors who are concerned about a stock's price falling too low. Using either a fixed dollar amount or a percentage, the investor sets a stop point; that is, a price at which the stock is automatically put up for sale. This is a good way to help lock in profits or prevent excessive losses, and it also takes the emotion out of making critical trading decisions. With a stop order, once your stock reaches your stop point, it becomes a market order.

ESSENTIAL

Company size, or market capitalization, is an important consideration when making an investment. Remember: To determine a company's market capitalization, multiply the number of outstanding shares of stock by the price per share. If a company's stock is trading for $25 per share and there are 10 million shares outstanding, the company's market capitalization is $250 million. Many blue-chip companies have market capitalization in the billions.

Stop Order Buy

You can also place a stop order to buy. Let's say Intel is currently selling at $19 per share. If the price climbs to $22, you want to buy because you think the price will continue to rise. Therefore, you put in a stop order to buy at $22. Once Intel hits $22 per share, your stop order automatically becomes a market order. Your order might be filled at your stop point of $22. However, since the stop order becomes a market order at your set stop point, you might also end up paying more or less for the stock. The price might rise to $22.50, for instance, before your order is filled. Conversely, the stock might hit $22 and then drop; you might end up buying it for $21.50.

Stop Order Sell

Let's say you bought that Intel stock at $22 per share. You can now place a stop order to sell if the stock price drops to $20. Once the stock hits your set stop point, your stop order to sell becomes a market order. Again, that means your order might end up being filled at a higher or lower price, depending on the market price at the time your order is filled.

Dividend Reinvestment Plans (DRIPs)

Dividend reinvestment plans offer shareholders a simple and inexpensive way to purchase stock directly through a company, without having to pay commissions. This type of investment plan does not require the services of a broker. Such plans enable investors to purchase small amounts of common stock right from the corporation itself—in many cases, as little as $25 worth of stock at a time. Depending on the company, there may be a small fee for handling your account. In most cases, you will have to already own at least one share of the stock (purchased through a broker) to be eligible to participate in the DRIP. And, as the name implies, this plan only works for stocks that pay regular dividends, which must be reinvested in the stock.

ESSENTIAL

Reinvesting dividends is kind of like compounding interest—you end up earning more money on your earnings. Here, dividends buy you extra shares (instead of being paid out to you in cash), and those shares earn more dividends. Dividends often aren't enough to buy full shares of stock. For example, if the stock is selling for $100 per share and your dividend payout was $25, the DRIP program would buy you one-quarter share of the stock.

Close to 1,000 companies, most of them blue-chips, have dividend reinvestment plans. If you are involved in ten different dividend reinvestment plans with ten different companies, you will get ten different statements. Dividend reinvestment plans may be a good choice for long-term investors who want to continue to buy shares of a certain stock on an ongoing basis. You can probably find a listing of companies that offer dividend reinvestment plans at your local library or on the Internet, or you can call a company directly to find out if they offer this service.

Keep in mind that, as with all dividend earnings, there will be a tax bill at the end of the year. Even though you don't actually receive any money (since your dividends are used to get you more stock), you will have to pay taxes on any dividends you earned. Along those lines, it's critical that you keep very good records of your DRIP account. When the time comes for you to sell shares, you'll need to know exactly how much money you've paid for them, including your reinvested dividends. That way you will be able to accurately calculate the capital gain (or loss) at the time of the sale.

Seeking Out Bargain Stocks

If you're like the average American consumer, you're on the lookout for a great bargain. You might clip coupons and watch for sales in your pursuit of a great deal on clothing, food, and cars. But the stock market works differently than other markets. Here, buying a stock simply because it's cheap (in terms of absolute dollars) is a terrible idea. The real deals are in stocks that are undervalued or underpriced (as in the case of growth stocks on the upswing that still have a fair way to climb), regardless of the actual stock price.

FACT

The average per-share price of the top-performing stocks of the last forty-five years was $28 per share before they took off and doubled or tripled (or more!). Though the actual per-share cost seems high, the earnings and growth potential make these top performers worth considering for your portfolio.

Lots of factors affect stock price, but the one that seems to impact price the most is earnings per share. Some other factors that contribute to stock price include public opinion of the company's product or service, its debt, its operating budget, and management changes. But company-related factors aren't the only ones that impact stock price. Overall market movement, the strength of the economy, and the prevailing political climate all have an effect. Sometimes, it's better to own just a few shares of a high-priced stock with strong growth prospects than a lot of shares of a cheaper stock with a dim outlook; that higher-priced stock may actually be the bargain. It may seem tempting to go for low-priced stocks; just remember that you get what you pay for.

Know Your Stock Symbols

Stock or ticker symbols are the abbreviations used to represent a stock or mutual fund. They are a necessary way to keep track of and find information about a security. Whenever you use a quoting service, you will be asked to type in the ticker symbol. Not all symbols correlate logically with the name of the company they represent. For example, the stock symbol for Internet America, Inc., is GEEK.OB. It's important that you learn the correct symbol for each company you invest in and each company you're researching for potential investment.

ESSENTIAL

Cedar Fair, L.P. is a publicly traded company with the seemingly unlikely stock symbol FUN. But the symbol is more appropriate than you'd think. Cedar Fair owns eleven amusement parks around the United States. You may have been to Dorney Park and Wildwater Kingdom (Pennsylvania), Kings Dominion (Virginia), or Knott's Berry Farm (California), all of which are owned and operated by Cedar Fair. No wonder their symbol is FUN!

The NYSE uses stock symbols of up to three letters for their listed companies. Companies listed on the NASDAQ exchange use four letters if the stock issued is common stock. Otherwise, they use five letters. The fifth letter has meaning. The table on the following page lists the fifth letter codes:

Code	Meaning	Code	Meaning
A	Class A	N	3rd Class Preferred Shares
B	Class B	O	2nd Class Preferred Shares
C	Issuer Qualifications Exceptions	P	1st Class Preferred Shares
D	New Issue	Q	Bankruptcy Proceedings
E	Delinquent in Filings with the SEC	R	Rights
F	Foreign	S	Shares of Beneficial Interest
G	First Convertible Bond	T	With warrants or with rights
H	2nd Convertible Bond	U	Units
I	3rd Convertible Bond	V	When issued and when distributed
J	Voting	W	Warrants
K	Nonvoting	X	Mutual Fund
L	Miscellaneous situations	Y	American Depository Receipt (ADR)
M	4th Class Preferred Shares	Z	Miscellaneous situations

Tracking Your Investments

Stock tables offer critical current information about stock prices. In order to monitor your stock investments accurately, it is vital that you become adept in understanding stock tables. Stock table information may vary slightly among different publications and websites, but the basic information is generally presented in a similar manner, with the stocks listed alphabetically.

There are a few things you should know about stock tables. For one, the date on a stock table is the date on which the trading activities occurred, not necessarily the date on which the information was published. Additionally, you will need to learn some stock table terminology, including the following:

- **High-low.** This is usually the first column in a stock table. It shows the highest and lowest prices for which the stock was traded over the past fifty-two weeks.
- **Company symbol.** This column lists the ticker symbol (the abbreviated name) of the corporation that issued the stock.
- **Dividends.** This column includes the dividends the corporation pays to its shareholders.
- **Volume (abbreviated VOL).** This column tells you how many shares were traded that day, in multiples of 100.

- **Yield (abbreviated YLD).** This column estimates the dividend yield, which is calculated by dividing the dividend (as listed in the Dividends column) by the closing price (as listed in the Close column).
- **Price-to-earnings (P/E) ratio.** This column shows you the P/E ratio, which is calculated by dividing the share price by the corporation's earnings per share.
- **Close.** This column indicates the last price at which the stock was traded during the day.
- **Net Change (abbreviated Net Chg).** This column records the difference between the previous day's closing price and the current day's closing price, measured in dollars.

Working with a Stockbroker

As an investor, you have multiple options for choosing a stockbroker. Before you make your selection, you need to evaluate your needs, comfort level, personal commitment, and available time for research, as well as your desire to be personally involved in your investment portfolio. Also be sure you are aware of any fees associated with your choice.

Discount Brokers

If you are ready, willing, and able to investigate potential companies on your own, then a discount broker may fit the bill. Many individuals find that taking charge of their investments is an empowering experience. Once they become acquainted with all of the available information, many investors feel like they are in the best position to handle their own investments, and are happy to be in the driver's seat.

Commissions charged by brokerage houses were deregulated in 1975, and this decision was truly the beginning of the ascent of the discount broker. Trades could be conducted for far less money than investors were used to paying at full-service brokerage firms like Smith Barney and Morgan Stanley. Discount brokers are now offering more services than ever before. Combine that with today's new and faster technology, and investors have all of the investment information they need right at their disposal.

With the explosive development of the Internet, the opportunity for self-education is virtually limitless. Beginning investors now have access to many of the same resources as full-service brokers. With this access to data, the demand for full-service brokers is diminishing. A little enthusiasm and determination on your part can pay off. With the wealth of online information, you can stay informed on everything from a company's new introduction to the ten most highly traded stocks on any given day.

ESSENTIAL

Ameritrade and other online brokers are available only on the Internet; there is no option to walk into a traditional broker's office and talk with someone face-to-face. Online brokers are expanding the range of services they offer over the Internet and are starting to catch up with full-service brokers in areas like float allocation and research distribution.

Some of the best Internet sites were created by financial institutions, and investors have access to everything with just the click of a mouse—from real-time quotes to analyst reports to stock market basics. You can even communicate with other investors, who may offer you some great investment ideas. The proliferation of online discount brokers has made it possible to trade around the clock for a nominal fee. In some cases, you can make trades for under $10. Trading online is ideal if you have done your homework and know exactly which stock you want to own.

Full-Service Brokers

If you want someone else to do most of the legwork, you might opt for a full-service broker. Of course, full-service brokers charge a premium for their input. There is no guarantee that a full-service broker will steer you in the direction of massive capital gains. It is also true that many such brokers tend to pay more attention to their large accounts (clients investing more than $250,000, for example) than the smaller ones.

Some experts believe that if you have investments totaling more than $100,000, you may want to explore the possibility of using a full-service broker. Find a broker who both shares your basic investment philosophy and gives you several investment options to choose from. Choose a broker with a minimum of five years of investment experience. You want someone who has traded in both bull and bear markets.

ALERT

If you want to work with a full-service broker, get a reference from someone you know and trust. Be on the lookout for brokers who engage in churning, a term for trades conducted purely to generate commissions. Churning is especially beneficial to brokers who work on commission—the more trades they make, the more pay they take home.

It's perfectly acceptable (and advisable) to interview potential brokers. Ask how long they have been in this business and about their formal education, their investment philosophy, and what sources they use to get the majority of their information. You may want to find out which investment publications they read regularly and which they find most helpful and why. Find out if they rely only on their brokerage firm's reports when making stock recommendations. You can also ask more pointed questions, like how their clients fared during the recent bear market, or what strategies they use to protect their clients from downturns. Also make sure the broker provides you with a written list of up-front fees you'll be charged, along with an explanation of when charges will be incurred. If the broker gives you the runaround or refuses to answer your questions, find someone else to work with.

Monitoring the Brokers

Becoming acquainted with the broker fee structure is crucial. In many cases, you may be charged for services you didn't know you were getting—and wouldn't use even if you knew you could. You also want to inquire about the fees associated with opening, maintaining, and closing an account; getting checks; participating in investment profiles; buying and selling securities; and attending various seminars. To circumvent potential discrepancies, it's important that you obtain this information in writing and in advance—and not after the fact.

The Financial Industry Regulatory Authority can answer your questions about the practices of a particular broker by looking up his past record regarding any disciplinary actions taken or complaints that have been registered against him. They can also confirm whether the broker is licensed to conduct business in your state.

FACT

> FINRA was created in July 2007 when the National Association of Securities Dealers (NASD) merged with the regulation committee of the NYSE. Before that, NASD took the lead with consumer-broker issues. The NASD also had primary responsibility for the running of the NASDAQ exchange and other over-the-counter markets, as well as administering licensing exams for financial professionals.

In addition to being the primary nongovernmental agency dedicated to protecting the investing public, FINRA also regulates every securities firm that operates in the United States—more than 5,000 firms. To get the job done, FINRA employs about 3,000 professionals throughout the United States, with its main offices in New York City and Washington, D.C.

Financial Planners

Another stock trading option is to hire a professional financial planner. These people go beyond handling just your investments—they can aid you in matters relating to insurance, taxes, trusts, and real estate. The cost of doing business with a financial planner can vary considerably. If you opt for a financial planner, it may be better to pay a set fee rather than commissions. If the planner works on commission alone, it may be in her best interest to encourage heavy trading. While some planners charge a flat hourly rate, others may charge a fee that is based on your total assets and trading activity. In this type of arrangement, you are responsible for paying the financial planner even if you do not follow any of her suggestions. Other planners operate with a combination of fee-based charges and commission. Here, you may pay less per trade, but you are also responsible for paying additional fees.

Working with an Investment Club

When a group of people get together, pool their money, and use it to make investments, you've got an investment club. Technically speaking, investment clubs are usually set up as partnerships. Each member plays his part by studying a specific investment (or two), then presenting his findings to the group. Then, the group votes to decide which investments to buy and which to sell. Generally, each club member actively participates in investment decisions. Club meetings are often fun as well as educational.

QUESTION

Does BetterInvesting host any events?
The group's many chapters hold a variety of learning events for members. The events include investors' fairs to give groups the opportunity to see presentations from corporations like Home Depot, General Electric, and Intel. Visit *www.betterinvesting.org* to see a schedule of events.

For more than fifty years, the National Association of Investors Corporation (NAIC)—which is now called BetterInvesting—has been helping investment clubs get up and running, and their efforts have certainly paid off. Due to the growing popularity of investing over the past several years, the organization has witnessed a dramatic increase in its membership. The Madison Heights, Michigan, not-for-profit organization provides members of the BetterInvesting community with an information-packed brochure called *How to Start an Investment Club* and the robust online 'Getting Started' curriculum. The organization's monthly magazine, *Better Investing,* covers a wide array of investment-related topics. In addition, members have access to sample agreements and brochures. There is a nominal annual fee per club to join, plus a fee for each club member.

Clubs normally meet about once a month, and members can include your neighbors, coworkers, friends, and relatives. Members should share similar investment philosophies. Recent NAIC statistics reveal that 67 percent of its members are women.

Some of the most successful clubs witness the best results when members develop a cohesive investment strategy and stick with it. In most instances, a long-term strategy of buying and holding stocks is the best approach. Such an undertaking is a great way for new investors to get acquainted with basic investing techniques and for experienced investors to sharpen their skills. Members can share ideas and learn from each other's mistakes.

Investment clubs tend to invest in individual stocks. It is suggested that members invest a set amount on an ongoing basis, reinvest dividends along with capital gains, and invest in a variety of different types of growth stocks. Such clubs make good use of dollar-cost averaging, investing a predetermined sum of money on an ongoing basis as opposed to making an investment in one lump sum. When a stock's price goes down, each investor gets more shares for his fixed investment amount. Conversely, the investor receives fewer shares for that fixed amount when the stock's price increases.

CHAPTER 7

Bond Basics

Bonds are like the geeky cousins of the hip and trendy stocks you've already learned about. However, bonds are part of a completely different asset class. Like the stock market, the bond market is heavily influenced by global economic and political trends—but to a much higher degree. In fact, the world bond market is considerably larger and more influential than the stock market, and much of the world economy depends on international bond trading.

What Are Bonds?

Bonds are marketable securities that represent a loan to a company, a municipality, the federal government, or a foreign government with the expectation that the loan will be paid back at a set date in the future. Like almost all loans, bonds also come with an interest component, which can involve periodic payments over the life of the bond or single payments at maturity. Bonds can be bought directly as new issues from the government, from a municipality, or from a company. They can also be bought from bond traders, brokers, or dealers on the secondary market. The bond market dictates how easily you can buy or sell a bond, and at what price.

A big part of the bond picture is interest: for lending them the money, the borrower (or issuer of the bond) agrees to pay the buyer a specific rate of interest at predetermined intervals. Bonds are sold in discrete increments (typically multiples of $1,000, with few exceptions), known as their par value or face value. Their maturities range from short-term (up to five years) to intermediate-term (generally seven to ten years) to long-term (usually around twenty to thirty years). Longer-term bonds typically will pay higher interest rates—averaging higher than 6 percent over the last fifty years—than short-term bonds. Though the bond's stated interest rate is a known factor, over the time its yield (or effective interest rate) will fluctuate along with changes in prevailing interest rates; this matters primarily if you are trying to sell a bond.

ESSENTIAL

Because bond values often move in the opposite direction of the stock market, bonds can be a key component in both the risk-reducing diversification and asset allocation strategies essential for good portfolio management. While bonds typically don't function as a complete substitute for stocks, they do make a strong complement, in addition to providing steady interest income to investors.

A bond will have a date of final maturity, which is the date at which the bond will return your principal, or initial investment. Some types of bonds—known as callable bonds—can be redeemed by the issuer earlier than that maturity date, which means that the lender pays you back sooner than expected. A $5,000 bond is worth $5,000 upon maturity (regardless of the price that bond would fetch on the open market), as long as the issuer does not default on the payment. The interest you receive while holding the bond is your perk, so to speak, for lending the money. Interest is usually paid semiannually or annually, and it compounds at different rates.

Bonds versus Stocks

Unlike a stockholder, a bondholder does not take part in the success or failure of the company. Shares of stock will rise and fall in conjunction with the company's fortunes. In the case of bonds, you will receive interest on your loan and get your principal back at the date of maturity regardless of how well a company fares—unless, of course, they go bankrupt. Bonds are therefore referred to as fixed-income investments because you know how much you will earn—unless you sell before maturity, in which case the market determines the price.

Corporate bond prices, like stock prices, can be affected by corporate earnings. However, they are often affected to a much stronger degree by fluctuations in interest rates. This is true even though the bond market itself often takes the lead in setting those rates. And both types of securities are subject to influences like terrorism, politics, and fraud.

ALERT

When you're considering a bond for your portfolio, remember to analyze these seven key features: price, stated interest rate, current yield, maturity, redemption features, credit rating, and income tax impact. Together, these factors can help you decide whether this bond fits into your portfolio and meshes with your personal investment goals.

Bond Risks

As a general rule, bonds, particularly U.S. government bonds, are considered less risky than stocks and are therefore considered a more conservative investment. Bonds also tend to provide a higher rate of interest than you can get from a bank account or CD, and this, along with a steady flow of interest income, usually makes them attractive, relatively safe investments.

There are drawbacks and risks inherent to bonds, which will also be discussed in more detail later in this chapter. The most basic risk is that an issuer may default, meaning you will not get your money back. You can also lose money in bonds if you are forced to sell when interest rates are high. And you may not see the type of high returns from bond investments that you can realize from more risky equity mutual funds or from a hot stock.

Bonds Fit in Every Portfolio

Adding some bonds or bond mutual funds to your investment portfolio is a good idea, especially if you have a lower tolerance for risk. For investors of every kind, bonds offer a wide variety of benefits.

Bonds can help stabilize a portfolio by offsetting the investor's exposure to the volatility of the stock market. Bonds inherently have a different risk and return character than stocks, so they will necessarily behave differently when the markets move. Also, bonds generally provide a scheduled stream of interest payments (except zero-coupon bonds, which pay their interest at maturity). This attractive feature helps investors meet expected current income needs or specific future expenditures such as college tuition or retirement income. Callable bonds and pass-through securities have less predictability, but investors are compensated for the uncertainty in the form of higher yields.

ALERT

You'll find dozens of bond investment calculators on the Internet, mainly offered by online brokers (and even some mutual fund companies). These calculators are easy to use—just plug in the variables— and can help you decide whether a bond will benefit your tax situation. This is a far superior option to guessing whether a bond is right for you and doing the math in your head.

Unlike stocks, bonds are designed to return the original investment, or principal, to the investor at a future maturity date. This preservation of capital provides stability to a portfolio and balances the growth/risk aspect of stocks. You can still lose your principal investment if you sell your bonds before maturity at a price lower than your purchase price, or if the borrower defaults on payment. By choosing high-credit-quality bonds, you can limit your exposure to default risk.

Another noteworthy advantage: certain bonds provide unique tax benefits. For example, you won't be paying any state or local income tax on interest you've earned on your U.S. Treasury bonds. Likewise, the interest on your municipal bonds (usually) won't be subject to a federal income tax bite, and in some cases, they'll also be free of state or local income taxes, too. A good broker or tax advisor can help you determine which bonds are best for you.

The Risks Unique to Bonds

As is the case with all investments, there is some degree of risk involved in bond investing. There are several types of risks that pertain specifically to bonds. Here are three of the most significant risks and how they affect the bond market.

ESSENTIAL

Other less common risks in bond investments include call risk, which means the issuer can buy you out of your investment before maturity. That can happen when rates drop and they want to call in high interest bonds so they can issue new ones at the new lower rate. But risks like these are less common, especially in a period of stable or rising interest rates.

Credit Risk

This is the risk of default by the company issuing the bond, resulting in the loss of your principal investment. This is why bonds are rated, just like people looking for credit. Government bonds—at least in theory— don't have this risk and therefore need not be graded; they are simply safe investments. As a potential investor, you need to compare the risk and the yield, or return, you will get from different grades of bonds. If, for example, you will do almost as well with a high-grade tax-exempt municipal bond than you will do with a lower-grade taxable corporate bond, take the safer route and buy the municipal bond. Buying riskier bonds, or lower-grade bonds, is only worthwhile if you will potentially see returns big enough to merit taking that credit risk.

Interest-Rate Risk

If you are holding a bond to maturity, interest-rate risk is not terribly significant, since you will not be particularly affected by changing interest rates. However, if you are selling a bond, you need to concern yourself with the rate of interest that ties in with the yield of the bond. Essentially, the risk is that you will be stuck holding a long-term bond that pays less than the current interest rate, making it hard to sell and reinvest your capital.

ALERT

Buy bonds based on your needs and financial situation. Plan to buy a particular bond and hold it to maturity. Don't be intimidated by a broker who asks, "But what if you need to sell the bond?" Buying just in case you need to sell is defensive buying, and you may regret it in the long run.

The longer the maturity of the bond, the more a change in yield will affect the price. You will better manage interest-rate risk by buying shorter maturities and rolling them over. However, if you are looking for higher returns over a longer period of time, you should go with the longer-term bond and hope you do not have to sell it.

Many financial brokers talk a great deal about the interest fluctuations on bonds. This is because they are in the business of buying and selling them. Many bond owners, however, tuck bonds away for years and enjoy the income generated. Therefore, before worrying greatly about the interest-rate fluctuations making your bond more or less valuable in the secondary market, decide on your plan. Are you buying bonds to sell them or to hold them to maturity? If you consider yourself financially sound and are simply looking to purchase a long-term bond for a future goal, then by all means go with your plan. Since the idea is to hold onto the bond until it matures, you will enjoy the higher yield. Even if you are forced to sell a fifteen-year bond twelve years toward maturity and you take a loss on the price, you will have still enjoyed higher yields than you would have with short-term bonds.

Income Risk

This is a double risk: first that should you sell, you won't get the full value (or par), and second that inflation will surpass the rate of income you are receiving from the bond (known as inflation risk). If you are reinvesting your interest income, you also will see less immediate income. However, you will be building your investments.

The best way to manage income risk is to stagger or ladder your bonds so that you can pick up the higher interest rates along the way. Inflation risk can be combated by simply re-evaluating your asset allocation and possibly moving to an investment that is higher than the inflation rate until it drops. If you already have an income-producing bond paying a rate of 3.9 percent, and inflation has gone up to 4.1 percent, you can reinvest the income in a higher-yield (perhaps slightly riskier) vehicle. An equity fund will more likely beat the inflation rate.

Credit Check: Know the Bond Ratings

Corporate bonds and some municipal bonds are rated by financial analysts at Standard & Poor's (S&P) and Moody's, among others. The ratings indicate the credit worthiness of the bond issuer and are, therefore, a report card of sorts on the company issuing the bond. Analysts look at the track record and financial situation of the company, the rate of income, and the degree of risk associated with the bond. All of this information is put together, and the bonds are graded. This is very similar to a personal credit rating, where people who are more likely to pay their debts in full and on time get higher scores than people who may not pay on time, or at all.

A rating or grade of AAA goes to the highest quality bond. Bonds rated AAA, AA, A, or BBB (Aaa, Aa, A, or Bbb in Moody's system) are considered high-quality. BB or B bonds are more questionable. Anything below B, such as C- or D-level bonds, are considered low-grade or junk bonds. However, if you pick the right rising company, a junk or high-yield bond can be very successful. But the risks are high, especially the default risk.

QUESTION

How do bonds pay interest?
A fixed interest rate is the most common, although interest can be paid at a floating rate, which changes based on economic conditions. Zero-coupon bonds pay no ongoing interest. Rather, they are sold at a deep discount and redeemed at full value, causing them to build up, through compounding interest, to their face value.

If you own corporate bonds that used to be solidly rated but have fallen on hard times, you have two choices: sell or hold. Part of your choice will be based on whether you believe the company will turn itself around and get back in the black; the other side of the decision is more immediately practical. If you don't believe the company will ever be able to pay its debts, get out while you can; if you believe the company will pull through—and maybe even emerge stronger—consider keeping the bonds. When the bond is in your portfolio primarily for income purposes (i.e., regular interest payouts that you count on as income), and that income stream is still flowing, it can make sense to hold on to it. On the other hand, if the bond is used as a hedge against riskier stocks or to give you a big lump of cash down the line, consider selling right away, before the bond price drops so low that you won't recoup a sizeable chunk of your investment.

Bond ratings for an issuer can change over time. A company issuing BBB bonds may become a much more stable fixture as a largely successful company, and their bonds may be A-rated next time they are graded. The opposite can happen as well: Highly rated corporations can fall on hard times and have their debt downgraded, sometimes substantially. It's a good idea to keep tabs on the grades of the bonds you own for the purpose of potential resale, as the grade does affect the bond's marketability.

Bond Yields

When it comes to bond investing, you need to know about the two types of yields: the yield to maturity and the current yield. They absolutely affect how much your bonds are worth on the open market.

One of the most (if not the most) important factors in determining bond yields, and therefore bond prices, is the prevailing interest rate. Essentially, the stated interest rate on your bond will be compared to the current interest rate for equivalent debt instruments. Whether this is higher or lower makes a big difference in the amount for which you could sell that bond.

Current Yield

Current yield is the interest (expressed as a percentage) based on the amount you paid for the bond (rather than on its face value). A $2,000 bond bought at par value (at $2,000) receiving 6 percent interest would earn a current yield of 6 percent. The current yield will differ if you buy the bond at a price that is higher or lower than par. For example, if you bought a $2,000 bond with a rate of 6 percent for $1,800, you have paid less than par and bought the bond at a discount. Your yield would be higher than the straight interest rate: 6.67 percent instead of the stated 6 percent. To calculate that yield, multiply the $2,000 face value by .06 (the stated interest rate), and you get $120 (the annual interest payment). Now divide that by $1,800 (the amount you paid for the bond) to get .0667 or 6.67 percent current yield.

ALERT

Historically, the average return on bonds, particularly on treasury bonds, is very low compared to the return on stocks. But this is not always the case. According to an article entitled "The Death of the Risk Premium: Consequences of the 1990s," by Arnott and Ryan (*The Journal of Portfolio Management*, Spring 2001), stocks could underperform bonds in the decades ahead by about 0.9 percent a year.

Yield to Maturity

Generally considered the more meaningful number, yield to maturity is the total amount earned on the bond from the time you buy it until it reaches maturity (assuming that you hold it to maturity). This includes interest over the life of the bond, plus any gain or loss you may incur based on whether you purchased the bond above or below par, excluding taxes. Taking the term of the bond, the cost at which you purchased it, and the yield into account, your broker will be able to calculate the yield to maturity. (You need a computer to do this; the math is extremely complicated.) Usually this calculation factors in the coupons or interest payments being reinvested at the same rate.

Knowing the yield to maturity makes it easier to compare various bonds. Unlike stocks, which are simply bought at a specific price per share, various factors will come into play when buying a bond, including term of maturity, rate of interest, price you paid for the bond, and so on. The idea here is to determine how well the bond will perform for you.

Importance of Interest Rates to Yield

Interest rates vary based on a number of factors, including the inflation rate, exchange rates, economic conditions, supply and demand of credit, actions of the Federal Reserve, and the activity of the bond market itself. As interest rates move up and down, bond prices adjust in the opposite direction; this causes the yield to fall in line with the new prevailing interest rate. By affecting bond yields via trading, the bond market thus impacts the current market interest rate.

The simplest rule of thumb to remember when dealing in the bond market is that bond prices will react the opposite way to interest rates. Lower interest rates mean higher bond prices, and higher interest rates mean lower bond prices. Here's why: Your bond paying 8 percent is in demand when interest rates drop and other bonds are paying 6 percent. However, when interest rates rise and new bonds are paying 10 percent, suddenly your 8 percent bond will be less valuable and harder to sell.

The Yield Curve

The relationship between short-term and long-term interest rates is depicted by the yield curve, a graph that illustrates the connection between bond yields and time to maturity. The yield curve allows you to compare prices among bonds with differing features (different coupon rates, different maturities, even different credit ratings). Most of the time, the yield curve looks normal (or "steep"), meaning it curves upward—short-term bonds have lower interest rates, and the rate climbs steadily as the time to maturity lengthens. Occasionally, though, the yield curve is flat or inverted. A flat yield curve, where rates are similar across the board, typically signals an impending slowdown in the economy. Short-term rates increase as long-term rates fall, equalizing the two. When short-term rates are higher than long-term rates (which can signal a recession on the horizon), you get an inverted yield curve, the opposite of the normal curve.

How Are Bonds Priced?

If you want to sell a bond or buy one on the bond market, you first need to know the latest in bond prices. For this information you can go online to a financial newspaper such as the *Wall Street Journal* or *Barron's,* or to the financial section of *USA Today* or your local paper. Bond prices do fluctuate, so the price you see quoted may change several times throughout the next business day.

Since there are far too many bonds to list—1.5 million in just the municipal bond market alone—there is no single complete listing. A single listing would not be practical, as many bondholders hang onto their bonds until maturity. Therefore, the listings you will see are benchmarks from which you can determine a fair price. Interest rates impact bond prices in a broad sense. Fixed-income securities, as a rule, will therefore be affected similarly.

In the bond listings you will find key information for treasury, municipal, corporate, and mortgage-backed bonds. The numbers you will see listed may vary in format from paper to paper, but will include the following:

- **Rate 6½ percent:** This is the yield that the bond is paying.
- **Maturity March 2011:** This is the date of final maturity—in this case, March of 2011.

- **Bid 103:12:** This means a buyer is offering a bid of $1,033.75 on a $1,000 bond, or a profit of just over 3 percent to the bondholder who bought the bond at a par value of $1,000. The numbers before the colon represent the percent of par value of the bond (in this case, 103% of $1,000 is $1,030). The numbers after the colon are measured in 32nds of $10 (here, 12/32 gives you $3.75 to add to that $1,030). This math works the same way for both the bid and ask.
- **Ask 104:00:** This is the seller's lowest asking price, in this case $1,040.00.

You might also see an Ask/Yield entry, which gives the bond's yield to maturity based on the asking price. This shows how much the buyer will earn on the investment based on interest rate, and the cost of the bond. A buyer who bought the bond at more than the face value will receive a lower yield-to-maturity value. The opposite is true if the bond was purchased at a discount, which means it was purchased for less than par.

ALERT

While the stock market sees consistent gains for long-term players, its volatility can be too much for some investors. During particularly volatile periods, more investors look to the bond market. Also, as more people reinvest money from plans like 401(k)s and pension plans, bonds become attractive places in which to invest. They offer income as well as greater security than equities.

Bond trading is brisk, so the price you see in the paper is likely to change by the time you make your decision to buy or sell. The price will also be affected by which broker can get you the best price on a particular bond. Don't forget that the dealers set their prices to allow for a spread, their profit on the transaction.

How to Buy and Sell Bonds

Bonds are almost always purchased through brokers and brokerage houses. All the major brokerage houses handle bonds and can get you the best bond rates. They trade bonds that are already on the market and will inform you about new issues. This is true for corporate and municipal bonds as well as certain types of government bonds, such as treasury bonds. Using a bond broker is a big commitment, though, as most demand a minimum $5,000 investment to get you started in the bond market.

If you're more of a do-it-yourself investor, you can buy treasury bonds directly from the U.S. Treasury Department through the aptly named TreasuryDirect service (*www.treasurydirect.gov*). Savings bonds can also be purchased from TreasuryDirect and also through most banking institutions. Savings bonds are inexpensive—you can invest as little as $25. You won't pay any state or local income taxes on the interest, and you can buy them without paying commissions.

CHAPTER 8

Types of Bonds

By now you've likely figured out that diversification is as important to your investment portfolio as the money that you invest in it. You'll continue to learn more about this as you read about the bond market. Stocks and mutual funds provide investors with a wide variety of options to choose from, and the bond market is no different. Bonds offer yet another means to bring diversity into your investment life. It's important that you understand the different types of bonds and their inherent risks and benefits.

Overview of Bond Categories

There are a variety of types of bonds, ranging from government issue to the more speculative and even foreign company and government bonds. They have different risk and investment characteristics, can create different tax situations, and may be used in a variety of ways to hedge stock exposure in a portfolio or to create an income stream for an investor. That's why it's so important to understand the critical role that bonds can play in helping you create wealth.

FACT

> There are five basic types of bonds for investors to choose among: U.S. government securities, mortgage-backed securities, municipal bonds, corporate bonds, and junk bonds (a.k.a. high-yield bonds). Each type has its own benefits and drawbacks, and some will fit into your portfolio better than others.

Investors use bonds for two main purposes: to receive the steady income of periodic interest payments or to protect and build up their capital stores. Bonds are predictable: you know when you're going to get your principal back, and you know when to expect your next interest check. For investors looking for reliable current income, the best choice may be bonds that have fixed interest rates until maturity and that pay interest semiannually.

On the other hand, investors saving for the future may fare better investing in zero-coupon bonds. You won't get regular interest payments with these bonds. Instead, you buy these bonds for a deep discount, a price that's much lower than their par value. Upon maturity, you'll receive one lump payment, representing the purchase price plus earned interest, compounded semiannually at the original interest rate; basically, it's the face value and the years of accumulated interest all rolled into one big payment.

The types of bonds you select to help you balance your portfolio should be based on your long-term investment goals. As you read on, you'll be better able to figure out which are the right bonds for your needs.

U.S. Treasury Securities

If the thought of watching a stock tumble in value makes you queasy, or if you have the need to invest in truly safe cash equivalents, consider U.S. treasury bonds. Uncle Sam's gift to U.S. investors, the treasury market offers a safe haven to battered stock investors looking for short- or long-term relief. Treasuries, as these bonds are known, are predictable and lower yielding on average than stocks, but they are also far more secure. Generally, federal taxes must be paid on the interest, but the interest is free from state and local taxes. Treasuries are also backed by the full faith and credit of the U.S. government.

What makes treasuries so desirable, though, is that they are highly liquid investments and can be sold quickly for cash. These securities are also easier to sell than other bonds because the government bond market is enormous. In fact, the treasury market is the biggest securities market in the world, with an average trading volume greater than $250 billion every day. Treasuries also make good hedges against interest rate fluctuations: Investors who buy them lock in a fixed, annual rate of return that holds firm even if rates change during the life of the bond. Treasuries come in three basic flavors:

- **Treasury bills** (T-bills) are very short-term securities, with maturities ranging from four weeks to up to one year. T-bills come in $100 increments with a minimum $100 purchase and are sold at a discount from face value; the discount represents the interest income on the security.
- **Treasury notes** come with intermediate-term maturities of two, five, and ten years. These notes are sold in $100 increments with a minimum $100 investment. They come with fixed interest rates and pay interest semi-annually.
- **Treasury bonds** are strictly long-term securities, with maturities of thirty years. They can be purchased for as little as $100. These bonds come with fixed coupon rates and pay interest every six months until maturity.

Municipal Bonds

Munis, as they're called, are very popular for their tax-free advantages. States, cities, towns, municipalities, and government entities issue them to build schools, parks, and numerous other important aspects of our communities. In exchange for your willingness to lend money to help with such worthy ventures, you not only receive interest on your loan, but your bond is usually exempt from federal—and often state—taxes. That last part is what catches people's attention, since most other investments have Uncle Sam camped on your doorstep waiting to take a bite.

ALERT

The yields on municipal bonds generally won't pay as much as those on their corporate counterparts. However, when you consider the yield after taxes are paid from corporate bond earnings, the munis often don't look too bad, particularly in states with high taxes. You do need to report tax-exempt interest on tax returns for record-keeping purposes.

Not unlike corporate bonds, many municipal bonds are also rated, and those with the highest ratings rival only the government bonds in their low degree of risk. Companies such as Standard & Poor's, Moody's, and other investment services grade the bonds in the same way they grade corporate bonds. AAA (S&P) or Aaa (Moody's) are the top grades. Look for bonds with a grade of at least BBB or Bbb. As with corporate bonds, the lower the grade, the higher the risk. To ensure safety, you can get your investment secured, or in this case insured, so that you cannot lose your principal and interest due.

Municipal bonds cost $5,000 or a multiple of $5,000. Yields vary, like other bonds, based on the interest rates. Actual prices for traded bonds will be listed in the financial pages. Prices will vary based on the size of the order of bonds traded and the market. Like other bonds, you can sell a muni on the secondary market and, depending on the current rate, receive a higher price than what you paid for the bond. However, if you sell a municipal bond and show a capital gain, the taxman will cometh.

If you are interested in munis, you should get to know the options available to you. Municipal bonds come in a few different types, including the types on the following page:

- **Revenue bonds.** These bonds are usually issued to fund a specific project, such as a bridge, an airport, or a highway. The revenue collected from tolls, charges, or in some manner from the project will be used to pay interest to bond holders.

- **Moral obligation bonds.** This is essentially a revenue bond offered by a state but with a unique twist. These bonds are typically issued when a state may not be able to meet the bond obligation through its normal revenue stream, which includes taxes and licenses. Just in case, the state forms a special reserve fund that can be used to pay the bond obligation, but there's no legal obligation for them to use that reserve fund; just a moral obligation. In most cases, this moral obligation—on which a state has staked its good reputation—can be even more powerful than a legal one.

- **General obligation bonds.** The issuer backs up the interest payments on these bonds by taxation. Known as GOs, these bonds are voter approved, and the principal is backed by the full faith and credit of the issuer.

- **Taxable municipal bonds.** Why would anyone want a taxable muni if nontaxables exist? Simple: They have a higher yield more comparable to corporate bonds, generally without much risk. Such bonds can be issued to help fund an underfunded pension plan for a municipality or to help build a ballpark for the local baseball or football team.

- **Private activity bonds.** If a bond is used for both public and private activities, it is called a private activity bond.

- **Put bonds.** These bonds allow you to redeem the bond at par value on a specific date (or dates) prior to its stated maturity. Put bonds typically come with lower-than-average yields in exchange for this flexibility, but they can make a good strategic purchase for active bond traders who expect a jump in interest rates. When rates rise sufficiently, they can cash in the put bonds (usually at par value) and reinvest in higher-yielding instruments.

- **Floating and variable-rate municipal bonds**. If it appears that the rate of interest will rise, then these are good investments because they will—as the name implies—vary the interest rates accordingly. Naturally, there's a greater interest risk involved with such bonds.

You can usually find prices of municipal bonds being traded in the financial section of a major paper or in a financial publication. Municipal brokers can then give you their own price quotes. The current market price will vary often, so if you want to buy (or sell), you need to stay on top of the current market price.

Zero-Coupon Bonds

Zero-coupon bonds can be issued by companies, government agencies, or municipalities. Known as zeros, these bonds do not pay interest periodically as most bonds do. Instead, they are purchased at a discount and pay a higher rate (both interest and principal) when they reach maturity.

ALERT

Don't buy zeros (or zero-coupon bonds) for liquidity in your portfolio. As for taxes, despite the fact that you do not receive any interest payments, you need to report the amount the bond increases each year.

The interest rate is locked in when you buy the zero-coupon bond at a discount rate. For example, if you wanted to buy a five-year $10,000 zero in a municipal bond, it might cost you $7,500, and in five years you would get the full $10,000. The longer the bond has until it reaches maturity, the deeper the discount will be. Zeros are the best example of compound interest. For example, a twenty-year zero-coupon bond with a face value of $20,000 could be purchased at a discount, for around $7,000. Since the bond is not paying out annual or semiannual dividends, the interest continues to compound, and your initial investment will earn the other $13,000. The interest rate will determine how much you will need to pay to purchase such a bond, but the compounding is what makes the discount so deep.

Corporate Bonds

When you buy shares of stock, you own a piece of a company; when you buy corporate bonds (or corporates, as they're also known), you are lending the company money for a specified amount of time and at a specific rate of interest. While corporate bonds are more risky than government or municipal bonds, long-term corporate bonds have outperformed their government and municipal counterparts over the past fifty years.

Unlike the U.S. government, however, companies can—and do—go bankrupt, which can turn your bond certificates into wallpaper. K-mart, United Airlines, and Enron are all examples of large companies that have declared bankruptcy in recent years. Therefore, the risk of default comes into play with corporate bonds. The rating system, described in Chapter 7, will guide you to the more secure bonds issued by the more stable companies.

Corporates are generally issued in multiples of either $1,000 or $5,000. While your money is put to use for anything from new office facilities to new technology and equipment, you are paid interest annually or semiannually. Corporate bonds pay higher yields at maturity than various other bonds—though the income you receive is taxable at both the federal and state level.

If you plan to hold onto the bond until it reaches maturity and you are receiving a good rate of return for doing so, you should not worry about selling in the secondary market. The only ways in which you will not see your principal returned upon maturity is if the bond is called, has a sinking-fund provision, or the company defaults.

Bond Calls

A call will redeem the bonds before their stated maturity. This usually occurs when the issuer wants to issue a new bond series at a lower interest rate. A bond that can be called will have what is known as a call provision, stating exactly when the issuer can call in their bond if they so choose. A fifteen-year bond might stipulate that it can be called after eight years. Reinvesting in a bond that has been called will usually involve lower rates. Since the call will change the mathematics, your yield to maturity won't be the same.

Sinking-Fund Provision

A sinking-fund provision means that earnings within the company are being used to retire a certain number of bonds annually. The bond provisions will indicate clearly that they have such a feature. Each year enough cash is available, a portion of the bonds will be retired, which are usually chosen by lottery. Whether the bonds you're holding are selected is merely the luck of the draw. Unlike a call provision, you may not see anything above the face value when the issuer retires the bond. On the other hand, since the company uses money to repay debts, these bonds likely won't default, making them a lower-risk investment.

There are a few other reasons why bonds can be called early, and those are written into the bond provisions when you purchase them. As is the case when you buy any investment, you need to read everything carefully when buying bonds. There are numerous possibilities when it comes to bonds and bond provisions. Again, read all bond provisions very carefully before purchasing.

High-Yield Bonds

Known in the financial world by their official name, high-yield bonds, but known to many investors as junk bonds, these bonds can provide a higher rate of return or higher yield than most other bonds. Junk bonds are risky investments, as investors saw in the 1980s debacle involving Ivan Boesky and Michael Milken. These two infamous financiers brought an awareness of junk bonds to the mainstream when their use of this risky debt to finance other endeavors came crashing down. The "junk bond kings" issued debt with nothing backing it up. When it came time to pay up, the money just wasn't there, and investors were left holding worthless pieces of paper—hence the term junk bonds.

High-yield bonds are bonds that didn't make the grade. They are issued by companies that are growing, reorganizing, or are considered at greater risk of defaulting on the bond, for whatever reason. These bonds are often issued when companies are merging and have debts to pay in such a transaction. They are used as a method of financing such acquisitions.

High-yield or junk bonds include a risk of default and a risk that their market value will drop quickly. Since the companies that issue these bonds are not as secure as those issuing high-grade bonds, their stock prices may drop, bringing the market value of the bond down with it. This will mean that trading such a bond will become very difficult, therefore eliminating their liquidity.

Before the 1980s, most junk bonds resulted when investment-grade issuers experienced a decline in credit quality, brought on by big changes in business conditions or when they took on too much financial risk. These issues were known as fallen angels.

Sometimes a company begins by issuing lower-grade high-yield bonds and does well, with their sales numbers going up. Eventually this company reaches a level at which they can issue higher-grade bonds. This means that in the short term, you can receive high yields from their original low-grade bonds. It also means that they will call the bonds as soon as they are able to issue bonds at a lower yield.

If you see a company with great potential that has not yet hit its stride, perhaps you will want to take a shot at a high-yield bond from that company. If you are not that daring, you might opt for a high-yield bond mutual fund, which diversifies your investment so that you are not tossing all your eggs into one high-risk basket. In this manner, if one company defaults you are still invested in others in the fund, some of which may prosper.

Mortgage-Backed Securities

A popular bond category since the 1980s, mortgage-backed securities (MBS) can be a highly profitable, extremely complicated, and highly risky investment option. The key word here, though, is complicated, and the intricacies of some of these securities (particularly the CMO, or collateralized mortgage obligation, variety) make them inappropriate for novice investors. In fact, they were largely implicated in the big financial meltdown of 2008. But the most basic form of these bonds, the MBS, can make a good addition to an income-focused portfolio.

Financial institutions help create mortgage-backed securities by selling part of their residential mortgage portfolios to investors. Investors basically buy a piece of a pool of mortgages. An investor in a mortgage-backed security sees profit from the cash flow (people's mortgage payments) generated from the pool of residential mortgages. As mortgage payments come in, interest and principal payments are made to the investors.

There are several types of mortgage-related securities available today, and one of the most common is the pass-through Ginnie Mae, issued by the Government National Mortgage Association (GNMA), an agency of the federal government. GNMA guarantees that investors will receive timely interest and principal payments. Investors receive potentially high interest payments, consisting of both principal and interest. The rate of principal repayment varies with current interest rates.

How to Choose Bonds for Your Portfolio

One of the keys to successful bond investing is diversification. Holding a range of maturities—a strategy commonly called laddering—helps ensure your portfolio won't take too big a hit when interest rates go wild. Your bond ladder should have an average maturity that meshes with your overall financial plan—and that helps diversify your portfolio as a whole. In addition, holding bonds with different risk characteristics can increase your returns with a margin of safety.

As you're deciding which bonds to buy, there are several more personal issues you'll need to consider. Taxes are first on the list. Some bonds, mainly government bonds, offer some tax advantages that may be very attractive to someone in a higher tax bracket. At the same time, though, holding tax-exempt bonds could cause the alternative minimum tax rules to kick in, increasing your tax bill. Another factor to consider is your inflation situation: If the rest of your income is relatively safe from the negative effects of inflation, you may not have to make risky bond choices to stay ahead.

Generally speaking, most people do best when the bulk of their bond investments are high quality, meaning treasuries, munis, and high-grade corporate bonds. Mixing these three types together is better than focusing on only one. These types of debt securities balance out the risk of the stock portion of your portfolio in a way that junk bonds cannot. And investors looking for big returns may be better off allocating a little more to the stock market than investing in high-risk, high-yield bonds.

CHAPTER 9

The Basics of
Mutual Funds

Though Americans generally get credit for creating the mutual fund, the idea was generated in Europe back in the mid-1800s. When the idea finally hit the States, some Harvard University staffers created the first American pooled fund in 1893. About thirty years later, the first official mutual fund was created. Called the Massachusetts Investors Trust, it was heckled by the investment community at the time. Little did they know how popular mutual funds would become. Currently, trillions of dollars are invested in mutual funds in the United States alone.

What Is a Mutual Fund?

A mutual fund provides an opportunity for a group of investors to work toward a common investment objective more effectively by combining their monies to leverage better results. Mutual funds are managed by financial professionals responsible for investing the money pooled by the fund's investors into specific securities, usually stocks or bonds. By investing in a mutual fund, you become a shareholder in the fund.

ESSENTIAL

Mutual funds can provide a steady flow of income or can be engineered for growth in the short or long term. The success of the fund depends on the sum of its parts, which are the individual stocks or bonds within the fund's portfolio.

Just as carpooling saves money for each member of the pool by decreasing travel costs for everyone, mutual funds decrease transaction costs for individual investors. As part of a group of investors, individuals are able to make investment purchases with much lower trading costs than if they did it on their own. The biggest single advantage to mutual funds, however, is diversification. Diversification, the easy accessibility of funds, and having a skilled professional money manager working to make your investment grow are the three most prominent reasons that funds have become so popular.

The History of Mutual Funds

Currently, the number of mutual funds exceeds 10,000, but as recently as 1991 the number was just over 3,000, and at the end of 1996 it was listed at 6,000. Stock funds are growing as a way to play the market because they don't require the investor to make purchasing and timing decisions.

Bond funds are also growing, partly because of the complexities associated with understanding individual bonds. Bond funds are also a way to hold more bonds than the average investor could afford by buying them on an individual basis. Money market funds offer a safe alternative to bank accounts (though they are not FDIC-insured), and provide higher interest rates.

As late as the early 1950s, fewer than 1 percent of Americans owned mutual funds. The popularity of funds grew marginally in the 1960s, but possibly the largest factor in the growth of the mutual fund was the individual retirement account (IRA). Legal changes made in 1981 let individuals, including people who already participated in corporate pension plans, contribute up to $2,000 a year into a tax-advantaged retirement account, which could be invested in (among other things) mutual funds. Mutual funds are now mainstays in retirement accounts like 401(k)s, IRAs, and Roth IRAs (which you can read more about in Chapter 20).

FACT

The first index funds were offered by Vanguard. And the first one they offered, created by Vanguard founder John Bogle in 1976 and originally called the First Index Investment Trust, is today's Vanguard 500 Index fund. In November 2000, it became the largest mutual fund, holding approximately $100 billion in assets.

By the end of the 1980s, money market mutual funds had become a bit of a cult. They offered decent returns, liquidity, and check-writing privileges. But would-be investors wanted more. Then, with computers and technology making information more readily available, the 1990s ushered in the age of the mutual fund. The Internet allowed financial institutions to provide a great deal more information than they could on television commercials or in print ads. They reached out to everyone, not simply those Wall Streeters who read the financial papers. People saw how easily they could play the market and have their money spread out in various stocks as well as bonds.

Mutual Funds Today

Every financial institution worth its weight in earnings has a wide variety of funds to choose from. In fact, in 2007, 48 percent of U.S. households owned at least one mutual fund. That makes for about 88 million mutual fund shareholders in this country. Among these 51 million households, the median fund investment is $100,000. And worldwide, there's over $26 trillion invested in mutual funds.

Purchasing funds today is as easy as making a phone call or sitting down at your computer. Fund families (large investment firms or brokerage houses with many funds) noted the surge in popularity of electronic trading. To make funds easily accessible to all investors, they created toll-free numbers and websites that make it easy for you to buy and sell mutual funds. Transactions can also be made by the old-fashioned method of snail mail.

ESSENTIAL

Another benefit of mutual funds is their liquidity, allowing you to convert shares to cash. A phone call allows you to sell your shares in the fund at its current net asset value (NAV, or posted rate per share). You should have your money in three or four business days.

Electronic trading has allowed investors to trade at all hours from the comfort of their own homes. It's not hard to find the top ten, twenty, or fifty funds, as rated by some leading financial source, and then buy them online. It is also not hard to get addicted to trading and find yourself overdoing a good thing. The accessibility and ease of trading online and through toll-free numbers has landed many overzealous investors in deep trouble. Many new investors, eager to see quick profits, need to develop the patience and research skills necessary for successful long-term investing.

Diversification

Investing in a mutual fund is less risky than owning a single stock. That's because the fund is managed professionally and is diversified. Mutual funds offer you diversification without making you do all the work. Funds can hold anywhere from a few select stocks to more than 100 stocks, bonds, and money market instruments. While some funds own as few as twenty or twenty-five stocks, others (like the aptly named Schwab 1000) own 1,000 stocks.

This diversity minimizes much of your risk. If you invest everything in a single stock, your investment is at the total mercy of that stock price. If you buy six stocks, you assume less risk, as it is less likely that all six will go down at once. If three go down and three go up, you would be even.

Mutual funds work on the same principle of safety in numbers. Although there are funds with various levels of risk, many mutual funds offer the investor limited risk by balancing higher-risk investments with lower-risk and thus safer investments. Diversity acts to your advantage as it protects you against greater swings in the market, be it the stock or bond market.

Further diversification can also come from buying more than one fund. You can allocate your assets into different types of funds. If you buy into a few funds in different categories, you'll have that much more diversification and that much less technical risk. For example, your portfolio might include the following:

- A more conservative bond fund
- A tech fund to cash in on a hot industry
- A higher-risk international fund
- A low-risk blue-chip fund
- A growth fund

However, keep in mind that it's usually not advisable to have more than six or seven mutual funds at a given time, or you can start to counterbalance your efforts to construct a strong portfolio.

The idea is to balance your portfolio between more and less conservative, or higher- and lower-risk investments. Your needs will guide how you diversify. One investor might have 10 percent in bond funds, 20 percent in growth, 30 percent in tech, and so on, while another has 5 percent in tech and 40 percent in blue-chip. That's why there is no one stock investment strategy that's suitable for all.

It seems odd to need to diversify your mutual funds since the job of the fund is to diversify the stocks, but it's all part of building a solid investment portfolio. Your mutual fund is the sum of many parts. Therefore, you may want another fund in your portfolio. Another significant reason for diversifying your mutual fund investments is to spread your assets out across sectors, industries, and asset classes. A fund manager, no matter how skilled, is limited by the goals and the direction set forth by the fund.

The Importance of Fund Managers

As the rock stars of the financial world, successful managers of the hottest funds appear on financial talk shows. They write books and are the talk of the financial community—that is, until their hot streaks end. In the mutual fund boom of the late 1990s, the successes and failures of fund managers were a phenomenon not only in the financial world but also in the mainstream media, which began to focus its attention on these people who made (or lost) investors so much money.

FACT

Here's an impressive tidbit about mutual funds: Not a single one has gone bankrupt since 1940. This certainly can't be said for banks and other savings institutions. It's just one more reason for the popularity of these funds. No bankruptcy in over sixty years—not bad, huh?

Professional fund managers are another reason for the popularity of mutual funds in the United States. Fund managers are well versed in the intricacies of the national and international fund markets.

To assess a good fund manager, look at his background over several years to determine if he's been consistent in management of the fund or previous funds. You also want to see that the fund manager is holding true to his fund's financial goals. For example, if you are looking at a more conservative growth and income fund, you don't want to find out that the fund manager is making high-risk investments and taking the fund in a different direction (known in the industry as "style drift"). Unfortunately, fund managers with roving eyes who look at and buy stocks that don't fit the fund's stated objective are more common than you might think. On the other hand, if a fund is struggling, you may appreciate a fund manager who starts drifting for the sake of keeping your investment afloat.

You should also look closely at a mutual fund's portfolio. While you may not be familiar with each and every purchase, you can ascertain whether they are following the latest trends or are bucking the system. If you have heard, for example, that a certain market, such as automobiles, is taking a downturn, and the fund manager is buying heavily in that area, it will mean one of two things. Either he is buying now for an anticipated turnaround (value investing), or he is not keeping up with market news.

You also need to check out changes in fund management. A new fund manager needs to show that she can work within the structure of the particular fund, holding true to the goal of that fund. Fund size and assets can matter as well. A manager who has handled a $2 billion fund successfully may not be as comfortable when dealing with $20 billion. You might also want to know whether this fund manager is working closely with a team of analysts or doing it all on her own. If the latter is the case, you could be in trouble when the manager moves to another fund and takes along her secrets.

ALERT

Check the fund manager's reactions to the down markets of 1997 and 2001. See how quickly their funds rebounded. Did she panic and make drastic moves or hold on tight and ride out the storm? Naturally, your assessment of the manager's actions should depend on the type of fund and the particular holdings.

Magazines such as *Forbes, Kiplinger's,* and *Money* and online sources such as Morningstar.com rate mutual funds and often give you the lowdown or profile on the fund manager. It's important to look for consistency. A fund manager who has bounced from one fund to another is not a good sign if you want to hold the fund for a long time. It is also not to your advantage to have a fund with a different manager at the helm every year.

Fund Families and Investment Styles

Fund families are a large group of mutual funds housed at a single company. You'll often pay lower fees for a fund family than you would if you had one fund at each company; the firm's higher overall investment usually comes with reduced expenses. However, if a fund family starts failing, your eggs are all in that single failing basket.

Each fund's investment style should be specific. You should know exactly what types of securities the fund will hold, the approximate proportions for each security type, and how actively the fund will be managed. Index funds, for example, are not actively managed, and hold essentially the same securities as the named index. Aggressive growth funds, on the other hand, are very actively managed and may change their holdings very regularly.

When you're investing in more than one mutual fund, it's important to make sure that their styles (and holdings) don't overlap. There's no point in holding a stock fund, a bond fund, and a balanced fund, for example, when the balanced fund already holds stocks and bonds. In addition, you want to make sure that any mutual funds you choose fit in with your overall portfolio strategy and that you're still maintaining your optimal asset allocation.

Load or No-Load?

A loaded fund charges a commission or fee. A no-load fund means you have bought the fund on your own.

There is certainly enough information available to support the choice of buying a no-load fund. However, if searching for the right fund is taking hours out of your potential income-earning time, you may be better off paying a commission with a load fund and using your time in other ways.

As is the case with everything these days, you have more than two choices. While no-loads have gained an edge on loaded funds, many companies have started offering loaded no-loads. Basically, this means you will be paying a fee somewhere down the line for the privilege of not paying a fee. Whether the costs are for some types of special benefits, a personal finance report, or some other accompanying service, the bottom line is that loaded no-loads are not commission-free funds. There are numerous ways that companies have found to slip fees and payments into their fund business, So read the prospectus carefully. If hidden costs start popping up, you might be better off looking elsewhere. In short, no-loads by any other name are essentially loaded funds. It's to your advantage as a new investor to stick with the basics, either loads or no-loads.

Fees, Expenses, and Operating Costs

While mutual funds certainly decrease the cost of investing for the individual, there are all sorts of fees and expenses attached to becoming a shareholder in any kind of fund, even a no-load fund. These fees can vary significantly, so it's important that you understand how to find and understand them.

Generally listed as the expense ratio, there are several costs that shareholders will pay for services and management of the fund. While the SEC closely monitors funds to make sure they make shareholders aware of all related expenses, it's important that you understand the basics behind these fees and have a sense of what to look for on your own. After all, there are thousands of funds. While some have devised new and inventive ways to bill you, the vast majority are fairly straight-forward about where the expenses are going. International funds often have higher expense ratios than domestic funds because they are deal-ing with companies overseas.

ESSENTIAL

One advantage of having funds in the same family is that you can save on commissions if you want to sell your shares of one fund and move your money into another in the same fund family. You can also avoid paperwork this way, and that alone can save you lots of time.

A mutual fund operates like a smaller business within the structure of the larger fund family. They share printed materials and costs, such as adver-tising the financial group, but from the perspective of the fund family, each fund is handled separately. In other words, the expense ratio you're paying for Fund A will not spill over to pay the manager of Fund B.

Typical fees include:

- **Service fees.** These fees are used for financial compensation of the planners, analysts, and brokers who assist customers with fund-related questions and provide information and advice regarding the fund. Accounting and legal services may also be included.
- **Administrative fees.** These are the fees associated with office staff, office space, and other fundamentals of running a business, including equipment. Sometimes these fees are absorbed into management fees. Office expenses incurred by a fund also include online support and information, check processing, auditing, record keeping, shareholders' reports, and printed matter.
- **Management fees.** This is the percentage that goes to the fund manager. This can be a flat percentage or one set up to coincide with the growth of the fund based on returns. Generally, the bigger the fund's assets, the lower the percentage.
- **12b-1 fee.** This fee (usually between 0.25 and 1.00 percent of annual assets) is used primarily for marketing or advertising the fund. Your fee is not just a contribution to the fund's advertising budget but will hopefully help the fund to grow. In fact, some funds report that because of advertising, their overall expense ratios have gone down as the funds have grown.

Operating costs are also part of mutual funds. This is the money spent to keep the fund afloat. Along with administrative expenses, this includes advisory fees for the fund's analysts and manager. Expense ratios range from less than .25 percent to more than 2.5 percent. It is important to take note of the operating costs to determine how much of a bite they are taking out of your profits. This is an area that more savvy investors are taking note of as they compare mutual funds. In their favor, mutual funds buy in vast amounts and save you on broker fees, which would be accumulating if you were buying stocks individually.

Decoding Fund Reports

Your mutual fund's annual or semiannual report is a tool used to measure how the fund is performing. Among the most significant information within the report is the fund holdings section. Look over this list carefully to determine whether the fund manager is "style drifting." In other words, a fund that is supposed to be buying small-cap stocks may suddenly be investing in larger companies; or a corporate bond fund may suddenly be stocking up on treasuries.

Some questions may arise: Is the fund satisfying my level of risk, or is it becoming too aggressive or too conservative for me? Is the fund becoming less diversified by moving more strongly into similar stocks? Does their current asset allocation negatively impact my asset allocation plan? The holdings will also tell you which companies the fund believes are strong. Look them over, and see if you agree. You may not know all of the companies held, but you should investigate a few.

When looking at the portfolio holdings, you want to find out this important data:

- **Familiar names**. A household name like Coca-Cola won't show up in a small-cap fund, but you are looking for smaller companies that belong in that fund. Just because you own a fund doesn't mean you no longer have to follow the activities of companies and their stocks. If you see holdings in your fund that you don't like, you can look at other funds that have shares of stocks that you feel are more promising.
- **Portfolio concentration.** Besides showing what is in the portfolio, the report will tell you how much, or what percentage, the fund is investing in each area.
- **Performance.** Not surprisingly for funds that perform well, this information sometimes jumps off the page. It can be harder to decipher in a fund that is not performing well.

You should know how the fund has performed in both the short and long term. How well the fund has performed compared to a specific (and relevant) index should also be included for analysis purposes. There should also be an explanation of why the fund has performed well or poorly. Which factors have made an impact on the fund? The report should describe what management has been doing and should include some indication of future plans.

After reading the annual report, you should feel either confident in holding onto the fund or determined to sell your shares. If you are left feeling unsettled as to what you should do—because you do not feel you have adequate information or the report is not easily discernible—you should consult print or online sources such as Morningstar.com, *Kiplinger's,* or the *Wall Street Journal* for a discussion of your fund. Check your fund's performance online as often as you like; if you feel dissatisfied, you can sell at any time. You should also call the fund or fund family and let them know you have some questions; after all, you are paying an operating fee that includes service charges, so let them serve you by providing some answers. If a fund does not help you feel comfortable, then it's not the right investment for you. Remember, it's your money!

Trading Mutual Fund Shares

Now that you're better acquainted with the pros and cons of mutual fund investing, you can take the next step. There are many factors to evaluate in light of each investor's goals. But as with all investment opportunities, there's one very important question you need to address: How will you make money in mutual funds?

ESSENTIAL

Despite common complaints about high operating costs and commissions, mutual funds have shown some tremendous results in recent years. How long the trend will continue depends on a wide variety of factors, including among others the economy, the stock market, and the number of successful fund managers.

You can profit from investing in mutual funds the same way you profit from stock investing: If you sell shares of your mutual fund at a higher net asset value (NAV) than you paid for them, you've made a profit. The fund acts as a single unit, and its total return is based on the performance of all the stocks, bonds, and other securities held. So if some stocks within the portfolio aren't performing very well, you can't simply get rid of those losers. The same goes for high performers within the fund; you can't sell them off to cash in on a strong market price. What you can do is sell off your shares of the fund as a whole, and hope that it's current value is more than what you paid at the outset. You may also profit from the fund's performance, and strong performance increases the NAV.

To get started, you can buy and sell mutual fund shares directly from a mutual fund company. All you have to do is call (or e-mail) the fund company, and request an application kit. You fill out a few forms, write out a check, and mail the whole package off to the company. When you're ready to sell, you call or write to the company to let them know exactly which fund and how many shares you want to sell; then you just wait for the check (or direct deposit) to come.

For people who plan to invest in several different funds—especially if they're in different fund families—it may be easier to go through a discount broker. Yes, you'll pay a fee (usually a fairly small fee), but you won't have to slog through reams of paperwork on your own. Rather, you'll fill out a single account application. Another benefit: instead of getting several account statements from all the different fund companies, you'll get an all-in-one statement from your broker, which is very handy at tax time.

Consider Dollar-Cost Averaging

One strategy that can work well with mutual funds is dollar-cost averaging. Essentially, you invest a fixed sum of money into the mutual fund on a regular basis regardless of where the market stands. Retirement plans and 401(k) plans are generally built on this principle, except they have restrictions on the withdrawal end.

Frequently, an investor will decide to have the same amount of money automatically withdrawn from her account and invested into the mutual fund on a consistent weekly, or monthly, basis—not unlike a 401(k) or retirement plan. Over time, a fixed amount invested regularly, as opposed to buying a fixed number of shares, will reduce the average cost per share. By putting in the same amount, you are buying more shares when the prices are low and fewer shares when the prices are high.

Dollar-cost averaging also eliminates the problems of "timing the market," which can devastate a portfolio. The volatility of the market in recent years has made this method particularly difficult. Fund managers, however, spend a great deal of time trying to time the market—with varying results. And market timing is definitely not advised for novice investors.

Dollar-cost averaging can be emotionally difficult at times, though. By investing on a regular basis, you will also be investing during bear markets. But that can be a good thing, especially when you know that effective fund managers will be filling the portfolio with securities that will best weather a market downturn.

CHAPTER 10

Many Types of Mutual Funds

The most commonly discussed mutual funds on the market are stock (or equity) funds, but they are certainly not the only funds available. They're not even necessarily the best funds. Regardless of the primary fund asset, your profit potential often comes from a successful fund manager, one who has accumulated more winners than losers in the funds—and more shares of the winners. And, as with any investing, your job is to understand what you're investing in, even when you have a fund manager to do the heavy lifting for you.

Benefits of Mutual Fund Stock Investing

Mutual fund investing can be much easier than investing in individual stocks, especially for beginners. For starters, you'll get the services of a top-notch mutual fund manager at just a small fraction of the cost of a personal investment advisor. This person is usually an expert in the field or sector you are investing in, which means you don't have to be.

Then there is the "getting in" factor. In short, investing in mutual funds is cheap—quite often you can invest in a fund for as little as $25 or $50. Add to the mix flexibility, choice, ease of management, and generally positive performance from stock mutual funds over the years, and you begin to see why these are so popular.

In an age where there are numerous types of Coca-Cola—Classic, Diet, Cherry, Caffeine-Free, Caffeine-Free Diet, Zero, and so on—it should not be surprising that there is also a wealth of mutual fund categories. As the market continues to grow, more and more types of funds are created, which adds further confusion. This chapter will help you clear this up.

When choosing a stock fund, you first want to know its overall goal. For example, does it aim for conservative long-term growth or aggressive short-term growth? Before purchasing a fund, you should ask to look at a listing of the stocks currently owned so you can see if the fund managers are indeed following the plan of action they have listed as their goal. Whether you're interested in index investing, current income, capital growth, good value, or superstar sectors, you can find it in the world of stock mutual funds.

Index Funds

Index funds strive to match a specific index, and they do that by holding the same securities as the one the named index tracks. These funds are passively managed, meaning that there's not a lot of trading going on, and that translates to lower expenses for you. The investment objective of this fund type is to mirror an index, the most popular of which is the S&P 500. From 1987 through 1997, the S&P 500 performed better than 81 percent of general equity funds. Then from 2001 through 2007, the S&P 500 trailed about half of actively managed funds. Index funds proved their worth during the down markets of 2008 as well, disproving the commonly held belief that active management does better in bear markets. In fact, S&P indexes outperformed managed funds in all categories but one (large value stocks) during the 2008 bear market. That includes the gold standard itself: The S&P 500 index outperformed 54.3 percent of all large-cap funds in 2008.

ESSENTIAL

Vanguard founder and indexing guru John Bogle claims that index funds will beat 70 percent of managed funds over time. If this claim is true, that means there are plenty of funds out there that can outperform the index.

Index funds offer an easy way to stick with a successful benchmark that everyone uses—and they are not limited to popular benchmarks. There's an index to track virtually every kind of investment there is, from micro-cap stocks to South American stocks to natural resource stocks. They allow you to be in specific sectors and to invest in both growth and value stocks, giving you maximum diversification. If the benchmark is the standard, after all, why not go with it?

Growth and Income Funds

You've entered the investing world to make money, and there are two primary ways to do that: growth and income. Growth securities you buy today will be worth more tomorrow. Income securities will pay you interest or dividends at regular intervals right now. And there are funds designed for each, even for both.

Growth funds don't focus on the current price of a stock; rather, their concerns center on the sales and earnings of the company and the expectation that both will grow, which will cause the stock price to rise. The idea is not the traditional "buy low, sell high" principle; rather, it is "buy at whatever price and watch the company build momentum, get on a roll, and grow." Growth investors seek out companies that have tremendous potential, based perhaps on new products, unique services, or excellent management. Long-term growth funds seek to capitalize on larger, steadily growing companies like Microsoft. Aggressive growth funds involve smaller companies that are taking off fast like Amazon.com.

Aggressive Growth Funds

Sometimes called capital appreciation funds, these are the funds that generate the most press. When they go well, they go very well. Some of these have produced tremendous results—but the opposite is also true. Investors should know that this volatile category can turn around very fast. Aggressive growth funds look for companies poised to grow in the short term, which is why they are riskier investments.

Income Funds

Income funds are best for investors who want to see results right away, in the form of steady income. These funds hold dividend-producing stocks and pass those dividends along to fund shareholders. Some of these funds may also hold interest-paying securities, like bonds; these earnings are also passed on to the fundholders. Even though that income is yours right away, you can choose to reinvest it rather than receiving a regular check. Be aware, though, that these earnings are taxed whether you take the cash payment or reinvest it.

Straight income funds are considered conservative by nature, seeking as their primary objective to pay you dividends from consistently well-performing companies. One of the nicest aspects of an income fund is that the companies that pay dividends, hence those in the portfolio, are usually not affected greatly by downturns in the market.

Combination Growth and Income Funds

You might also choose to go with a fund that specifically seeks out companies whose stock is not only expected to grow but also pays dividends. Such a fund provides steady income, which is attractive to anyone who likes to maintain cash flow even during major dips in the market. A growth and income fund can also work very well for an individual who may be retiring but still wants to have money in the market. Such a fund will provide cash toward living expenses while allowing the investor to maintain some capital.

Value and Sector Funds

A value mutual fund invests in stocks that are undervalued. These are companies that—for one reason or another—are struggling, and while the stock prices are low, the actual value of the company may be much higher. Sometimes it's a matter of too much market competition; in other cases a company may be lagging behind in the latest technology or has not made a major impact of late. However, if the P/E ratio and book value of the stocks in the portfolio are good, the fund can be worthwhile. Although in recent years value funds have been outperformed by growth funds, they adhere to the old adage "buy low, sell high." A stock that is valued at $40 but selling at $20 allows you more room for error. Even at $30 per share you would still come out ahead.

Sector funds concentrate their holdings in one industry. Rather than spread your investment around among various types of industries, they choose stocks from one particular industry, such as oil, health, utilities, or technology.

Like market timing, the idea behind buying a sector fund is to select an industry that you foresee taking off in the next few years. For example, new health-related technologies have people looking at stock in companies doing new and innovative things in medicine. Internet sector funds may also generate more attention, but be careful that an overabundance of Internet providers doesn't bring prices back down to earth. A sector fund can give you a bumpy ride if you are planning to stay there for the long haul.

International and Global Funds

Many investors assume international and global funds are the same. They're not. While global funds include securities from the whole world, international funds do not include securities from the home country of the investor. So, to an American, an international fund would not include U.S. securities, but a global fund might.

Many international funds spread your investment around, buying into markets worldwide, while others look at the economic potential of one country. International specialized funds have not fared well over the past three or even five years. Recent returns are also down, largely as a result of the worldwide financial crisis that started in 2008.

FACT

International funds can be further focused as regional or single-country funds. Regional funds put your investing dollars in a specific geographical area, such as Asia or South America, offering you broad access to a small region. Single-country funds, as the name clearly states, buy up securities issued in a single country. Mexico, Japan, and Germany are among the most common.

Usually not the place for a beginning investor, international specialized funds can be risky because of the high volatility of many overseas markets. For that reason, it may be best to strictly limit your holdings in these funds to a small portion of your total portfolio. Remember, other funds you hold may already be investing a small portion into overseas investments, thus dabbling in the arena and letting you have some foreign diversification. Changes in currency and politics make it hard to assess, even for fund managers, what the future investing climate will be on a global basis.

Balanced Funds and Asset Allocation

Balanced funds are characterized by their balanced approach to investing, just as the name suggests. They derive capital gains from a mixed bag of investments, primarily consisting of stocks and bonds. This is ideal for those investors who do not want to allocate their own portfolios. Balanced funds provide maximum diversity and allow their managers to balance more volatile investments with safer, low-risk investments such as government bonds. Naturally, since this type of fund can have a wide range of investments, it is important to look over the fund's portfolio and get an idea of what makes up the balance in your balanced fund. The combination of good returns and nice yields makes these funds worthy of your attention.

Like a balanced fund, an asset allocation fund maximizes diversification. The fund is managed to encompass a broad range of investment vehicles and asset classes. If managed correctly, an asset allocation fund will include a mix of stocks, bonds, and short-term instruments and distribute the percentage of holdings in those areas providing better returns.

Whereas a balanced fund tries to maintain a balance between stocks and bonds, an asset allocation fund can be 75 percent stocks one year and 75 percent bonds the next. This is largely dependent on the market. If the economy slides into a bear market, the percentage of bonds will rise; in a bull market, the percentage of stocks will be higher. Factoring in each type of investment, the fund manager has a wide range of choices across asset groups. In a broad sense, this is a matter of market timing. These fund managers have more leeway, as they are not locked into a set percentage allocated to one type of investment.

Large-Cap, Mid-Cap, and Small-Cap Funds

In the world of mutual funds, "cap" means "capital," and it indicates the size of the companies the fund invests in. Large-cap funds invest in the major corporations; small-cap funds seek out smaller, often growing companies; and the investments of mid-cap funds are somewhere in between. The larger, more established companies usually present less risk and therefore large-cap funds tend to make safer investments. Small-cap stocks can take off and have often fared better, but present a greater risk since these companies are trying to establish themselves. While some small-cap companies have become huge quickly, others have moved along slowly or vanished into oblivion.

Small-cap funds can sometimes be deceiving. A company that starts out small and continues to grow is ultimately no longer a small-cap company. Yet it still may remain in the fund. After all, why throw out your ace pitcher even though he's no longer playing in Little League? E*TRADE was a small-cap company found in many small-cap funds, but as it grew and brought the funds high returns, fund managers and investors enjoyed reaping the rewards, so it stayed.

Investing in different types of cap funds primarily serves to diversify your investments. You don't want companies that are all the same size because success does go in cycles. In 1998, large-cap funds sitting with

Coca-Cola, General Electric, IBM, and other giant companies performed better than the small-cap mutual funds. One of the possible reasons is the tremendous growth in investing by a much wider sector of the population. As more and more people get into the stock market and buy into funds from their home computers, they tend to be more comfortable—at least in the beginning—buying stock in larger, more familiar companies. There's nothing wrong with this. After all, unless you've taken the time to sufficiently study some new, small-but-growing plumbing supply company, you too might lean toward the more familiar Wal-Mart or Disney.

QUESTION

What is a mega fund?
This is a fund that buys into other funds. Like a big fish eating smaller fish, it looks at the smaller funds and lets you diversify your diversification. As the number of mutual funds grows, you may see more mega funds buying mutual funds much the way mutual funds select from the thousands of stocks at their disposal.

Some small-cap companies, such as those in the technical sector, are also very well known to the computer-friendly population, which is why companies like Intel or Dell Computer can also shine. As the newer online investors become savvier, they too will branch out from safer, more familiar territory and explore the many growing companies.

Bond Funds

Bond mutual funds are generally less risky than stock mutual funds, but they generally do not yield the same high rates of return as stock mutual funds. When you purchase a single bond, your money is tied into the bond until maturity. You can sell the bond, but sometimes bonds can be more difficult to sell because they trade in the bond market. Buying and selling the bonds is the job of the fund manager. A bond fund, thanks to interest, can provide a monthly check, which can also be reinvested into the fund.

Remember that your principal is not secured in a bond fund. Should the fund price drop, you could lose some of your initial investment. The price of the fund dictates the worth of your investment rather than the underlying bond holdings. The value of the bonds in the portfolio will fluctuate until they reach maturity, based inversely on the interest rate.

While looking through bond funds, you will notice the three primary types of bonds represented: municipal, government, and corporate. International bond funds also exist. As is the case with stock funds, there are different levels of risk associated with different types of bond funds. The greater the risk (when dealing with junk bonds, for example), the greater the potential returns, and vice versa. When dealing with low-risk government bond funds, the rate of return is relatively low.

Municipal Bond Funds

These are bond funds that invest in either intermediate or long-term municipal bonds. Such money is often allocated to worthwhile projects, such as building new roads, repairing older ones, upgrading sewer systems, or other projects that both produce revenue and add to the community. An incentive of such munis, as they're often called, is that they generally offer you income that is not taxed. The tax-free bond funds, while paying lower yields, are often paying as much or more than many taxable bond funds because you are not paying those ugly federal—and, in many cases, state—taxes. Municipal bond funds can be national, investing in municipalities nationwide; statewide, investing in specific state municipalities; or local, investing in local municipalities. If you are in a state with high taxes, you may find these funds to be appealing because you avoid such taxes. Crossing state lines, however, may require you to pay taxes. In other words, you may be taxed in your home state if you buy a municipal bond from another state.

U.S. Government Bond Funds

You want low risk? Invest in the government. Despite high deficits and outstanding loans to countries that no longer exist, the U.S. government has never defaulted, and there is no risk in the securities in a government bond fund. These funds hold treasury securities, bonds, and notes, as opposed to savings bonds. There is some volatility because the fund managers do trade on the market, but for the most part this is a very safe route, and many people will use a government bond fund to balance out other funds they hold. Since there are not as many choices in regard to government bonds, and since the risks are significantly lower, many investors do not bother looking for such a fund. Instead, they simply purchase their own government investment vehicles from the government directly, since it is so easy to do.

Corporate Bond Funds

The majority of the holdings in this type of fund are, as the name implies, in corporations. Like equity funds, there are a variety of types of corporate bond funds, and they differ depending on the corporations from which they are purchasing bonds and the length of the holdings. Bond funds that buy high-grade (or highly rated) bonds from major corporations are safer on the fundamental risk scale than other corporate bond funds. They also tend to produce slightly better returns than government bond funds over time.

ESSENTIAL

Specialty funds describe funds that don't quite fit into any other category. These funds often hold more unusual investments, like precious metals, currencies, commodities, and stock options. These funds come with a higher risk, but they also carry potentially higher rewards.

However, some of these funds cheat a little, albeit legally, by owning a small percentage of lower-grade bonds to balance out their portfolio and—if they pick the right ones—enhance the numbers slightly. As is the case with most funds, there is some flexibility beyond the category in which the fund falls.

Beware of bond funds that buy from corporations issuing bonds that are below investment grade. These junk bonds produce a high-yield fund that can be more volatile than many equity funds. The risk of the company backing this bond is higher and, therefore, the yield is also higher to compensate.

In short, junk bond funds mirror junk bonds (which are high-risk bonds), only the fund contains more of them.

Choosing Bond Funds That Work for You

Just as you would consider the track record of a mutual fund before buying, you need to examine a bond fund's history before making your investment decision. In addition to learning the fund's track record, you need to ask some key questions when it comes to picking bond funds:

- Is the fund picking bonds with long or short maturities?
- What quality bonds is it selecting?
- Am I in the market for taxable or nontaxable bonds?
- Who is doing the picking?
- What do interest rates look like today?
- How will the current interest rate environment impact my investment?

Bonds with longer maturities and bonds of a lower grade, or lesser quality, are more risky, which taps into your risk/tolerance equation. Risk tolerance is always a key factor in your investment selection process. Although bonds are generally perceived as a less risky alternative to equity investments, there are risks in the bond market and in bond funds. Since bond funds do not hold onto most of their bonds until maturity, longer-term bonds will have more time to fluctuate and may therefore be more risky. If the bonds were held until their final maturity, these changing rates would not matter.

FACT

Many people select bond funds to round out an equity fund portfolio, with perhaps two stock funds and two bond funds, or one balanced fund and one bond fund. The inclusion of a bond fund is often meant as a conservative safeguard in the portfolio.

The taxable/nontaxable question reflects primarily on municipal bonds. Why in the world would you want a taxable bond if you could own one and pay no taxes? Well, a 12 percent yield on a junkier bond, after taxes, still earns you more than a 5 percent yield on a tax-free bond. Also, if you are buying the bond fund in a tax-free vehicle, such as your IRA, why purchase a tax-free fund? You are already not paying taxes on your IRA investment, so it's a useless advantage. Depending on your current investment strategy and the amount of time you have remaining until retirement, consider holding taxable bonds (to preserve principal) or a bond fund (to balance out an equity-laden portfolio) in your tax-free retirement vehicle.

As for management, you must once again evaluate how the fund is run. Bond funds generally have fewer operating costs than equity funds. However, they generally have fewer high payoffs.

Just like the equity fund player, however, someone who is primarily investing in bond funds may allocate a certain amount to safer funds while putting the rest in lower-grade or riskier funds. The higher-yield funds do have their share of successes, and with the right fund manager, they, like a good equity fund, can be profitable. Unlike owning one junk bond, a high-yield fund will consist of a carefully balanced portfolio. If one or two of the issuers default, you will still be fine due to the great deal of diversification in that area.

Like all other areas of investing, bond funds offer higher rewards for higher risk. While there are many funds to choose from, it's also to your advantage to understand more about bonds in general.

Socially Responsible Funds

The identity of these funds depends largely on the fund manager's definition of social responsibility. Some funds steer clear of products that use animal testing; many do not invest in companies involved with the defense industry, guns, or tobacco; others concern themselves with child labor issues. Some funds use all of the above or other criteria. You need to match those investing criteria with what you consider to be socially responsible and find funds that are earning money. They are out there, but they require that you take time to look beyond the marketing and the numbers of the fund management.

ALERT

When it comes to socially responsible funds, the intentions are good and the funds are profitable. However, exactly how closely any of these funds stick to their overall criteria is hard to judge, even with a concerted effort. While a company may clearly not be manufacturing weapons, it may be inadvertently polluting the environment.

Dreyfus Third Century Fund and PAX World are two of the most successful, best-known funds this area. They look for protection of the environment and natural resources, occupational health and safety, life supportive goods and services, and companies that do not sell liquor, firearms, or tobacco products.

CHAPTER 11

Maintaining the Right Fund Combination

There's an old joke about the key to success: Put aside eight hours a day for work and eight hours a day for sleep, but make sure they're not the same hours. This is especially true with your investments. Investment gurus agree that finding the right mix of funds is a combination of feeling comfortable with your investment goals and tolerance for risk, and finding funds that meet those objectives and limitations. If you're losing sleep over your investments, something isn't right.

Risk Tolerance and Your Fund Portfolio

Chapter 2 directed you to think long and hard about your personal tolerance for risk in your investment strategy. By now, you have decided whether you are a conservative, moderate, or aggressive investor. Now it's time to apply what you've discovered about your risk tolerance to your fund portfolio objectives.

Knowing your own risk tolerance is critical in determining the best investing strategy for you and which mutual funds suit your style. Your risk tolerance informs your overall portfolio, each investment you choose, and your asset allocation plan. Even though mutual funds are by nature less risky than individual securities, they still come with their own forms of risk and you can still sustain losses.

Risk in mutual funds usually refers to the fluctuations in the price of a fund, as opposed to the dividend risk and market risk associated with stocks, or the default and interest-rate risk that comes with bonds. As risk increases, both price volatility and total return potential increase proportionately. On the other side, risk declines along with decreases in price volatility and total return.

ESSENTIAL

If you've decided that you have a conservative level of risk tolerance, you will accept lower returns on your investments in order to minimize price volatility. If you're an aggressive investor, you'll seek out the highest returns regardless of price volatility.

Regardless of your risk tolerance level, you can achieve your investment goals with mutual funds—whether they're categorized as growth, balance, or income—as long as you keep your money invested over the long term. The shorter your investment horizon, the fewer options you have in the mutual fund market to achieve your end goals.

Risk tolerance can be the most important element in determining mutual fund selections. Two investors with the exact same investment objectives and investment capital will enter into two dramatically different portfolio scenarios if they have different tolerances for risk.

Using Diversification to Minimize Risk

Diversification in an investment portfolio is absolutely necessary to achieve a well-rounded investment strategy. The point of diversification is to hold enough distinct funds to achieve your objectives while minimizing your overall investment risk. Though a fund innately offers diversification, owning disproportionate amounts of single asset categories—even in fund form—still opens you up to a lot of risk.

ALERT

Most fund families let you exchange shares in one fund for the shares of another fund managed by the same advisor without charging a fee. You can find out more about this in the company's fee schedule; look to see if there's an exchange fee. You might be able to make a move that would benefit your portfolio without spending any money.

Different fund types (growth stock, municipal bond, value stocks, balanced, etc.) provide different risk/return objectives. As the number of risk/return combinations in your portfolio increases, so does your overall diversification. Sounds good, but you need an action plan to help you really achieve this critical goal. These guidelines can help you hit the right diversification target:

- **Set clear investment goals.** Your time horizon, risk tolerance level, earnings needs, and portfolio size all matter when it comes to your investment strategy. When the funds you choose match your goals, your investment plan is more effective.
- **Opt for quality, not quantity.** The important point here is how diverse your fund choices are and how well they fit your investment strategy, not how many funds you own. Don't think of diversification as a challenge to buy as many funds as possible or you'll end up with a portfolio that does not match your strategy.
- **Value fund category above fund style.** A fund category defines its objectives; the fund's style is the method used to pursue those objectives.

- **Avoid duplication.** It is a waste of your investment monies to own multiple funds with identical objectives. It's best to own just one fund in any particular fund category.
- **Fewer is better.** When it comes to mutual funds, less is more. Use as few funds as you can to achieve the diversification you desire. Since most mutual funds hold between fifty and 150 individual securities, you can meet your diversification objectives with a small number of funds.

No matter how many funds you hold in your portfolio, the key to real diversification is to make sure that each fund contributes a unique means to secure your investment goals.

Reading the Prospectus

Obtaining a prospectus should be as easy as calling the fund's toll-free number. Examining a mutual fund's prospectus will most likely not be the highlight of your week, however, even if returns are spectacularly high. A prospectus can be dense and wordy, even hard to decipher. The average investor's information needs are not considered in the organization or the wording. Important information is in there somewhere, but it can be hard to find in the midst of the legal jargon. In this highly competitive market, however, some funds are actually trying to soften the legalese in which the fund's prospectus is written. In fact, many now publish easy-to-read newsletters to supplement the information in the prospectus—or at least translate some of it. However you get it done, it's to your advantage to read the prospectus with an eye for specific areas of importance.

The Fund's Objective

The fund should have a clear statement of the objective. Is it aggressive growth? Current income? While it may be clear-cut in bond funds, a fund's objective is not always as obvious when reading the prospectus of a stock fund. If the objective is unclear, the mutual fund manager has more leeway. It also means your intentions in choosing that particular fund may not be carried out. If the fund objective is not clear, you can seek out a fund that is more clearly defined, ask someone in the fund's investment information department, or follow the old rule of thumb and do your homework. Look up the fund's current holdings.

The Investment Risks

The mutual fund prospectus should discuss the level of risks the fund will take in conjunction with its objective. Stock funds should discuss the types of stocks they are buying. Are they talking about speculation? Are they telling you about the volatility of particular stocks? Look at the warnings they're giving you. Are they telling you about the currency and political risks involved with their international holdings?

ESSENTIAL

One of the most common errors investors make when buying mutual funds is simply buying at the wrong time. Don't put your money into a mutual fund right before its yearly capital gains distribution. Even if you buy the fund one day before gains are distributed, you'll owe taxes as if you owned the fund all year.

The prospectus should specify the risks associated with its portfolio. As an investor, you should be aware of the risks of investing and how those risks mesh with your risk tolerance. To make the best possible investment choices, it's important to understand how different investments perform under different economic scenarios. For example, aggressive growth stock funds typically perform best as the market is emerging from a long downward trend. Bond funds, on the other hand, often do well during periods of slow growth, as interest rates fall and bond prices climb. By combining your knowledge with the information in the prospectus, you'll be able to make better, and better-informed, investment choices.

Investment Breakdown

The fund should clearly lay out the percentage of holdings they are committed to in each asset group. The prospectus should state, for example, that the management is required to hold at least 70 percent U.S. bonds, or 80 percent in common stocks, or no more than 20 percent in international investments. The breakdown and parameters of the fund give you an idea where your money will be invested. Other types of investments, such as cash instruments, may also be included.

A fee table should outline all the fees associated with that fund. Read them carefully, and make sure you are left with no surprises. Operating costs, loads, and any other fees should all be included.

Financial History

A prospectus will also give you the history of that mutual fund. The financial information should provide the per-share results for the life of the fund—or at least the past ten years if your fund has been around for a long time. You can use this to gauge the total return of the fund on an annual basis. You can also look at the year-end net asset values, the fund's expense ratio, and any other information that will help you gauge how the fund has performed over time. You can check on dividend payments if it is an income fund, or see the types of holdings the fund has sold and purchased.

Look at (But Don't Rely on) Past Performance

Judging past performance of a fund can be trickier than it might seem by glancing at five- and ten-year returns. Sectors or industries that are in vogue during one period may not be during the next. One spectacular year of 90 percent growth followed by four years of 10 percent growth, will average 26 percent growth per year. This average would not be a good indicator of how that fund is performing at the end of the fifth year, when you are thinking about buying. Also, a sector that has not fared well over a stretch of time may be on the upswing due to new products, consumer needs, or public awareness (for example, socially responsible stocks). This won't show up in past performance.

The same holds true for the large- and small-cap companies. A fund that invests in small companies will not see large returns when the trend leans toward the large corporations, as it did in the late 1990s. The best you can do is look at each measure of past performance, read up on future expectations, and try to make an informed decision. Remember this: long-term five- and ten-year returns are important, but they are only part of the larger picture.

ESSENTIAL

> A mutual fund's past performance is less important than you might think. Sales materials—like ads, rankings, and ratings—almost always highlight just how well a fund has performed in the past. But studies show that future performance has no tie to the past. Last year's top fund can easily become this year's loser.

The long-term success of your mutual fund investments is partially dependent on several factors, including:

- Each fund's operating expenses, fees, and sales charges
- Any taxes due based on the fund's distributions
- The size of the fund
- The age of the fund
- Any changes in fund management or operations
- The fund's volatility and risk profile

When selecting a fund family, it is often suggested that you look for one that has been around a while. The one exception concerns emerging industries, such as tech stocks, an area in which all of the newer fund families have been around for about the same length of time. The better-established fund families can show you ten-year returns, which you can compare against funds in other fund families. They can also give you an indication of how the fund has fared during the bear markets and how long it took them to recover. Naturally, some of this will depend on the fund manager, but you have a better chance of finding a fund manager with ten years of experience at the helm of a fund at an older, more established company. Look at the ten-year returns and see if the same fund manager was there over that time period. If you look at ten-year returns and see that the current manager has only been on board for three years, those ten-year returns won't mean as much. It's like looking at the last ten years of a baseball team that only acquired its superstars in the past three years; management experience makes a big difference.

Additionally, you should compare the mutual fund that interests you with other comparable funds. If the fund you like had a 10 percent return last year and other similar funds were also around 10 percent, then the fund is performing as expected. However, if the fund is bringing in 10 percent and comparable funds in the same category are bringing in 12 and 15 percent, you can do better without changing your goals or choosing a more (or less) risky fund. All you have to do is find another fund in the same category.

ALERT

Liquidity is a key benefit of mutual funds. You can sell a fund on any business day, and you'll get that day's closing price—unless, of course, your order comes after the closing bell (4:00 P.M. ET), which counts as placing the order on the following day.

Once you finally make a decision, expect to be in the fund for at least one year, usually five or more. Mutual funds are not generally thought of as a short-term investment, but sometimes market conditions can dictate change earlier than you had planned. If you've invested in a fund that was on the upswing and now it's heading back down (or "correcting"), you may be better off selling before share prices drop lower. You'll almost always have the opportunity to revisit the fund after it stabilizes, when you'll have a chance to benefit from the next round of growth.

Six Fund Investment Strategies You Can Swear By

As you head into the world of mutual funds, here are six strategies that will help steer you through the murky depths of what can sometimes be a confusing investment genre. Don't let yourself become overwhelmed; simply take your time and cover your bases.

Start Now

Nothing will build your nest egg like time, and it's never too early (or too late) to start taking care of your financial future. Every study in this area shows that the sooner you start investing, the more money you'll have later, thanks to the power of compound interest.

Max Out

The more money you invest, the faster you'll become a successful investor. Put as much money as you can possibly afford into your investment plan, even if it means sacrificing some of life's luxuries.

Learning is Earning

When you know enough about the holdings in your portfolio to make all the decisions that impact them, you've seized control of your financial future. Read everything you can about investing and finance, and make sure you understand all the ins and outs of every mutual fund prospectus you read. The reward for all that hard work will be a nest egg you can draw from for a more financially comfortable life.

Be Aggressive

Caution is a good approach when you're at or very near retirement, but it's a disadvantage for other investors. Time and again it's been proven that to grow your money faster, a hefty portion of your portfolio should be earmarked for high-performance stock funds. If you only buy conservative investments like bond or money market funds, your chance of seeing inflation-beating returns is virtually nonexistent.

Keep the Money Working

Don't be tempted to take money out of your investments or borrow against them in order to meet short-term financial crises at home. It's important that the money you've invested be allowed to do its job over time so that you can meet your long-term financial objectives. If you hit a financial stumbling block, try to find other ways to get over it before you even think about tapping your investment monies.

Keep an Eye on the Market

Don't ignore market trends as you're evaluating your holdings or making new investment choices. No matter how well a fund is managed or how well it's performed in the past, changes in the overall geopolitical and economic climate can turn the markets upside down. Wise investors keep an eye on the overall trend of the markets and adjust their investments accordingly.

Tracking Your Funds' Performance

Tracking your investments starts with the orders you place. Every time you buy or sell mutual fund shares, you'll get a confirmation slip from the fund or from your broker (depending on how you placed the order). Make sure each trade was completed according to your instructions and at the quoted price. And make sure the commissions or fees are what your broker (or the fund's customer service associate) said they would be.

ALERT

Beware of unauthorized trades in your portfolio account. If you receive a confirmation slip for a transaction you didn't authorize, contact your broker immediately. The trade could have been made in your account in error. If this occurs repeatedly or if your broker won't correct the problem, call the SEC or your state securities regulator.

The longer your time commitment to your investment portfolio and the broader the range of your investments, the less active you'll have to be in monitoring them. If you've decided (against the best recommendations of this book) to place all your investment eggs in one basket (even if it's one mutual fund), you'll have to watch that basket very closely. At the minimum, mutual fund investors should check performance, costs, and fees once or twice a year and re-examine their contribution schedule.

Tracking fund performance isn't enough, though. To make sure your money continues to work as hard as it should, compare your funds' performance against appropriate indexes and against similar investments for the same time period. It also makes sense to compare the fees and commissions that you're currently paying to those available through other options, like different fund families or different brokers.

ESSENTIAL

To help keep track of your investments and trends in the market, you can subscribe to the *Wall Street Journal* or *Barron's*. Both are available in print and on the Internet (at *www.wsj.com and www.barrons. com*). These publications will provide you with specific data related to your investments and keep you on top of news that might affect your portfolio.

Monitoring your mutual fund holdings is critical to your overall investment success. When you keep an eye on your funds, you'll be able to prevent minor snafus from evolving into portfolio-busting problems. The following ten investment tracking tips will help you make sure your money is invested in the best places and bringing in the best returns:

- Verify every document you get pertaining to your investments. If you find an error, contact the sender (be it mutual fund company, stockbroker, or investment advisor) immediately, and request a written correction confirmation.
- When you talk with your financial advisor, either in person or over the phone, make some notes of your discussion. Be sure to jot down any actions you've authorized so you'll have a record of the conversation in case problems crop up.
- Make sure that all account paperwork, especially trade-related documentation, is sent directly to you and not first to your financial advisor. If the paper trail is too cumbersome for you to follow, have the papers sent to someone you trust who is not connected with the account: your accountant, a competent relative, or your family attorney, for example.
- If you don't receive transaction confirmations or account statements, follow up right away. You have every right to receive this information

regularly and promptly. And if you don't get these documents regularly, it could be a warning sign.

- When something unexpected shows up on your investment account, address it right away. If there's a transaction that doesn't make sense, call your advisor and ask about it at once.

- Even if you don't trade online, consider getting online account access. Internet access to your account lets you look at your account any time, whenever the impulse strikes. You can also immediately verify trade information and account statements. And to cut down on the mountains of paperwork that needs filing, you can ask for confirmations and account statements to be sent to you via e-mail.

- Never make checks (or other payment forms) for investment purchases payable to an individual. Rather, payments should be sent to only to the brokerage firm or another financial institution.

- If you decide to use a broker, meet with him in person, in his firm offices. Investing is a huge financial undertaking, and you should exercise the same degree of skepticism and caution as you would with any other major purchase.

- Know your investments. Don't rely on canned information from someone else—do your own research. The materials are out there and are easily available; all you have to do is read them. Before you make a trading decision, check out the following documents: annual reports (Form 10-K), quarterly reports (Form 10-Q), prospectuses, independent research reports, and even the company website.

- Periodically review your portfolio. Make sure the pieces that comprise your portfolio still meet your investment objectives. Also make sure you understand and are comfortable with the risks, costs, and liquidity of your investments. As part of this review, you may want to check the information that is on file at your brokerage firm regarding your accounts. You have a right to know what is on file about you.

Know When to Sell

The best reason to sell a fund is the same best reason for buying it—your investment plans. Even the best performing fund can and should end up on the selling block if it does not meet your investment needs any longer. Just as you should make your buying decisions based on how the fund in question can contribute to your long-term financial goals, your selling decisions should be made with the same ideas in mind.

ESSENTIAL

Timing matters. Someone nearing retirement might want to get rid of more aggressive funds and stock up on more conservative, cash-preserving investments. Sometimes you'll need to sell a fund because you need the money for something else: a new house, a new car, or your daughter's college tuition.

In addition to the main driving factor—your overall financial plan—many other factors can tell you that it's time to sell a fund. Sell reasons can include a fund's unsuitability for your portfolio (which can happen due to style drift of the fund, for example), poor performance, a change in the fund's holdings, a change in fund management, or inefficient service from the fund family. Taxes can provide another motive for selling a fund: Taking a loss on a fund and switching to another may allow the government to share in your loss through an income tax deduction.

You should also sell a fund that is performing poorly because it isn't sticking to any real style. Keep your eyes open when you look at your funds. Are they still doing what they said they would do? If not, you should sell, and you should also question whether the investment concept you bought into is worth buying into again.

And, equally important, there's the ulcer factor. You may want or need to get rid of a fund when you just can't take its ups and downs anymore. The aim of investing is to hit your key financial goals, not develop ulcers. If a fund in your portfolio is so volatile that not even the prospect of spending your profits on a dream vacation in Hawaii can keep you from reaching for the antacids, it's time to sell. Be positive you will never again buy that particular fund.

CHAPTER 12

All About Exchange-Traded Funds

With the popularity of index mutual funds, it was just a matter of time before a spin-off investment appeared. Back in the early 1990s, the first exchange-traded fund (ETF) was created and sold. Since then, this innovative investment vehicle has grown by the billions (though they still pale in comparison to mutual funds held), more often becoming the security of choice around which to build a portfolio. Strong performance and flexibility keep these securities among investors' favorites – and more new ETFs are being introduced all the time.

What Are ETFs?

ETFs are exactly what they sound like: funds that trade on open exchanges. Just like buying stock, you'll need to place a brokerage order to buy ETF shares over an exchange. The very first ETF, which tracked the S&P 500 Index, was traded in 1993 on the Amex. Though at first investors were confused by these new securities, they soon caught on among investors and brokers alike.

Today, ETFs claim more than $500 billion of investing dollars. Sounds huge, but it's not when compared with the total mutual fund market, which starts counting in the trillions. Given the very real advantages of ETFs, though, they may eventually outpace mutual funds as the diversified investment of choice.

Each ETF tracks a specific index (like the Dow Jones Industrial Average or the Russell 2000, for example), meaning that it holds the same basket of securities as the index. Some ETFs represent stock indexes, other represent bond indexes. There are also more specialized ETFs that allow you to invest in real estate, commodities (like gold), or international securities.

QUESTION

Why would anyone buy an ETF matching an index when a mutual fund can beat the index?
Managed mutual funds offer hit-or-miss performances. They do sometimes outperform their relevant index, but they also underperform; there's no guarantee either way. On top of that, managed mutual funds usually charge hefty fees, and that always eats into profits.

ETFs are virtually the same as index mutual funds, but with some very important differences, the most important of which is that they trade like stocks on the secondary markets while mutual fund shares have to be bought from and redeemed with mutual fund companies. Other differences include trading choices, tax treatment, fees, and transparency.

ETFs Versus Mutual Funds

The first big difference between ETFs and mutual funds is how they are traded. ETFs are bought and sold over exchanges, like stocks, at any time during the trading day. Mutual fund shares can only be bought from or sold to the mutual fund company, and only at that day's closing price. On top of that, there are no minimum ETF purchases, as there are with many mutual funds. But—and it's a big but—every time you buy or sell shares in an ETF, you will incur brokerage fees, and that can cut deeply into your investing dollars.

Another difference is the fees and how they work. Sometimes you'll fare better with an ETF, and other times you'll have lower expenses with an index mutual fund. ETFs will often have lower expense ratios because they're designed to incur minimal operating costs. That doesn't mean they will always post lower expenses. While the lowest-expense ETFs charge about 0.07 percent fees, there are plenty that charge much more. In fact, some charge as much as 0.50 percent, which is higher than the average index mutual fund charges. As with mutual funds, though, you need to read through the ETF's fund information to find out exactly what fees are charged to shareholders. And while many mutual funds come with no load (meaning no sales commission), ETFs must be bought through a broker, and that means a commission of some sort.

ALERT

Because of the high trading cost, ETF investing makes more sense when you're making bigger purchases. If you have a $7 trading fee, and you buy $50 worth of ETF shares, you're losing 14 percent of your investing dollars. If you invest $700 in ETF shares, that $7 takes up only 1 percent of your investment, for a lower effective fee.

Income tax impact is another big difference between ETFs and index funds. Because of the way they're set up, ETFs don't have the internal capital gains issues that index funds do. When index mutual funds rebalance their portfolios, investors get tagged with the capital gains resulting from the sale of holdings. ETFs, on the other hand, use a different process to rebalance called "creation/redemption in kind," which means that you won't be hit with a tax bill as no security sale has occurred. Bottom line: ETFs create fewer taxable events than mutual funds, and that means you get to keep more of your money. (Of course, whichever type of investment you hold, when you sell your shares for a gain, you will be hit with the capital gains tax.)

Transparency is another area where ETFs hold the advantage over mutual funds. Investors can always see exactly which stocks are being held by their ETF. This is in stark contrast to mutual funds, which are only required to report their holdings twice a year. Why does this matter? Knowing exactly which securities your funds are holding makes it much easier for you to avoid fund (or portfolio) overlap, meaning you won't be holding the same securities in two different funds (or in a fund and singly in your portfolio).

Covering Every Corner of the Market

Like mutual funds, ETFs encompass virtually every type of investment you'd want for your portfolio. From equities to debt instruments, from rapid growth to stable income, you can find what you're looking for in an ETF.

ESSENTIAL

More adventurous investors can tap into their risk-loving sides with leveraged ETFs. Leveraged ETFs track U.S. market indexes, but with added volatility, as they hold options and futures on the underlying securities rather than the securities themselves. These funds can help aggressive investors tap into short-term market movements.

Equity ETFs cover the stock markets from every conceivable angle. There are broad-based, total U.S. market ETFs, such as those tracking the S&P 500, the Dow Jones Industrial Average, and the Russell 3000. You can also find global (with or without U.S. stocks included) ETFs, such as those tracking the MSCI All Country World Index (ACWI). More targeted international ETFs track more focused indexes, like the MSCI EAFE (Europe, Australia, Far East) index or the MSCI Emerging Markets Index. If you want to keep your money in U.S. securities with a more narrow focus, you can look into sector ETFs, which track niche portions of the stock market (like utilities or technology). If value investing is your passion, there are ETFs for that, such as those tracking the S&P 500 Value Index (a subset of the whole market index). Same goes for growth investing, where you can get an ETF that tracks, for example, the Russell 3000 Growth Index.

Fixed-income ETFs allow investors to capitalize on the benefits of bonds with the convenience of stocks and the inherent diversification of bond mutual funds. These ETFs are a little different than the equity variety, as they hold portions of bonds that are included in their tracking index (whereas equity ETFs hold whole stocks). Investors get their bond interest as dividends (though it still usually counts as interest for tax purposes). You can invest in total bond market ETFs, which hold corporate and government bonds of varying maturities. You can also invest in more specialized bond ETFs, such as those that focus on specific maturities (like only tracking bonds with maturities of less than three years), or inflation-indexed bonds.

Finally, there are highly specialized, alterative-investment ETFs available. These allow investors to dabble in commodities and currencies, or to take a more risky investing approach. Commodities ETFs will hold either the goods themselves (like gold) or futures on the goods. They may track single commodities, a basket of several commodities, or shares in companies that produce commodities. Currency ETFs track money movement, holding either foreign currencies themselves or future contracts. You'll find single currency ETFs (such as those focusing on the Japanese yen or the Euro) as well as currency basket ETFs (which hold several different currencies). Inverse ETFs allow investors to bet against the market — these funds move opposite to a major market index, basically by short selling the index components. For example, an inverse S&P 500 ETF would go up 1 percent for every 1 percent the index itself went down and, of course, the ETF would drop every time the real index increased.

Spiders, Diamonds, Vipers, iShares, and Cubes

SPDRs, the very first U.S. ETFs, were created by State Street Global Advisors. These funds tracked the S&P 500, and gained the nickname spiders, which comes from SPDR (Standard & Poor's Depository Receipts). SPDRs trade on the NYSE, with SPY for their ticker symbol. Along with the broad index ETF, you'll also find SPDRs that track specific market sectors, aptly named Select Sector SPDRs.

When you buy a share of a Diamond (NYSE: DIA), you are buying a fraction of each of the stocks in the Dow Jones Industrial Average. Like SPDRs, Diamonds are exchange-traded funds bought and sold on the NYSE, and sponsored by State Street Global Advisors.

VIPERs are ETFs issued by Vanguard, a leading mutual fund provider. VIPERs (which are formally known as Vanguard Index Participation Receipts) cover the U.S. stock and bond markets, as well as some international equity markets.

Barclays Global Investors launched their own version of ETFs under the iShares name. At last count, Barclays was the world's largest ETF source. Investing in the iShares family gives investors immense diversification opportunities, as these ETFs cover everything from currencies to emerging markets to fixed income securities.

Cubes, which trade under the QQQQ symbol, track the very popular Nasdaq 100 index. They are brought to you by PowerShares, a relatively new player on the ETF block. This company offers investors the opportunity to invest in more than straight indexes. Rather, they focus on "dynamic indexing," which allows them to hone in on the best-performing securities within an index.

Fitting ETFs into Your Portfolio

ETFs can be used to enhance diversification in your portfolio. With just a few strategically selected ETFs, you can create a well-diversified set of core holdings, covering virtually every corner of the market. For far less than the cost of holding individual stocks, your ETF can give you exposure to all the major equity classes: every size of market capitalization and every market sector.

You can round out your holdings with one or two fixed-income ETFs. These offer you the benefit of steady income, just like you'd get by holding individual bonds or bond funds, with the flexibility of stock trading; bond ETFs trade over exchanges, whereas bonds can only be bought through brokers or TreasuryDirect.

For more portfolio protection, you can branch out into foreign ETFs. These offer you a hedge against problems in the U.S. markets, as other countries may be doing well when the U.S. markets are down. Global ETFs let you stick your toe in international securities, so you don't have to figure out which securities—or which countries—to invest in.

ALERT

Think plastics are going to go sky-high this year? Interested in the biotech sector? Depositary receipts (or HOLDRs) allow you to invest in niche market sectors. HOLDRs can only be traded in increments of 100 shares. This form of investment, originally created by Merrill Lynch, allows investors to trade 100-share blocks of HOLDRs for the actual underlying securities.

Holding ETFs does not mean you can't also hold mutual funds. Managed mutual funds are designed to outperform the markets, while ETFs aim mainly to match the markets. A combination of core ETFs and some more aggressive mutual funds can keep your portfolio profitable without risking too much stability.

Choosing the Right ETFs

When it comes to figuring out which ETFs make sense for your portfolio, the process is very similar to mutual fund selection. The first thing you need to do is revisit your financial plan. Your immediate and long-term goals, your current holdings, and your feelings about risk will all inform your ETF choices.

You'll also want to consider the expense situation. If you choose a broad-based ETF that holds basically the same securities as an index mutual fund, carefully measure which one will cost you the least to own, remembering to take trading costs into account. There's no reason to buy the ETF if a no-load mutual fund will offer you the same returns at a lower cost. You'll also want to check the current trading prices; while mutual funds are bought and sold at their net asset value, ETFs often trade at premiums or discounts to the NAV, based on the day's market activity.

Also consider the different fees charged by different ETF families. Competition among ETFs is increasing as more players come into the market, and one way to draw new business is to lower fees. Compare like ETFs to see which offers the best expense ratio, especially if you plan to add only one of these securities to your portfolio.

FACT

Asset allocation ETFs can take all the guesswork out of investing. Just like their mutual fund cousins, these relatively new ETFs hold more than one class of securities, such as stocks and bonds. That allows investors to hold a single ETF for a fully diversified portfolio.

As you're looking into different ETFs, you also want to make sure that you're putting your investing dollars into good hands; not all ETF sponsors are alike. Make sure the ETF you're considering holds a least $10 million in assets, as smaller offerings may not be as liquid (meaning you may have trouble selling when you want to). Also, look into the trading volume of the fund you're interested in, as that will also tell you how easy it will be to sell when you're ready. Popular ETFs see volume in the millions every day (meaning more than one million shares exchange hands daily), while others may see virtually no trading activity at all.

How to Buy and Sell ETFs

Trading ETFs is just like trading stocks—literally. You place a buy or sell order with your broker, and he fills the order for you, adding the securities to your account when the transaction is closed. Whenever the market is open, you can make a trade. And just like stock orders, you can add conditions to your ETF trading orders. For example, you can place a limit order for an ETF, just like you would for a stock. In fact, everything you can do to order a stock trade, you can do to order an ETF trade, from time-sensitive to price-driven orders.

Many investors take an active approach to ETF trading, which is much less common with mutual fund holders. Though the ETFs themselves take a passive investment approach, simply tracking an existing index, traders can buy and sell ETF shares in the same way they would with individual stocks. People who do this are typically trying to beat an index, but their profits can be eaten up in trading commissions—and their strategy may turn out to be less profitable than simply following the index.

Tracking Your ETFs

Keeping track of your ETF holdings is as easy as—you guessed it—keeping track of stocks. Every financial reporting service, from the *Wall Street Journal* to Reuters to the ETF sponsor, maintains current pricing and yield (for income ETFs) information for the ETFs on the market.

ESSENTIAL

Morningstar.com is a great resource for learning more about exchange-traded funds. This website posts voluminous amounts of information about ETFs, including tutorials directed at beginning investors. In addition to fund information and price tracking, Morningstar also offers ETF ranking and screening options for investors.

To track your ETFs, you'll need to know their trading symbols. Then all you have to do is look at a current price table, whether in the newspaper or online, to find out everything you need to know. Most ETF price tables contain data like closing price, the dollar and percent change from the previous trading day's closing price, and trading volume. Some also include the year-to-date price change, the day's high and low prices, and the annual high and low.

CHAPTER 13

Green Investing

Perhaps you consider yourself an environmentalist. Do you talk to your friends and relatives about how important it is to recycle? Do you bring a reusable bag with you to the grocery store? Maybe you avoid avid consumerism and get books (including this one) only out of the library rather than buying them at the bookstore. Or perhaps you keep your thermostat low in the winter for more than money-saving reasons. If so, you might also be interested in making a positive environmental impact through your investment decisions, too.

What Are Green Investments?

Everyone is jumping on the green bandwagon, and corporate America is leading the way. Even the blackest companies—the ones with the worst environmental records and practices—are looking for ways to paint themselves green. That's where the money is, after all, as green investing is attracting more green (dollars) than ever before.

True green investments are those that put money into companies that are truly helping the environment. It's not only the negatives that count here, though those are important: no pollution, no toxic waste dumping, no resource gluttony. True green companies actively strive to make the environment better than it was before.

ALERT

Investing is an area in which you will benefit significantly from using your intelligence. Investors often cite a gut feeling, and that feeling is usually based on something they know but either consciously or unconsciously don't want to divulge. Emotions alone should not guide your investments, but a message from your gut is always worth listening to.

It's not enough for a company to simply limit negative environmental and social practices. Social investors notice and move their money to companies that make conscious efforts to improve their performance. Mainstream investors want to do good in the world and for their portfolios, and corporate leaders are learning how to coordinate socially responsible practices with long-term profits. More and more, corporations that pair social and environmental responsibility with good stock value are attracting more long-term investors. Indexes and actively managed mutual funds—as well as several ETFs—track these kinds of stocks, as well. And both municipalities and green corporations may issue bonds to raise money for environmentally sound projects.

While money is the bottom line in any investment, green investors emphasize the importance of supporting their personal values in the process. As you educate yourself about green investing, you'll find plenty of options you can choose from that will support your values and put money in your pocket, from mutual funds to individual corporations to community projects. This will also help you make decisions as a consumer as well as an investor.

Green Stocks

Green stocks allow you to be part of the solution. As part owners of corporations that are working to better the planet, you can both contribute to and profit from a healthier world. It's not all about global warming, either, but also about preserving and protecting our natural resources, keeping our water clean, making sure the rain forests aren't completely razed, and that millions of species don't die out. Companies can help achieve this change in positive ways by developing safer, cleaner technologies, or by providing alternatives to environmentally destructive products. They can also impact the environment in less negative ways, like cutting back on toxic waste dumping and emissions or creating products out of recycled or recyclable materials.

ESSENTIAL

When it comes to detective work, the Internet is a great source of information to aid your green investigation. For example, you can search the EPA website (*www.epa.gov*) to learn whether the company you're considering is being investigated or has existing black marks against it.

Many of these pure play (singly focused) corporations trade on the major exchanges. While some of these cutting edge companies are considered start-ups, they need to have substantial funds and plenty of outstanding shares to be listed.

In addition to the standard information you should gather about any security you want to invest in, green investments call for a bit more scrutiny. This is especially true of companies claiming to have new planet-saving technologies in their pipelines. Before you put your money into any so-called green corporation, consider the following questions:

1. Does the corporation have an actual product or is everything still in the conceptual stages?
2. Is there a reasonable time frame set for development and testing?
3. Is there a defined niche market that the company plans to penetrate?
4. Does the company talk about how it expects its product to evolve?
5. Does the corporation talk in specifics (target markets, real-world applications) or generalities?
6. How do the corporation's ideas and technologies stack up against others in the industry?

If the materials you're privy to don't spell out the answers to most of these questions, you may want to consider putting your greenbacks somewhere else.

Green Bonds

Bonds are simply ways to borrow money without getting a bank loan. Instead of borrowing from just a single institution, the borrower asks for money from the general public. The borrower can be a municipality (a city or a town) or a company. And when that money will be used for environmentally sustaining projects, the bond turns into a green bond.

FACT

Community investing can be a great way to get involved and grow your nest egg. Community investing means lending money locally, and it's practiced in large part through four main types of institutions: community banks, community credit unions, community loan funds, and microenterprise lenders.

From a corporate bond standpoint, you have two issues to deal with: default risk (as you would with any bond) and your green meter. Once a corporation has passed your green test (which can be done using the same criteria listed in the green stock section above), you still need to make sure that investing your money with them makes good financial sense.

Official green bonds (actually called Qualified Green Building and Sustainable Design Project Bonds) are tax-exempt securities issued by companies or municipalities for projects that come with the qualifying federal stamp of approval. To qualify for the moniker, the funds must be used to develop brownfield sites, which are land parcels that are underdeveloped, underutilized, or hold abandoned buildings. The often polluted or contaminated land is reclaimed and made healthier.

Green Funds

Green funds include both traditional mutual funds and ETFs. While both types of funds cover this fast-growing sector, ETFs may hold a slight advantage for diehard green investors: You will always know *exactly* which stocks are held by the fund. In contrast, mutual fund holdings are only published occasionally, meaning you won't know if they add in (or fail to sell off) a company that you don't consider green. Green funds come in three basic flavors: eco-friendly, alternative energy, and sustainable resource funds.

Eco-Friendly Funds

Mutual funds that focus on eco-friendly corporations have a broader range of investment options than more targeted green funds. These funds can include companies that strive to improve the environment, produce environmentally friendly products, or take steps to minimize their negative impact on the environment.

One such mutual fund is the Calvert Large Cap fund, which invests in less risky large-cap stocks but still screens for green. The fund actively seeks out corporations that have environmentally conscious reputations and bring in decent returns.

When looking into eco-friendly funds, be extra diligent in your screening. Corporations may paint themselves green to look better to investors, and some mutual fund companies may be more interested in posting big returns than truly vetting their holdings. Make sure you read the most recent list of holdings, then decide for yourself whether those holdings match the stated philosophy of the fund.

Alternative Energy Funds

Alternative energy funds hold baskets of securities of corporations that are actively involved in researching or producing alternative energy sources. They search out corporations that are involved with technologies like solar and wind power, biofuels, hydro power, and other sustainable and renewable energy sources. Right now, these alternative energy sources supply only about 20 percent of global energy. But as the most popular forms (oil, coal, and natural gas) are neither renewable nor sustainable, that balance will have to shift in the future. In addition, as oil prices climb higher and higher, alternative energy funds grow in value.

ALERT

Eco-friendly funds may hold shares of companies that are making minimal changes in order to qualify as green investments, but may still be less than green in reality. For example, Exxon is working to ensure its oil transport is safer. However, it spent nearly twenty years in court fighting against paying damages for the infamous 1989 Exxon Valdez spill.

An example of an alternative energy ETF is PowerShares WilderHill Clean Energy (NYSE:PBW), a fund that invests exclusively in the stocks of companies that produce cleaner, renewable forms of energy. All of the companies in this fund fall into the small-cap category, which are generally considered higher risk than mid- and large-cap companies, so take that into consideration when adding such a fund to your portfolio.

Sustainable Resource Funds

Sustainable resource funds invest in companies that strive to maximize returns while ensuring the survival of natural resources. Examples include sustainable water, which includes everything from water distribution to treatment to consumption, and sustainable climate, which looks at companies that try to delay or moderate global climate change.

There are actually a few indexes that track the water industry, which is, in fact, a huge industry. After all, even though water covers about 70 percent of the earth's surface, only 1 percent of that is considered drinkable. And as the global population grows, that resource gets ever more precious—and precious resources tend to generate big profits. You can invest in sustainable water with an index fund, such as one that tracks the Dow Jones U.S. Water Index (which includes fewer than twenty-five companies) or the S&P 1500 Water Utilities Index (which includes just two companies).

ESSENTIAL

When you are socially responsible in your investing, you have a double bottom line. You want your money to support your morals and values at the same time it brings you financial profit. This additional bottom line is generally rooted in strong moral and ethical beliefs or in personal principles that you apply to other areas of your life.

There are also nonindex funds specifically devoted to sustainable resource investing, like the SAM Sustainable Water Fund (which trades under the symbol SMWNX). This fund seeks long-term capital growth for its investors, and it carefully selects investments related to a sustainable world water supply.

Socially Responsible Funds Lean Toward Green

In addition to specifically green funds, many socially responsible funds hold investments in green companies. These funds hold both environmentally friendly investments and those that proffer socially important values. Examples of other types of socially responsible investments that may be held by these funds include organic farming and food companies, companies that offer aid to impoverished areas, and companies that treat their employees and communities exceptionally well. Socially responsible funds may also screen out undesirable companies, such as those involved in weaponry, tobacco, alcohol, or other destructive products or services.

You can find a comprehensive list of green funds in the *National Green Pages*, a service of Co-Op America (*http://coopamerica.org*). And you can find more information about funds you are considering by searching through the archives of the GreenMoney Journal (*http://greenmoneyjournal.com*). You can also check out the investment options at companies like Green

Century Funds, which has been focused on environmentally responsible investing since 1991.

Avoid Scams: Look Beyond the Green

You've seen the TV commercials: A man wearing jeans walking through a field or a forest, taking in the sights and sounds of nature. The scene is full of green, and the man seems to be protecting the land. But then you find out he works for a big oil company, a company that's trying to help save the planet by making vague changes. You know it doesn't make sense—but it does all look convincing.

Listen to your inner skeptic. Just because a company has wrapped itself in green doesn't mean it's really green. They're just greenwashing the ugly truth and trying to convince you that they care about the environment.

QUESTION

How common has greenwashing become?
The practice is widespread, and the term is so widely used that it actually made it into the Oxford English Dictionary. You'd be hard-pressed to find a company that isn't trying to green up its image. So take off your green-colored glasses and take greenwashing with a grain of organic sea salt.

This new trend toward greenwashing comes to us courtesy of Madison Avenue, whose goal it is to make their clients appear benevolent and kind and environmentally friendly. These days, going green brings in more green (money, that is). Consumers and investors alike are attracted to companies who claim to be affecting environmental change. So being thought of as green makes a company seem better and better poised for future success. The problem is that the changes themselves are often created out of thin air or out of marketing spin.

How can you tell what's real? Start with the sniff test. If something smells fishy (like an environmentally friendly oil corporation), it probably is. Take British Petroleum, a corporation that even changed its logo (now a green and yellow sun) to make it look like a friend of the environment. Its corporate website also spouts green ideals and talks about a cleaner future, but it doesn't highlight the fact that in 2007 the company won a hard-fought battle to gain a permit to dump even more toxic waste into Lake Michigan. Or consider Archer Daniels Midland, a company that prides itself on creating biofuels but skims over the fact that creating biofuels actually produces so much pollution that it effectively erases any environmental savings. It also doesn't mention that planting all the palm and corn needed to make biofuels involves clearing land (often by setting fire to it), which emits more than a billion tons of greenhouse gases into our air.

Bottom line: Expect greenwashing, and look past the spin. Do a basic Internet search on any green company you're looking to invest in and focus on the news stories. It's easy to make your corporate website look like an environmental sit-in, but it's a lot harder to greenwash the Internet. You can also search dedicated not-for-profit websites that call out offenders, like CorpWatch (*www.corpwatch.org*), Corporate Accountability International (*www.stopcorporateabuse.org*) and Multinational Monitor (*http://multinationalmonitor.org*).

Building a Profitable Green Portfolio

Green is good for the environment—but that doesn't necessarily mean that a green company is good for your portfolio's earnings and growth. Luckily, you can marry the two concepts, environmentally friendly and profitable, with some careful research and planning. Many traditional investors (i.e., those investing solely based on profit potential) used to turn their noses up at all forms of socially responsible investing, but they're looking much more closely at it now. Turns out that a lot of people care about the world as much as they care about the bottom line—and that translates to a boon for green investors. The more money that pours into green, the more profits will be taken by environmentally conscious investors.

On top of that, truly green corporations have as much profit motive as any other corporation. These companies are in business to make money, pure and simple. Sure, they're doing it in a way that helps the world, but the bottom line is the bottom line. And as the industry takes off, green companies are poised for substantial growth—which means capital gains for savvy investors.

Should you decide to dedicate your entire portfolio to green investing, you will still need to follow basic investing principles to ensure success. Assessing your current personal financial situation, time horizon, and risk tolerance comes first; this directs every investment decision you will eventually make. Next, you must determine the optimal asset allocation for your portfolio, allotting your investment dollars toward stocks, bonds, funds, and other assets. And within each allocation category, you want to make sure to diversify your holdings.

ESSENTIAL

There are plenty of resources available to help you build an environmentally conscious (and profitable) portfolio. Helpful websites to visit include Good Money (*www.goodmoney.com*), the Social Investment Forum (*www.socialinvest.org*), and Social Funds (*www.socialfunds.com*). You can also check out Appendix C for more great investment websites.

A successful green portfolio will hold some stock, some bonds, and some other investments, such as precious metals or real estate. You will need to monitor your green portfolio in the same way that you would a standard portfolio, weeding out losing investments and seeking out more profitable ones. By following these essential investing principles, your green portfolio will provide you with a nest egg that can make you both wealthy and proud that you've contributed to a cleaner, safer planet.

CHAPTER 14

Ground Rules: Investing in Real Estate

Real estate generally holds steady against inflation and any lows the stock market might suffer, but it can lose value during deflationary periods or in areas that are affected by housing slumps. Because the market has such a particular focus, the average investor faces some hurdles. Not everyone will want to deal with all the rates real estate brings with it—interest rates, occupancy rates, vacancy rates, construction rates—but those who have a mind for it can find real estate investment a profitable experience.

Real Estate Investing Basics

The details of real estate investment can be overwhelming. There's a whole new language to learn: closing costs, resale value, liquidity, and inspections. But if you're willing to overcome your apprehensions, you'll find that real estate can be a wise investment. If you are considering investing in real estate, it's important that you do your research so that your investment will turn into a profitable venture. It's harder to get out of real estate than a stock or bond purchase, so educate yourself and make sure you understand exactly what you're doing.

A real estate investment is generally tangible—you buy land or property that you can actually see. Think about how stocks and bonds work. You invest your money in a company you do not physically own. By buying shares, you are in essence lending the company your money and hoping for a profit. With real estate, you own the "company," so you need to sell "shares" of it to see a profit—by selling or renting the property.

You must consider inflation when investing in real estate. Believe it or not, a real estate investor can reap profits from inflation alone. Check out this example. An investor has $30,000 worth of equity in a $100,000 property. With a 3 percent inflationary increase in property values, her holdings are now worth $103,000—a $3,000 increase. That $3,000 increase on her $30,000 investment translates into a 10 percent return—due solely to inflation.

The Power of Leverage

Leverage, plain and simple, is debt; it's using other people's money to buy what you want, which actually allows you to use less of your own money to get more property. In real estate investing, leverage can make or break your portfolio. With the right amount of debt taken out on the right lucrative properties, you can make a killing in real estate using very little of your own money. But there's a downside: too much debt or unaffordable debt coupled with shrinking property values can spell financial disaster. There's a pretty fine line between the two, and as long as you stand firmly on the profitable side, real estate investing can provide solid returns—but it will take a lot of legwork on your part to pull this off.

Here's the key to success: You have to be smart about your borrowing. Never borrow more than you can afford to pay back. Always understand all the terms of your loan contract, particularly if you take on an adjustable interest rate (also called a variable interest rate). Don't let anyone talk you into a loan that doesn't make sense.

When you borrow wisely, you can use the bank's money to acquire and improve investment properties. At the same time, you can invest your own money in other ways. This means more money is going to work for you, which increases your portfolio's profit potential. When everything goes your way—you quickly flip a property for a profit or immediately land a golden tenant who always pays the rent on time—you can pay back the loan with your investment cash flow and keep a tidy profit for yourself.

Of course, there's a downside. When circumstances are less favorable, as they usually are, you may end up struggling to pay the investment property loan. That's why it's critically important to only get a loan you can afford to pay back even if you don't get a tenant or can't sell the property right away.

Fix-Up and Flip Properties

Real estate is a risky business, and there are no guarantees on every piece of land or property. Be careful and educate yourself before dropping a big chunk of change on any property. First, you need to know the difference between speculators and investors.

Real estate speculators aren't the same as investors. Speculators buy and sell quickly in order to make a fast profit. Investors seek out long-term gains and look for what they can afford to keep for the long haul. You must consider your finances carefully to determine which option is right for you. If real estate investing is new to you, hold off on speculation until you're more familiar with the market. And consider consulting a property specialist to help you get your feet wet without getting soaked.

For the novice real estate investor who wants to own physical property, there are two good options: small rental properties (like single- or two-family homes, or four-apartment buildings), or a house that requires some fixing up. Of all the ways you can invest in real estate, single-family houses may offer the clearest opportunities for new investors, mainly because they're very easy to acquire and usually easy to sell.

FACT

> If you take a day to paint instead of hiring a painter, do you really save that much? If you hire a painter, you can spend the day finding another bargain property—perhaps one with a $20,000 profit margin. If it takes you 100 hours to find, fix, and sell this property, you have, in essence, paid yourself $200 an hour!

You may be able to reap big profits by buying older, run-down homes and restoring them for resale. This is a very common way for investors to approach real estate, and while it can bring in some tidy profits for some, it's not for everyone. Here are some factors that you'll need to consider before making the decision to invest in a fixer-upper:

- **Expertise.** You'll need to know at least something about building design and construction in order to have an idea of how much work (and money) it will take to get the house into good shape. Figure out what you can do yourself and also how much it will cost you to hire someone else to do it. Remember to factor costs for building materials, contractors, and your time into the property's purchase price.
- **Staying power.** Do you have the patience to withstand the problems that are bound to crop up as you restore the property? Real estate can be a bigger commitment than many people expect. Plus, in down markets, property—even fixed up, premium property—can be difficult to sell for a profit, and you may have to wait for prices to go up again.
- **Inspection.** Hire a professional home inspector to do a comprehensive inspection of any property before you agree to purchase it. It's critical to be fully informed of all the potential pitfalls you might encounter once you start rehabbing the property, but keep in mind that no inspector will be able to spot all the problems.
- **Location.** The location of the property is the most important factor to consider. Study the neighborhood, shopping, and transportation facil-

ities. Think about how the property can be used based on its location and zoning. Residential rental property in a good school district will attract young families. Property with easy highway access could be very valuable for commercial purposes.

If you want to invest in commercial property or executive rentals, look for property within thirty miles of a city. If you are willing to look outside the cities, you can usually find inexpensive land. If you discover a tract of land that appeals to you but is not listed for sale, you might be able to track down the owner by visiting the county register or calling the county appraiser's office. You can always try to contact the owner with an offer—she just might be willing to sell.

ESSENTIAL

If you decide to rent your investment property, be prepared to get rental insurance and property insurance. Your homeowner's policy most likely won't cover renters, and you need protection against any damage done by your tenants. This also covers you if tenants try to blame injuries on you.

Most real estate professionals will tell you to stay conventional in your real estate investment strategies and not to buy white elephants. Of course, you must also look for hidden defects in the property before you buy. If you find any problems after the purchase, you will be the one who has to fix them, especially if you're trying to make the property attractive for resale. Pay attention to what's going on locally, and be sure your planned purchase makes sense. Will there be a demand for this kind of property in five or ten years? Always be on the lookout for things that make a sale easier, like a bargain property or extraordinary features.

Potentially profitable real estate opportunities exist during good economic times and bad, but it is critical to make wise decisions and pick carefully to get the best deals. This can be a tricky proposition for any investor, especially when property values are at their peak, or when a tight credit market makes securing a loan seem harder than winning the lottery. The following example illustrates why you should take demand and location into account in purchasing a property. After watching their children grow up and go off to college, a couple decided they did not need such a big house any longer, so they bought a beautiful place in upstate New York that needed some work. They made improvements and additions, and after just two years the house had increased in its appraised value. However, the house next door was empty. The bank had foreclosed on it, and the structure sat empty and unkempt. Furthermore, an important local industry was laying off workers. To make a long story short, the couple saw that if they wanted to sell, they would have to drop their asking price substantially.

A house with an empty property next door in an economically depressed area is not desirable enough to sell for its appraised value. Any property is only worth what the buyer is willing to pay for it.

Building Wealth with Rental Properties

If you are considering making a real estate purchase for rental purposes, you will choose between commercial and residential property. You need to assess your own financial situation first, as this is not the most liquid investment. It's important to determine how much money you will need up front, how much money you can borrow, and what the terms of the loan will be. Investment capital is the first item on your agenda. If you do not have it, you'll need to borrow it. New investors are usually advised not to borrow for the purpose of buying real estate. Unlike stocks or bonds, you cannot start out with a $100 investment.

ESSENTIAL

Real estate investing can come with a big tax benefit. Special tax incentives for real estate investors can make a big difference in your ultimate tax liability. Rental property deductions may be used to offset other income. In fact, tax breaks can transform real estate losses into profits.

Make sure you do all your homework about a property's location even if you think it's a once-in-a-lifetime deal. A house that seems like a steal today may not seem like such a great deal in a few months when a major highway construction project comes through its front lawn. Find out from the local municipality what building projects are slated nearby—particularly projects like schools, highways, shopping centers, and industrial or commercial centers. All of these developments can impact traffic issues and property values. Sometimes a great property offered at a great price means the seller knows something you don't about an upcoming event that will impact the resale value of the property. If you are purchasing a commercial or residential property with the idea of renting it out or selling it in the future, you need to consider the following:

- Is this a prime location? Remember, location still means everything in real estate.
- Has this property been rented successfully before?
- How old is the property?
- Has it been thoroughly inspected and given a clean bill of health? You may need to arrange for this yourself, thoroughly inspecting and fixing electricity, plumbing, and the foundation and roof. Everything must comply with local safety ordinances.
- How much renovation and work needs to be put into this property? This will follow, in part, from the inspections. Changing the interior to fit your business or rental needs is an important cost factor.
- How much will it cost to maintain the property? Do you need gardeners? Will a janitor be needed on the premises at all times? Upkeep is important in evaluating the potential resale or rental value of the property.
- What are the zoning laws in the area? This is particularly important if you are opening a new type of business in a commercial property.
- What is the accessibility to and from the property? You may find the perfect little hideaway for a summer rental, but a business property will need to be accessible.
- What plans are being made for the future of the area? Is a new highway coming through that would help your business by providing high visibility, or will it ruin the vacation value of your secluded villa?
- How much insurance will you need? What are the rates for that property in conjunction with the purposes of your investment?
- What property taxes are applicable? What can be deducted?

If this list hasn't scared you off, you might be the ideal real estate investor. Not unlike investing in stocks, there is an issue of timing when it comes to investing in real estate. The stock market, over time, tends to end up ahead. Real estate should as well. However, the economic climate can change, so real estate, like any other investment, can be risky.

Managing Your Rental Properties

In addition to the money, there are other complex aspects of buying real estate for the purpose of renting or selling. It's important that you have good management skills and an eye for detail, as there are numerous details involved with any property. You need to be able to maintain the property, which means proper upkeep. You have to factor that into your costs. Unless you are very handy, you will need to know how and where to find the right electricians, plumbers, and contractors. Maintaining a property is a major responsibility; unlike stocks or bonds, you are responsible for keeping this investment in good condition.

If you decide to make the leap and purchase a rental property, you will be entering the world of the landlord. If you have been a renter, you know a good landlord can make life easy, while a bad landlord can make life miserable. How you act as a landlord will have a great impact on the well-being of your investment.

ALERT

Always check a renter's credit history, background, and references. If you don't screen your tenants and select them carefully, you could encounter numerous problems later: a tenant who's always late with the rent, damages your property, moves in objectionable friends, or worse.

Problems will arise in any rental situation, and the way you handle them is important to maintaining the property at a reasonable cost. It's far easier to make the effort to maintain a property when it's your own residence. However, you'll have to do as much work—if not more—to protect your investment. If the investment is taking up too much of your time, you are basically losing income. That's time you could be spending earning money somewhere else. If you are spending hours maintaining a property, you are cutting into your income-earning time and losing money in the process. People choose stocks, bonds, and mutual funds as investments partly because they require little work to maintain.

Good communication with your tenants is crucial to your ability to be a good landlord and to protect your valuable investment. Tenants need to understand your expectations, as well as your rules and regulations, in advance of entering into an agreement to lease your property. Any changes in the rules need to be expressed and explained in writing with sufficient notice to tenants. Make sure all communications with tenants are done in writing and that you can prove the communication was delivered to the tenant.

No matter what shape it's in, you cannot expect to buy a rental property, immediately find tenants, and then just walk away and let the monthly rental checks roll in. If you aren't prepared to manage your rental property, or if you just don't have the time, hire a professional property manager. Property managers take care of daily repair and upkeep issues, landscaping needs, tenant concerns and complaints, and collecting rent. Fees vary based on the level of work required and size of building involved. You can hire an individual to do this work or contract with a management company. If you think you're going to need a professional manager to handle your rental property, make sure you factor that cost into your decision to buy the property and the rental costs you pass on to your tenants.

Choosing the Most Profitable Real Estate

Now that you've decided to invest in real estate, you have to decide which properties to purchase. Your long-term plan, whether you plan to rent the property or flip it, will in part dictate which kinds of properties you investigate. An investor looking to flip single-family homes faces a very different marketplace than an investor who wants to rent office space to professional firms.

One of the best things a potential real estate investor can do is look for an area that is marked for revitalization. A careful examination of the local political scene can help you determine an area's development future. See what significant changes are being made. A major theme park opening up might mean it's advantageous to buy the family restaurant down the road or transform a property into such a place. Perhaps you find out that a major New York City–based company is buying property in Tenafly, New Jersey, for its corporate headquarters. Is there property for sale in that area? It might be valuable with the influx of 20,000 people every day. Look for commercial property in places people are moving to or visiting frequently. People bring money into an area.

ESSENTIAL

Because it's close to everything New York City has to offer, a modest one-bedroom apartment in midtown Manhattan can sell for more than a nine-room house on a three-acre property just outside Kansas City. It's simply that supply and demand dictate property value. The same holds true for rental property.

If you want to invest in a residential property, the same principle applies, but the needs are different. Families buying homes are concerned about things like shopping, good schools, transportation ease, and low crime rates. It's important to see the property from the perspective of a potential resident. If you were going to be living at this address, would the area have what you need? To get the best price for your property or the highest rent from your tenants, you'll need to be sure that the whole package works, not just the home itself.

Investing in Real Estate Investment Trusts

If you're not quite ready to jump into a real estate investment as an owner or landlord, there is another option that allows you to reap the benefits of real estate investing without all of the negatives of property ownership. A real estate investment trust (or REIT, pronounced "reet"), offers investors a way to invest in commercial real estate in much the same way they would invest in the stock market. In short, a REIT lets you invest in real estate without having to actually buy property or land. There are more than 200 REITs to choose from, and shares of REITs are traded much like shares of stock. In fact, you can find REITs listed on the stock exchanges.

Less popular than stocks, funds, and even bonds, REITs are not new. They were established more than thirty years ago as a safe way to get into the real estate market. They are more liquid, and therefore more attractive, than direct investments in real estate; selling shares of a REIT is as easy as selling a mutual fund or stock. Since you don't actually own the real estate, you don't suffer the hassles that come with property ownership. On the other hand, a REIT gives you none of the rights that come with property ownership, either.

REITs share the characteristics of both stocks and mutual funds. A REIT is a publicly traded company, so owning shares is similar to owning shares of stocks. On the other hand, REITs were created to follow the paradigm of the investment companies, or mutual funds. Since most small investors cannot invest directly in income-producing real estate, a REIT allows them to pool their investment resources and is, therefore, like a mutual fund. This investment type is called a pass-through security, passing through the income from the property to the shareholders. The income is not taxed at the corporate level but at the investor level.

What's in the REIT?

Unlike mutual funds, which purchase stock in companies, REITs focus on all types of real estate investment. These investments usually take one of two forms. An equity REIT buys actual property (with the property's equity representing the investment). A mortgage REIT invests in mortgages that provide financing for the purchase of properties. In the latter, the income comes from the interest on those mortgages. Of course, like everything else, there's always one option that fits in the gray area in between. In this case that's known as a hybrid REIT, which does a little of each.

What does all this mean to you? It means that REITs can be attractive investments. As with any investment, you must do your homework. The National Association of Real Estate Investment Trusts offers a great deal of information on REITs at *www.reit.com* or by phone at 1-800-3NAREIT. Many REITs have their own websites as well. Brokerage houses also have

REIT information. Since REITs are not as common as corporate stocks and mutual funds, however, not all brokers have the expertise to provide you with good guidance. Be sure you choose a broker who is familiar with this type of investment.

Comparing REITs

When comparing REITs and deciding which is best for you, you need to consider several factors. Here are some important areas to look at when you start comparing different REITS:

- **Dividend yield.** Review how much the REIT offers when paying dividends and how that compares to the price of the stock. Dividend yield is the dividend paid per share divided by the price of the stock. So if the price goes down, the dividend yield goes up. Dividends in 2004 averaged 4.7 percent for REITs—compared with 1.7 percent for S&P 500 companies (according to *www.realestatejournal.com*, run by the *Wall Street Journal*). And even with the highly depressed real estate market in 2008, REITs still offered better dividend yields, paying out an average 7.56 percent compared with a paltry 3.11 percent for the S&P 500 companies.
- **Earnings growth.** With REITS, the magic earnings number is called funds from operations, or FFO. The FFO indicates the true performance of the REIT, which can't really be seen with the same kind of net income calculation used by standard corporations. A REIT's FFO equals its regular net income (for accounting purposes) excluding gains or losses from property sales and debt restructuring, and adding back real estate depreciation.
- **Types of investments held.** Identify what properties the REIT invests in. REITs can invest in office buildings, shopping malls, and retail locations; residential property, including apartment complexes, hotels, and resorts; health-care facilities; and various other forms of real estate.
- **Geographic locations.** Check out where the REIT invests. Some REITs invest on a national level and others specialize in regions of the country.

- **Diversification.** There's that word again. Whether you choose a REIT that diversifies across state borders or buy several REITs with the idea of investing in everything from small motels to massive office complexes, you should always favor diversification when investing, and that includes investing in REITs.
- **Management.** Much like buying shares in a mutual fund, you are purchasing an investment run by professional management. You should look at the background of the manager. In this case, you'll be looking for someone with a real estate background. REIT managers often have extensive experience that may have begun in a private company that later went public as the person continued on with the company.

Just as you investigate a company issuing shares of stock, you have to investigate the company behind your REIT. You must also look at the real estate market and the economic conditions in the area or areas where your REIT is doing business.

ALERT

Over the thirty-year span ending December 31, 2008, the compound annual total return for equity REITs was approximately 11.9 percent. Compare that with the S&P 500 return during the same stretch of time, which came in lower at 10.8 percent (data from *www.nareit.com*).

Tracking Your REITs

You'll see share prices for your REIT quoted daily, so you can follow your investment pretty much the same way you would track a mutual fund. The best measure of your REIT's performance is its FFO, which is often referred to simply as earnings. The FFO differs from corporate earnings mainly in the area of depreciation. For corporations that have assets like computers and tractors, all physical assets (except land) depreciate, meaning they record a decline in value. That makes sense because they really do lose value over time. However, real estate typically maintains or increases its value. A company whose main holding is real estate calculates its earnings, or FFO, by starting with the standard net income number, adding back depreciation on real estate and other noncash items, and removing the effect of some capital transactions. This way, you can see a clearer picture of what kind of cash the REIT is really generating.

All in all, if you are a beginning investor who believes the time is right to invest in real estate, the best choice is a REIT. This form of investment provides a cost-effective way to invest in income-producing properties that you otherwise would not have the opportunity (or the capital) to become involved in. Regardless of how you get into real estate, whether through a REIT or as a property owner, it can be a lucrative and worthwhile investment strategy.

CHAPTER 15

Alternative Investments for Risk Lovers

Risky investments, those where you're as likely to lose your shirt as score big gains, make many investors cringe. Along with the risk of devastating loss comes the possibility (albeit a pretty small possibility) of staggering returns, and profits beyond your wildest dreams. There are quite a few ways to score such big returns, though each comes with its own unique risk characteristics, including the chance of losing *more* than you invested!. Are you willing to risk it all for the chance of spectacular gains?

Risky Strategies: Enormous Returns or Devastating Losses

Most investors are content to sit back and let their investments grow over time. Others love the roller-coaster ride of sharp ups and downs that come with more aggressive investing. These risk-lovers are willing to accept the chance of failure and loss in exchange for the very real (but hard to pin down) possibility of enormous returns.

Risk lovers have two basic ways to capture these sky-high returns: by investing in unusual and complex securities, or by using aggressive and chancy investment strategies. Alternative investments include things like IPOs, commodities, currencies, options, and futures. Alternative investing strategies include short selling, margin buying, and hedging. Aggressive investors can employ both methods to ramp up portfolio returns, though even the most risk-friendly investors keep a generous helping of safer buy-and-hold securities among their holdings as a safety net against total loss.

That's what the risk is here: total loss. At best, that means losing every dollar you invested. At worse, it means losing even more than you invested (and, yes, that can really happen). But for some investors, the gamble is worth it, and this type of investing gamble gives them the same rush they'd get by going to Vegas and putting it all on red.

Short Selling and Margin Buying

When it comes to investing, you can divide the whole pie into two pieces: long and short. Long investing means you're expecting the price of a security (usually a stock) to go up. Short investing means you're betting the market price of a security will go down. Most people go long, but risk lovers often go short, knowing that they may reap spectacular returns when a corporation falls.

Short Selling

Short selling is the practice of selling a stock (usually a borrowed stock) before you've bought it, and hoping the share price will drop so you can replace the borrowed shares with shares that cost less than the ones you sold. It sounds tricky because it is tricky, but an example with numbers will make it more clear.

FACT

When the stock market experiences a sudden, sharp decline, the government may put the kibosh on short selling. Since short investors want share prices to drop, their activity can actually cause further declines in an already falling market. To stop a market crash (and to boost investor confidence), short selling may be temporarily suspended until market equilibrium can be restored.

Let's say Joe thinks shares of Exxon will go down very soon, and he wants to profit from it. Joe borrows 100 shares of Exxon from his broker and sells them for the current market price of $100. That means Joe just brought in $10,000. But he still owes his broker 100 shares of Exxon. If he's lucky, Exxon shares will drop. If they do drop, let's say to $90 per share, Joe can pick up the 100 shares for just $9,000, scoring a quick $1,000 gain. (We're also assuming there are no transaction fees here, to keep the numbers simple.) If the price doesn't go down, Joe buys the shares at $100, hands them over to his broker and breaks even. But if Exxon rallies, and the shares climb to $101 per share, Joe's out of luck. Now he has to pay $10,100 for those same shares, netting an instant loss that comes directly out of his pocket, and directly out of his portfolio.

Margin Buying

Margin buying is related in the sense that it involves borrowing, and can also cause devastating losses that deplete an investor's portfolio. The investor who buys on margin buys stock using a little of his own money and a lot of his brokerage firm's money. To buy on margin, you first have to have a margin account set up with your broker. Once you make a buy, the shares remain in the account as collateral on the loan. Sounds like a good deal, right? You get to buy more shares than you ever could on your own, and the shares themselves count as collateral for your loan.

If everything goes your way, and the stock price goes up, it is a great deal. But if the price drops, you're in a lot of hot water. Not only did you lose money on your investment, but you still owe the brokerage firm the money you borrowed to buy the stock, plus interest. Of course, the stock could rebound, but that doesn't fix the current situation. You see, to maintain a margin account, you're required by law to have what's called a maintenance margin. Federal law requires a maintenance margin of at least 25 percent; the balance of your margin account has to be equal to at least 25 percent of the value of the stocks you borrowed.

ALERT

If there's anything an investor dreads, it's a margin call from his broker. Those come when a stock the investor has bought on margin drops in price. The shares in the margin account are no longer worth enough to cover the account's collateral requirements, and the investor has to scramble to make up the difference.

An example with numbers will clarify. Suppose Jane wants to buy $10,000 worth of shares in IBM and wants to use only $5,000 of her own money. She buys the shares through her margin account, using $5,000 of the broker's money, and the IBM shares are held in the account. The next week, IBM has dropped in value, and Jane's shares are only worth $7,000. The balance in her margin account has now fallen to $2,000 (the current share price of $7,000 less the $5,000 loan), which is $500 less than the 25 percent maintenance margin. Jane either has to pony up $500 (which she'll do if she thinks the shares will rebound) or sell the shares for a loss and pay off the loan.

Initial Public Offerings

Initial Public Offerings (IPOs) are exciting and frightening propositions, both for those involved in managing a company as it enters an IPO and for those who choose to invest in one. A company launches an IPO when it chooses to go public as a way to raise money, which means it will be issuing stocks to the public for the first time. By selling shares of its stock, a growing company can raise capital without taking on debt. Investors, in turn, expect to earn profits by purchasing stock in a company they hope will grow, eventually making the stock worth a lot more than they paid for it.

An investment bank—Deutsche Bank, for example—usually handles the detailed process of issuing stock. A company works with the investment bank to determine how much capital is needed, the price of the stock, how much it will cost to issue such equities, and so forth. The company must file a registration statement with the SEC, which then investigates the company to ensure that it has made full disclosure in compliance with the Securities Act of 1933. The SEC then determines whether the company has met all the criteria to issue common stock and go public.

FACT

If a company has already gone public and issued stock, it can hold another primary offering during which additional new stock is issued. This is still a public offering because the stock is being sold directly to the public by the company, not among investors in the secondary markets. And while this is a public offering, it does not count as an IPO.

How to Get in on an IPO

The best way to find out about an IPO is to have a broker who is in on all breaking financial news. *Investment Dealers' Digest* (*www.iddmagazine .com*) lists all IPOs that are registered with the SEC. Once the stock is issued, the publication will print an IPO update. Companies awaiting an IPO often call the leading brokeley.vierage houses and/or brokers they are familiar with, who will inform their clients about such an offering. As is the case with anything new, these stocks can be very risky due to their potentially volatile nature. It's a good idea to wait until the stock settles before you determine whether it would be a viable investment. The vast majority of stocks that you will be researching have probably already been actively trading.

An IPO Example

In August 2004, one of the most highly anticipated IPOs in more than a decade took off with a resounding thud. The founders of Google, the Internet search engine company, took their brainchild public, using a Dutch auction system to price the company's stock in an effort to revolutionize the way Wall Street handles IPOs. This goal may have been worthwhile given Wall Street's past methods of handling IPOs (not always popular). However, Google still managed to upset both institutional and individual investors.

ESSENTIAL

Before the company has its initial public offering (IPO) and its stock goes public, the SEC must make sure that everything is in order. Meanwhile, a red herring is usually issued, informing the public about the company and the impending stock offering. When the stock is ready to go public, a stock price is issued in accordance with the current market.

Individual investors who were supposed to benefit from the offering were turned off by the overly high suggested share price, which Google set at $108 to $135. (The stock ended up trading at $85.) Google's decision to issue two classes of stock also turned individual investors off. The founders got stock that gives them ten times the voting power of the hoi polloi. Google said it wanted to be democratic, but the way it structured its IPO told individual investors that management, not investors, would continue to have the primary say in how to run the company. And what of the investors who did participate, despite some dissatisfaction with the methods? They saw quick profits, as the stock hit around $200 a share within just a few weeks.

Commodities and Precious Metals

When investors want to go straight to the source, they can invest in commodities or precious metals. These raw materials feed the production supply for every industry in the world, from basic needs like food to high-tech needs like virtual reality games. While these goods are plentiful and replaceable, their prices may remain low. Scarcity, though, drives prices higher. Even fear of scarcity (like we've seen with oil) can drive prices up. Savvy investors look at the growing resource demands of the world, and put their money into those commodities that they expect the world to consume at the greatest rates.

This market has come leaps and bounds from where it started, while hardly changing at all. Hundreds of years ago, farmers would drag their corn and wheat to the markets, selling them to the highest bidder. While no one lugs commodities into the marketplace anymore, their producers may still hold out for the highest price they can get.

ESSENTIAL

The commodities market has its own unique lingo. The commodities themselves are called "actuals." "In sight" means the actuals underlying a commodity futures contract are about to be physically delivered. And a "break" refers to a natural occurrence (like a tornado or an unseasonal frost) that negatively affects the commodities underlying a futures contract.

Though this class of investment is riskier than other classes, holding commodities in some form (even in a mutual fund) adds diversification and some inflation protection to a portfolio. In fact, as emerging nations begin to gobble up resources, prices of commodities keep rising, sometimes even outperforming stocks.

Commodities

Some investors prefer to go straight to the base of the production chain, buying resources directly rather than investing in the companies that use these resources—or commodities, as they're called in the investing world—to make consumer products. Commodities are natural resources, the raw materials used in all means of production. Examples of commodities include the items on the following page:

- Lumber, which is for much more than building houses.
- Oil, which impacts more than just transportation costs.
- Cotton, which is used in many items, from clothing to coffee filters.
- Wheat, the main ingredient in hundreds of foods.
- Corn, which can be found in foods, building materials, and biofuels.
- Gold, a precious metal used for much more than making jewelry.

Commodities are traded on commodities exchanges. These exchanges include the Chicago Board of Trade (CBOT) for trading agricultural products; the Coffee, Sugar & Cocoa Exchange (CS&CE) for trading those three goods; and the COMEX (Commodities Exchange) for trading futures and options on precious metals only. Commodities may also be traded at spot markets, so called because these are markets where buyers can buy these goods for cash on the spot.

While commodities themselves can be bought and sold directly, they are often the underlying investment for futures contracts. And while most individual investors don't buy bulk commodities, they can invest in commodities through mutual funds and ETFs.

Precious Metals

Precious metals, gold in particular, are exceptions to that individual investing rule. Millions of investors throughout the world buy and sell gold, though many more invest in this commodity through stocks (in mining companies, for example) and precious metals funds. Investors who buy and hold gold, believing that the metal will maintain good value over time, are called "goldbugs."

FACT

Gold is a lot more than a beautiful shiny metal that looks good around a neckline or surrounding precious gems. Gold is also used in many other types of products, from medical machinery to aerospace equipment to glass. And, of course, it's been used as currency for more than 3,000 years.

Investing in straight gold can take a few different forms, such as buying gold bars or bullion coins. Gold bullion is pure, raw gold, before it's ever been shaped into a bar or a coin; very few (if any) individual investors hold straight bullion. Gold bars are what most people think of when they think of gold: stacks of gold bricks. Gold bars must be made of at least 99.5 percent pure gold bullion, as measured in karats. Most gold bars weigh a uniform 400 Troy ounces (which is the standard used to weigh gold), though you can find them as small as a single standard ounce. Gold coins, or bullion coins, are real currency made out of solid gold. Though they're rarely used as currency any more, these coins have definite value, usually more than just their worth in gold. Most investors choose to own gold coins, often taking great pride in their collections.

People can invest in other precious metals as well. Silver, platinum, and copper (just to name a few) are also bought and sold by investors, often in coin form. These metals don't have the same trading value as gold, though they are much sought after by industry for production purposes.

Trading Currencies

The idea that trading money can earn you money seems counterintuitive, but there's a lot of money to be made in currency trading. Lots of people engage in this trade without even realizing it, as a matter of fact. Every time you visit another country and swap your dollars for the local coin, you're involved in currency trading. In investing terms, currency trading is known as foreign exchange, or forex (FX). And, believe it or not, the forex market sees more than $2 trillion dollars worth of trading every day.

The bulk of trading involves the currency of eight major players, those with the most robust and sophisticated financial markets:

1. United States (U.S. dollar, also called the Greenback)
2. United Kingdom (pound, also called Sterling)
3. Japan (yen)
4. Europe (euro)
5. Canada (Canadian dollar, also known as the Loonie)
6. Switzerland (Swiss franc, also called the Swissie)

7. Australia (Australian dollar, sometimes called the Aussie)
8. New Zealand (New Zealand dollar, nicknamed the Kiwi)

Of course, other currencies trade as well. But those listed are the most liquid and the easiest to trade profitably. The most important thing to remember is that currencies have relative value. For example, trading U.S. dollars for Japanese yen will get you a very different result than trading U.S. dollars for euros. That's because the currency pair you're trading is based on each currency's worth in relation to the other.

Currency Trading Is Different

Many of the investments we've discussed until now trade on formal exchanges. Not so with currency trading. Unlike virtually all stocks, ETFs, and options, currencies don't trade in a regulated forum. There's no central governing body (like the SEC). There's no official body to guarantee or verify trades.

FACT

One basis point is equal to 1/100 percent. So, for example, a currency that trades with a rate of 700 basis points is trading with 7 percent interest. A currency trading at 50 basis points comes with interest of 0.5 percent.

This often seems crazy to novice forex investors, but the system (or, rather, nonsystem) works. Because it's a free market system, the forex market is self-regulating, thanks to competition and cooperation among traders. However, if you're planning on testing the waters of currency trading in the U.S., make sure you use an FX dealer that's registered with the National Futures Association, as those dealers agree to engage in binding arbitration in the case of a dispute (meaning you have recourse if a deal doesn't go down the way it was supposed to).

Another notable forex difference: you can trade currencies 24 hours a day during the week. From 5:00 P.M. on Sunday to 4:00 P.M. on Friday, trading is continuous.

Rates Drive Return

If there's one golden rule in the currencies markets, it's that rates drive return. This concept is simpler than it seems. When you buy and sell currencies, they always trade with an interest rate attached: buyers earn interest, sellers pay interest. That seems like the opposite of what you'd expect, but it's how the system works.

From a procedural point of view, you are first selling one currency, then using the proceeds to buy another (though the transactions happen simultaneously). When you sell a currency, you have to pay interest on it (sort of like a bond issuer pays interest); when you buy a currency, you earn interest along with it.

Each currency has a unique interest rate attached to it, computed in basis points. Your net return is the difference, in basis points, between the currency you're selling and the currency you're buying. So if you were selling a currency with a rate of 400 basis points and buying a currency at 600 basis points, your net return would be 200 basis points (or two percent).

Deciphering Derivatives

Derivatives are investments that derive their value from something else. On their own, they really aren't worth anything. Their value comes from an underlying asset and changes in its value. For that reason, every derivative is the same thing as a bet. Derivative traders are gambling, usually on minute movements affecting the assets that lie beneath them.

FACT

Have you ever seen the movie *Trading Places*? The two men who make Eddie Murphy and Dan Aykroyd trade places are derivatives traders who invested heavily in orange juice futures. When a fictional cold snap hit Florida and those futures became worthless, those traders lost it all.

Every derivative is a contract agreement between two parties. The most common derivative contracts are options, futures, swaps, and forward contracts. And these contracts aren't written only on other investment securities, although that's the norm. Derivative contracts can be written on things like weather data (will it rain in Florida in August?), holiday retail sales, or interest rates. But most derivatives are written on investment-related items: stocks, bonds, currencies, commodities, and even on market indexes.

All About Options

An option is a marketable security that gives the holder the right, but not the obligation, to buy or sell another security at a specific price by a certain date. The essence of the option is that it's a bet; option holders are betting that the price of the underlying security will move as they expect, and as much as they expect. They don't necessarily care which way the price moves, as long as it moves. And though most people associate options with stocks (i.e. stock options), options can be written for virtually any kind of security that exists. However, since stock options are by far the most common, this chapter will focus on them.

FACT

Listed options are those that trade on the Chicago Board Options Exchange (CBOE) or another national options exchange. These options all come with fixed expiration dates and strike prices. In addition, every listed option represents a contract to buy or sell 100 shares of stock.

Before we get to the ins and outs, you need to learn the basic language of options. The two most important terms are *put* and *call*. A put option is for selling. A call option is for buying. Both types of transactions are carried out on the asset underlying the option. When you decide to buy or sell, you'll be exercising your option. The security price specified on the option is called the *strike price*. Long-term options are called *LEAPS*.

Stock Options

A stock option comes with a specific stock as the underlying asset. Stock options give you the right to buy or sell (depending on the type of option) a specific number of shares of named stock for a preset price within a preset time period. For example, you could buy a call option that would allow you to buy 300 shares of ABC Corp. for $50 one month from today. If the market price of ABC is $60 in a month, you would exercise your option and buy 300 shares of ABC at $50 (then turn around and sell them at $60 for a nifty $3,000 profit, $10 times 300 shares). On the other hand, if the stock price is only $45 next month, you would let your option expire. After all, why would you pay $50 for shares you could snap up for $45?

ESSENTIAL

Investors can also create, or write, options, as opposed to buying them. In that case, the option writer offers someone else the opportunity to buy or sell an underlying security at a named strike price. If the option holder chooses to exercise the option, the writer is obligated to fulfill the options contract.

If you have an option, you have virtually unlimited profit potential, and your losses are limited to what you paid for the option. A stock option's value is determined by five principal factors: the current price of the stock, the strike price, the cumulative cost required to hold a position in the stock (including interest and dividends), the time to expiration (usually within two years), and an estimate of the future volatility of the stock price.

LEAPS

Some investors prefer a long-term view, and they may purchase longer term options known as LEAPS (long-term equity anticipation securities). LEAPS typically don't expire for two to three years, sometimes as long as five or ten years. Other than that key distinction, LEAPS trade like regular options.

Though they trade just like standard options, they are not as widely available. You can get them on most heavily traded stocks, but they are not written on as many different stocks as short-term options are.

Employee Stock Options

You may have heard about—or even received—employee stock options. These stock options are given by a company to its employees (usually top-level employees as part of their overall compensation packages) based on the company's own stock. In some industries, even lower-level employees may be offered stock options, especially in the fast-growing sectors like bio-tech. These options give employees the incentive to work harder and help make the company even more profitable. They are often used as an incentive to lure quality employees to the corporation.

FACT

The U.S. futures markets came about to help farmers stabilize grain prices, both in times of surplus and times of shortfall. That way, when crops are scarce (during the winter, for example), prices won't get prohibitively high. And when crops are plentiful, farmers won't have to sell their produce so low they can't buy supplies for the next year.

Employee stock options are different from regular options in that there's no third party writing the contract. Instead, it's a direct agreement between the issuing corporation and the option holder. In addition, employee stock options are often tax-advantaged, an added benefit for both the company and the employee. Another key difference is in the time frame under which these options can be exercised: Employee stock options usually must be held for a minimum time period (often more than a year) and can be exercised over long time periods, even as long as ten years.

Trading Futures

Futures contracts are among the riskiest investments in existence. While buying futures is (in practice) as easy as buying stock—you just call your broker, place an order, and pay a very hefty commission—the potential consequences are nowhere near the same. Unlike options, when you purchase a futures contract, you become obligated to buy or sell the asset (usually a commodity) named in the contract, by a predetermined time for a set price. Futures contracts are most often written on agricultural products (like pork bellies and corn), energy products (like oil), precious metals (like silver and gold), or currencies.

Futures traders stand to make piles of money when things go their way. But the downside can be financially devastating. If you guess wrong on which way prices are heading, you could end up on the hook for much more money than you invested in the futures contract. Remember, you will be contractually obligated to fulfill the terms of the agreement. For this reason, even the most risk-loving individual investors should stay away from the futures market unless they are confident that they have a comprehensive understanding of the underlying commodity, its market, and the way its market moves.

CHAPTER 16

Teaming Up: Working with a Financial Advisor

You may wonder why an entire chapter of a book about self-directed investing would be dedicated to working with a financial advisor. The reason is simple. Before you've gained some solid knowledge and experience, you can benefit from the wisdom of someone who's been doing this for years. Think of your financial advisor as a mentor, someone to guide you through the rough spots as you begin investing. When it comes time to make your first purchase decisions, you'll be in the driver's seat—but it can be comforting to have a seasoned navigator sitting next to you.

What Kind of Advice Do You Need?

You may like to do things yourself, but is this a wise choice in the complex world of investing? Often it is, particularly after you've gained some experience managing your money and trading securities. For example, if you know you want to allocate half of your investing dollars to growth stocks, another 25 percent to international securities, and the rest to long-term bonds, you don't really need to pay someone else to figure out those proportions for you. However, if you're not yet comfortable making those decisions on your own, a financial advisor can come in handy.

ESSENTIAL

Your financial advisor assumes the role of a true consultant, assisting you in developing long-term investment plans and determining asset allocation strategies for your investment portfolio. Your advisor can also help you prepare a budget, plan for college education savings, and even help with taxes and estate-planning issues. If you decide to do without an advisor, the consultant's responsibilities all fall on your shoulders.

Before you decide whether you will team up with a financial advisor or strike out on your own, take some personal inventory. Emotions play a major role in any investment plan, and building your own financial security is no small job. Ask yourself if you have qualms about the financial markets, especially when they're in a downturn—which can bring excellent buying opportunities for careful investors. Does the thought of crunching numbers and poring over statistics make you cringe, or are you excited at the prospect of diving headfirst into market analysis? Do you jump for the business section (even before the sports section) to see how your investments are doing? Are you willing to devote a solid amount of time to investing? If you find yourself answering more in the negative—if these questions feel like too much—then you may fare better by working with an experienced financial professional.

In the go-go information age, time is a big factor. Essentially what you're buying from a financial advisor—apart from her expertise—is time. In other words, your financial advisor has the time to scour the world for the best investment opportunities and the best fund managers, even to run different options through the computer to figure out the best choice. Maybe you don't have that kind of time. If not, it's a good idea to hire a financial advisor to take the time to help you make the right decisions for you and your family.

Let's assume that you want to work with a financial advisor. In order to appreciate the real value of this unique approach to investing, it is important to understand the financial advisor's role, which can vary based on the type of advisor you choose and on your comfort level with personal financial decisions. Financial advisors run the gamut from simply helping you find potentially profitable investments to actually making all of your investment decisions. As you gain confidence and experience in the financial arena, you can modify the role of your advisor. But when you're just getting started, having an expert in your corner can not only help you make good choices, it can also keep you from making bad ones.

ALERT

Unlike the impersonal relationship you have with your stock brokerage firm, discount trader, or mutual fund company, you should expect to develop a direct and lasting relationship with your financial advisor. As with all close long-term relationships, it's important that you feel comfortable talking with and questioning your advisor.

It is especially critical for a new investor to establish a good relationship with a financial advisor who has the expertise and experience needed to grow and preserve assets. The whole idea behind wealth creation in the Information Age is that individuals and smaller investors have the same opportunities as institutional investors. Job one for your financial advisor is to know the market better than you do, even if you are somewhat market savvy.

What Can You Expect from a Financial Advisor?

Taking an active role in your finances not only increases your chances of becoming wealthier, it also makes you a better investor. But that doesn't mean you have to go it alone. The best financial advisor for you is one who complements your existing knowledge and skills, and helps you gain insight and confidence in making financial decisions.

To that end, there are several types of financial advisors, and each type puts a slightly different spin on their roles. The type of advisor you choose will dictate the services you'll receive. Financial advisors include:

- The most encompassing is the money manager, who actually makes all decisions for you once you've agreed to a general style and purpose; with these professionals, you will have virtually no part in the day-to-day decision making process, though you will be kept abreast of the activity in your portfolio.
- Financial planners help map out long-term strategies and advise you on all aspects of your personal finances, but you make the final call about what actions are taken.
- Investment analysts and advisors focus primarily on trade recommendations and don't really look at your overall financial picture; again, here you have the final say-so as to which trades are made.

When you work hand-in-hand with a financial professional, regardless of the type, you will receive frequent reports regarding both your personal financial status and current market activities. More frequent personal interaction with your advisor will help you build a better relationship with your money and, by extension, your financial life. Your participation level is up to you, but the more involved you get, the sooner you'll be able to captain your own financial ship. For this reason, it's critical to work with a professional who's available to you and willing to work with you. Avoid those financial professionals who try to keep you at arm's length and are hard to connect with.

Two key pieces of your decision are control and access—the advantages traditionally associated with institutional investors. When you invest in a no-load fund, for example, your access is basically limited to a toll-free telephone number and you have no control over the underlying investments. When you hire a financial advisor, though, you're engaging an investment consultant with whom you can interact, ask questions of, and learn from.

Your financial advisor should monitor your portfolio's performance, help you change your asset allocation strategies when appropriate, and alert you to major changes in the markets. Additionally, your advisor should help you stay focused on the long term. Many investors get emotionally involved with their money—which is certainly understandable, given the high stakes involved. But a good advisor will stop you from buying high and selling low, or making unsure, emotional decisions based on short-term results.

This makes working with an experienced professional financial advisor even more critical when the markets are in decline. Everyone can make money during bull markets, but advisors who can get you through bear markets with your nest egg intact—or even bigger than it was before—are well worth your money. You should expect your advisor to help you preserve your wealth (as much of it as possible) even when the markets are crashing. He can employ emergency investing tactics, with your knowledge and approval, to keep your financial goals on track.

Shopping for a Financial Advisor

Once you've decided to use a financial advisor, and in what capacity, it's time to start looking for a good fit. Many investors make the mistake of choosing a financial advisor based on performance track record alone. Equally important, though, are the investment style, the organization the person works for, the levels of service provided, and the fees. It's also vital to consider how comfortable you feel with the advisor and whether her philosophies mesh with yours. You will need to do some investigating to make sure the advisor and the company she works for are trustworthy, experienced, and solvent. Look for evidence of an efficiently run, profitable organization with an attention to client servicing. Look into how much insurance coverage the firm has for possible fraudulent acts of its employees. Ask about the investment successes, setbacks, and strategy changes that came about from market turnarounds. And check whether there have been any complaints filed with the SEC by going to their website at *www.sec.gov*.

When it comes to credentials, acronyms abound. It's important to understand the distinctions among the various designations and certifications.

That knowledge will help narrow your search to the type of advisor who will work best in your situation. Read on for information on some of the most common advisor designations and the skills each brings to the table.

Certified Financial Planner (CFP)

An advisor with "CFP" tacked on to his name has proven competency in virtually every area of financial planning. The education required is extensive—more than 100 crucial topics are included, from the ins and outs of stocks to estate planning. After completing their studies, those seeking the CFP designation have to pass a rigorous certification exam and then obtain qualifying work experience. The licensing agency (the Certified Financial Planner Board of Standards, Inc.) then monitors its licensees to make sure they adhere to strict ethical and professional standards. In addition, the CFP board posts information about their professionals, including any whose licenses have been revoked.

ESSENTIAL

Don't be afraid to ask for references. Any advisor worth hiring will be happy to provide references or testimonials from both clients (only with the client's permission, of course) and industry professionals (like insurance agents and accountants). If the advisor seems insulted or refuses to provide references, go somewhere else.

CFPs can make excellent financial planners. They can help you develop an overall financial strategy from the ground up, either long or short term. Then they'll advise you on the best ways to achieve your financial goals. If you're looking for someone to help you develop a portfolio to serve your short- and long-term needs, a CFP makes a good candidate.

Chartered Life Underwriter (CLU)

A chartered life underwriter starts out where the name implies—insurance. These professionals have undergone demanding study programs in the insurance field and other areas. Licensed by The American College, prospective CLUs have to pass eight courses, meet minimum experience standards, and adhere to a strict code of ethics to get their licenses. Once they are licensed, they must also keep up with continuing education requirements.

While the main focus here is insurance, CLUs know about a lot more than just life policies. They're typically well versed in overall financial and estate planning, and often work heavily in retirement planning. When it comes to current investment selection, though, these people probably aren't your best choice. Use a CLU if you have insurance planning questions, maybe even to help you formulate an overall comprehensive long-term financial plan. But for stock picking and the like, you may be flying solo.

Chartered Financial Consultant (ChFC)

Also certified by The American College, many chartered financial consultants are also CLUs—but with a lot of extras. The ChFC program covers virtually every area of financial planning from the client's perspective. Students are taught how to assemble a true picture of each client's financial know-how, position, and goals. The coursework goes on to make sure each candidate knows how to turn that basic information into a comprehensive plan, as well as how to set the plan in motion and keep it on track.

Once they've completed the program and passed the requisite exams, potential ChFCs must demonstrate evidence of three years industry experience before they can append the initials to their business cards. When they receive the designation, you can be sure they are well versed in everything from income taxes to stock analysis. What does that mean to you? You'll have the ear and advice of an expert who can take you from square one all the way to the finish line.

Personal Financial Specialist (PFS)

Personal financial specialists are certified public accountants (CPAs) with additional financial planning qualifications. On the plus side, they're starting out with an intimate knowledge of the tax code and may also have vast experience with tax planning; this can come in handy when you're looking for ways to add income without increasing your income tax bill. In order for a CPA to become a PFS as well, she must either complete additional education as demanded by the American Institute of Certified Public Accountants (AICPA) or already have a CFP or ChFC designation.

To maintain both the CPA and PFS designations, the professional must keep up with continuing education requirements and adhere to strict ethical guidelines. PFSs can be very helpful in determining your current net worth, your future needs for retirement, and appropriate investment strategies. Plus, you get the added benefit of expert tax planning to help minimize your current and future tax burden.

How Much Will You Pay?

The short answer is: that depends on the advisor you choose. Financial advisory services don't come cheap, but it's important to know ahead of time how much you'll be paying and that you'll get what you pay for. There are many fee arrangements out there. You must discuss this issue with the advisors you're considering before you make your final choice. Remember: While you don't want to nickel and dime when you're paying for expert knowledge and advice, you also don't want to be taken to the cleaners. Any advisor who won't discuss fees with you before you sign, or won't show you a preprinted fee sheet, is not the right advisor for you.

There are basically three ways fees are determined: commissions, flat fees, and percent of assets, although this is mainly seen with money managers. In addition to base fees, there may also be other charges associated with your account (for example, transaction fees, below-minimum-balance charges, and account maintenance fees), so make sure to ask about all related expenses. You don't want to pay for services you won't use and don't need. Keep in mind, though, you will be charged standard brokerage fees every time you make a trade using a broker, regardless of the way you're paying for advice.

Commissions

Advisors who get paid commissions rather than flat fees earn more money with active accounts than passive (or buy-and-hold) ones. And although there are many scrupulously honest commission-paid financial advisors out there, you may also encounter some who place their own financial interests above yours. Because of this, novice investors often feel more comfortable with fee-only advisors.

Flat Fees

Fee-only advisors are paid a flat annual fee. They get paid (by you) the same amount no matter how much activity your account sees, and no matter how much they grow your wealth. However, these advisors may get commissions from their firms or from mutual fund companies based on which assets they buy and hold in your portfolio. Make sure you know whether that's the case, as it can influence which investments the advisor directs you toward. You can expect to pay at least a few hundred dollars—and as much as thousands of dollars—every year for basic advisory services.

Percent of Assets

If you decide to go the money management route, you can expect to pay for this heightened level of service. The total cost for a money management service averages out to between 1 and 3 percent of assets managed on an annual basis with flat fee advisors. This fee percentage often drops with the size of the account. For example, if you have an initial investment of $25,000 you might pay a slightly higher rate than the person who's bringing $100,000 to the table. The discounts usually get bigger the more money you toss into the asset pot. On the plus side, the manager will earn more as your portfolio grows, giving him incentive to make your holdings profitable. Pricing schedules may include trading, money management, custody, and financial consultation. The bottom line here: The more services you receive, the more you'll pay.

What's Best for You

If you go with a commissioned advisor (but not a money manager), insist on approving every trade before it's made—and actually take the time to understand the advice before acting on it. If you go with a fee-based advisor, find out who she's really working for: you, or the company whose investments she tries to sell you. If you go with a money manager, make sure you know all the fees your account will be charged, not just the advisory costs.

The most important thing to take away from this discussion: Get the fee structure in writing before you sign on.

Where to Find an Advisor

It's not too difficult to find the right financial advisor, but it may take some time. As in romance and matrimony, finding the right advisor for you can be a real trial-and-error process. If you can, get a referral from a trusted family member or friend with financial holdings similar to yours. Then you'll be starting out with somebody with a proven track record of performance productivity and a reputation for playing well with others.

If that doesn't pan out, try going directly to the organizations and associations that have access to good financial planners. You have several resources at your disposal, including the Financial Planning Association, the National Association of Personal Finance Advisors, the American Institute of Certified Public Accountants, the American Society of Financial Service Professionals, and the International Association of Registered Financial Consultants. Talk to as many professionals as you can until you find the right advisor for you.

CHAPTER 17

DIY Investing

Believe it or not, Wall Street's fastest form of broker-to-investor communication in the eighteenth century was through carrier pigeons. Things have come a long way since then. It's amazing to think that just twenty years ago, no one imagined how integral the Internet and computers would become to almost every aspect of life, including investing. Think of the speed and ease of modern-day online investing. In about five minutes, you can log on to your online account and put in a limit order for a certain stock.

How Much Will You Do Yourself?

Investing seems like a very simple process: pick a stock (or bond or fund), buy it, make a profit. Sometimes it really does work that way, but not all investments (or investment strategies) are winners.

When you're just getting started, it's a good idea to enlist professional help, in at least a minor advisory role. In fact, you may want to call on more than one professional: a CPA to guide you through tax implications, for example, and a financial planner to help you design a portfolio and create the right asset allocation strategy for you.

Some people will prefer more guidance at the outset, until they become comfortable researching and choosing securities for their own portfolios. Other people may decide to hand their money over to a financial professional, then just get regular reports and occasional dividend checks. If you're reading this, though, you probably want to take your financial future into your own hands. As long as you face this challenge with your eyes open and a wealth of research behind all the securities you invest in, you should be able to build a thriving nest egg.

DIY Investors Hit the Internet

There are quite a few advantages to Internet investing, including lower service and transaction fees.

ESSENTIAL

Be forewarned. You can get addicted to online investing. People who trade stocks online use the Internet for an average of 11.6 hours each week, as opposed to the rest of the population, which spends 8.34 hours a week online.

The Internet has revolutionized investing. Superior services are now available to more customers than ever before. Anyone can now access financial planning tools that previously were available only to the very rich. Today, Americans with $1 million net worth—a population that continues to increase—can access services at a level that used to be reserved for those with $100 million or more.

The wealth of educational information is the most important of the services available to consumers. Investors are now able to learn about stocks, bonds, and mutual funds and how to properly incorporate them into an investment portfolio, all on their own.

Investment websites do a great job promoting basic investment guidelines, like the importance of investing regularly, investing for the long term, and creating investment goals. Thanks to the Internet, investors know more about things like mutual funds—something investors just twenty years ago basically ignored.

Best Practices of Internet Investing

Even though the Internet has made the practice of investing your money faster, more convenient, and less costly, you still need to take the time to learn some of the best ways to maneuver through the web and make your investment decisions.

ALERT

Be careful when you're placing orders online. Double-check your orders before you finalize them. Make sure you're using the right ticker symbol and trading the right number of shares. If you're distracted or in a rush, you could end up with 100 shares of ABC instead of 10 shares of BAC.

To make sure your online investing experience is easy, efficient, and successful, you'll need to keep a few things in mind. First, research is the key to trading success. Never invest in anything without doing plenty of research first. Virtually all online brokerage firms provide investment information and financial news in addition to current price quotes. Beware of any information you pick up from investment message boards and chat rooms. These sites are chock full of groundless and often ridiculous rumors. Don't bet the farm on any hot tips you read on message boards, since you can't verify the legitimacy of the postings or the people who posted them.

Know Your Orders

Know the details of market and limit orders. The prices of market orders depend on the time of day the order is placed. If the price of the security you want to buy is volatile, you may end up paying more for it than you planned. When you use limit orders, you can set a specific trading price, but your order might not go through if that price isn't attained. Get familiar with your broker's trading guide, so you can be sure you place the right order type to accomplish your goal. Finally, trade wisely. There are times when the buy-and-hold strategy works well, and times when you may need to trade a little more actively to grow and protect your nest egg. Keep abreast of general market conditions, especially those directly affecting your holdings, and revisit your strategy accordingly. No matter how carefully you choose a stock, when it drops below your stop point (typically 10 percent), it's time to sell.

The Advantages of Online Investing

There are many advantages to investing online, and the more you invest online, the more Internet investor resources you'll find. Here are just a few of the benefits of managing your fund portfolio through an online broker:

- **Control.** You don't have to rely on your broker's schedule anymore. If you're confident in your decision-making process, control over your portfolio should be an advantage. It's your portfolio, and you should ultimately be responsible for making it grow. You do the research and initiate trades. And with online services, you won't have to call your broker, wait for a call back, or deal with him droning on about the mutual fund his company is pushing.
- **Access to information.** The Internet provides you with previously unavailable information on financial products and services. Investors interested in trading online can receive breaking industry news, analyst's reports, and real-time stock quotes and account updates, all from one website. You can take stock of your

investments, check up on your trading activity, and make a trade at any time.

- **Convenience.** The Internet gives you the ability to access your financial information from anywhere at any time. By employing the Internet, consumers are no longer restricted to making financial transactions at a physical location or during a firm's hours. And if you travel frequently, the Internet is the most convenient and reliable way to stay up to date.
- **Efficiency.** The web gives you a platform for managing all of your finances. With the click of a mouse, consumers have access to past account statements and transaction histories without stockpiling paper. And the Internet now gives consumers the ability to review information from multiple financial providers on one site.
- **Economy.** Increasing competition among online brokers means lower fees and commissions for you. Thanks to online investing, you can buy fifty shares of stock for $10 or $15, compared to a whopping $80 fee with a traditional broker. By using the Internet, you can put more of your money into your investments—and that means your nest egg will grow faster.

Is There a Downside?

Online investing has gained a lot of acceptance among individual investors, with its instantaneous trading and low fees. The Internet offers investors a new kind of freedom and personal empowerment, but Internet investing also carries risks.

Network Crashes

If you've experienced the horror of having your computer die in the middle of a workday, you know computers are not infallible—and neither are the networks that drive them. Traffic overloads can lead to network breakdowns, something that's become more common as more investors choose Internet brokers. Online brokers can have a hard time keeping up with investor demand on busy trading days, and sometimes they find that they can't meet the immediate needs of the many investors trying to access their sites.

When the markets are performing poorly, history shows us that investors will run to the Internet, and Internet brokers may not be able to keep up with the activity level. For example, online brokers were vilified when a one-day crash on October 27, 1997, caused trading to halt on the New York Stock Exchange and for several brokerages as well. Too many devastated investors clamored to access their accounts at one time, and brokerage sites were overwhelmed by the demand. In recent years, major Internet brokers have worked hard to increase their network capacity. They are now strong enough to cope with emergency conditions, but you must realize that online brokerages may not be available when you really need them.

ESSENTIAL

Online chat rooms offer investors communities that discuss just about every investment opportunity around the globe. At every hour of every day of the week, some new investment is being primed and pumped in an Internet chat room. To minimize fraud, the SEC says it will hold website owners liable for what they say when they engage in online chat sessions.

You're Flying Solo

If you commit to online investing, you will no longer be the wingman to your broker. You are in command of the flight, with no professional advisor to guide you along the way. For the most part, online brokers are strictly do-it-yourself ventures. Sometimes you may have access to live brokers on demand, but that's not the same as working with someone regularly, someone who's well versed in your personal financial history, resources, and objectives.

Even if you do make your trades online, a financial advisor can still help you make good investment choices and help you make sure that your choices are in line with your big-picture goals. And if you would rather let a professional make your investment decisions, the Internet can still be a great tool. It offers information and resources that will increase your knowledge of the investment world as well as allowing you to evaluate the professionals handling your money.

Beware of Internet Scams

Searching the Internet for hot stock tips? Be very skeptical of everything you read. Be aware that the analyst who claims she's discovered the next Starbucks may be a paid publicist for the stock she's endorsing. Touts-for-hire thrive in the shadow world of stock-tip web pages, where they can write whatever they want, and you can't look them square in the eye to assess their character.

It's tempting to listen to apparently objective financial analysis from a source that seems reputable, especially if she says all the right things and asks nothing in exchange for the hot tip she's giving you. All you have to do is click your mouse a few times to buy the stock, then you can sit back and await a big payday—which will probably never come. By the time you realize that you've been had, your investment dollars have already vanished—and so has the "financial professional" who gave you the tip and is now enjoying her big payday from the executives who cashed in on your investment naiveté. This happens so often that there are names for it, like "pump and dump" (where "analysts" talk up a lackluster stock that they own, then sell it off when the price hits a peak and leave you with a worthless security).

Did You Hear the One About . . . ?

The SEC takes investment fraud very seriously. On its website (*www .sec.gov*), you can find plenty of stories about their successful investigations. Check out the case of Matthew Bowin, for example. According to the SEC, Bowin raised $190,000 solely from online investors. He solicited Internet investments for his company ("Interactive Products and Services"), then turned around and spent the money on himself. The SEC got wind of the scam and had Bowin prosecuted. He was found guilty on fifty-four felony accounts, and sentenced to ten years in jail.

That's just one example, and there are many more. That's why you have to be especially vigilant when you're investing online, especially when someone comes to you looking for money. In addition, the SEC warns online investors about the growing threat of identity theft, particularly through the act of phishing. Phishing happens when a thief uses a copycat website to steal your personal information. For example, the thief creates a fake Bank of America website that looks very similar to the real one and entices you to log on with your account and password information. He then takes that information to access your real account—and steal all your money.

What You Can Do

You are not helpless here; you have the resources to fight back. Investors can help the SEC track and catch securities scam artists. If you've been duped or if you've visited a suspicious investment advice website, take the following steps to make sure Internet criminals are stopped right away:

- Contact your state securities regulator or check the SEC's online database (follow the links from *www.sec.gov* to EDGAR) to see if a security has been properly registered.
- Ask your state securities office to find out whether the person or firm selling the security has a valid license to conduct business in the state and whether any complaints or fraud alerts have been filed.
- Assume the worst. Until you've done independent research that proves an investment worthwhile, assume any investments offered over the web are scams.

The SEC strongly encourages investors to report suspicious Internet activities related to securities fraud to its Enforcement Complaint Center. You can reach them at the SEC website (*www.sec.gov*) or e-mail them directly at *enforcement@sec.gov*. To learn more about avoiding Internet fraud, check out the Investor Information section of the agency's website.

What to Look for in an Investment Website

In order to get the full advantages that go along with online investing, look for websites that provide all the education and tracking tools you need to manage your portfolio successfully. Different site features and styles will appeal to different people, but a truly useful website will have these elements:

- An easy-to-access website with simple onscreen navigation
- A trading screen that's easy to get around and includes built-in safeguards against typing mistakes
- Current stock prices posted on the screen at all times
- The ability to trade a variety of securities, including stocks, bonds, mutual funds, and exchange-traded funds
- Immediate transaction confirmations
- Real-time account balances and portfolio updates
- Instant customer service access, both online and over the phone, available all day, every day
- A low minimum-balance requirement to open and maintain an account
- The ability to enter special buy and sell orders, like limit orders and stops, so you can automatically trade a security when it hits a specific price without tracking it all day yourself
- An automatic daily sweep of any uninvested cash into a money market fund

ESSENTIAL

Internet chat rooms can be informative places to meet with other investors and get the benefit of disparate advice. Use caution, though, when you're sifting through this information. You don't know the sources, and a lot of information exchanged on message boards is bogus.

The Ten Best Investment Websites

There are hundreds of investment-related sites out there in the ether. If you search around, you'll find plenty to choose from, although the quality can vary dramatically from site to site. Be careful whose advice you take, and make sure you know where their information comes from. To get you started, here is a list of the top ten investment sites, in no particular order:

- **E*TRADE** (*www.etrade.com*). This site offers a comfortable trading experience with lots of bonus features. Easy to use and navigate.
- **Schwab** (*www.schwab.com*). Serving more than 7 million investors, Schwab offers online investing with a personal touch, including easy-access research and reasonable fees.
- **TD Ameritrade** (*www.tdameritrade.com*). This site offers competitive pricing, abundant third-party research, and great human customer support.
- **Sharebuilder by ING** (*www.sharebuilder.com*). With commissions as low as $4 per trade, this site makes it easy to keep more of your money working for you and allows you to invest in more than 7,000 stocks and ETFs without any account minimums or inactivity fees.
- **The Motley Fool** (*www.fool.com*). A great place to get financial advice, analysis and commentary in plain English, as well as personal financial calculators and investing tutorials.
- **MSN Money** (*www.investor.com*). In just a few minutes, you can download a free portfolio-tracking program, which offers extensive portfolio management features, such as integrated charts and news to help you track your investments.
- **Morningstar** (*www.morningstar.com*). Morningstar offers superior securities and market analysis, as well as excellent portfolio management tools to help you make better investment choices.
- **Reuters Financial** (*www.reuters.com/finance*). This fast, easy-to-use site lets you see how your investments are faring anytime during the day and posts up-to-the-minute breaking financial and economic news.

- **CNET News** (*news.cnet.com*). This cutting-edge site provides IPO information, tech market updates, headline news, and much more for the investor who wants to play a little edgy.
- **Hoover's Online** (*www.hoovers.com*). A site designed to provide information to help guide the investor through the marketplace, Hoover's offers detailed research on more than 32 million companies, assessments of industry trends, and news and analysis from outside sources.

The websites of traditional newspapers and magazines are also good places to look. The *Wall Street Journal* (*www.wsj.com*), the *Washington Post* (*www.washingtonpost.com*), and *Forbes* (*www.forbes.com*) all offer trustworthy information.

CHAPTER 18

You, Your Portfolio, and Uncle Sam: Investing and Taxes

Naturally, you can't expect to get high returns from your investments scot-free. Uncle Sam expects a little compensation too. But think about it this way: If you weren't making money, you wouldn't be paying taxes. You can double your investment in just a few years if you make the right investment choices, and that includes some tax planning. Sure, taxes can be burdensome and the system could use some reform, but if you consider them just another investment expense, they may not seem quite so taxing.

How Taxes Impact Your Portfolio

Wall Street and the U.S. Congress have always been engaged in a tug of war, battling over the amount of money investors make and how much of that money should be taxed and given to Uncle Sam.

Naturally, Wall Street takes a minimalist approach to taxes—the less taken out of investor earnings, the better. Uncle Sam sees things differently and expects investors to dig deep and fork over a chunk of their profits.

As an investor, you might vehemently disagree with Uncle Sam, but there's no way around it—you'll have to pay taxes. This being the case, what's the best way for you to hang on to as much of your hard-earned investment as you can? You can actually do a lot to help control your tax burden.

QUESTION

How many people work for the Internal Revenue Service (IRS)?
For fiscal year 2008, the IRS scored a $11.4 million dollar budget. This supports approximately 90,000 employees, which encompasses such diverse careers as revenue agents, taxpayer advocates, and economists.

First, get a sense of the terrain—learn the types and workings of investment taxes, like capital gains and retirement plan taxes. Once you're a tax expert, you'll be ready to work with your accountant to prepare a tax strategy that keeps your wallet full.

You can owe taxes on a number of investments. Primarily, though, most tax-related events apply to American stocks, bonds, mutual funds, and other investments that you've bought and sold, as well as tax-deferred retirement plans like IRAs and 401(k)s. And don't forget your house—possibly your biggest investment of all.

Types of Investment Taxes

There are generally three ways in which investment income can be taxed: through dividends, capital gains, and investment interest. When a company profits, it distributes dividends to its shareholders. You can choose to receive the dividends as a check or have them invested directly in a dividend reinvestment plan, or DRIP. When you sell an investment security like bonds, stocks, or mutual funds at a profit, you generate a capital gain. When the opposite happens and you sell at a loss, it's called a capital loss.

With a capital gain, the holding period for the investment security will determine the tax rate. For holding periods of longer than twelve months, rates are 15 percent for qualifying taxpayers in the 25 percent and higher tax brackets. For those in the 10 percent and 15 percent brackets, the long-term capital gains tax rate is zero—that's right, nothing (at least through 2010 under current law). If you hold a security for twelve months or fewer, any gains are taxed at the same rate as your ordinary income. Capital losses, whether long-term or short-term, can be deducted against any capital gains. Should your capital losses exceed your gains, up to $3,000 can be used to offset your other taxable income.

ESSENTIAL

To keep your cash in your wallet, keep efficient tax records. These can equal big savings for you. For example, keep track of your tax credits and allowable deductions in order to use them, and you'll find that more of your money stays yours.

Most interest earned from your investments, mostly fixed-income investments like bonds, are considered taxable at your marginal tax rate. Some interest-bearing investments offer you tax-free income at the federal or state level. For example, municipal bond interest is normally not taxed by the state or locality that pays the interest and is usually exempt from federal income taxes.

Then there's the flip side: deductible investment interest. Even though many people believe that only mortgage interest is tax deductible, the current law lets investors deduct the interest they pay on loans (such as margin interest) they've used to make investments. Typically, you're allowed to deduct that interest to the extent of your taxable investment earnings. When you're figuring out your investment income for this purpose, you usually can't include capital gains that are treated specially under the law or nontaxable interest or dividends. Your tax professional can help you figure out how much of your investment interest expense is deductible for tax purposes.

Creating an Investment Tax Strategy

When it comes to any type of tax planning, the basic premise is this: Keep your taxes to the bare minimum and keep more money in your pocket. To make that goal a reality takes some planning on your part, best done in conjunction with your accountant or financial advisor. Remember, though, that while tax avoidance (i.e. minimizing your tax bill by every legal means) is legal, tax evasion is not.

FACT

Though it may seem like there's a tax for everything, some things in life are actually tax free! For example, some investment-related income, such as life insurance proceeds paid upon the policyholder's death and interest on municipal bonds, is not taxable by the IRS.

While the current U.S. tax code allows for plenty of tax shelters, which are ways to protect your wealth from current taxation, there are lots of illegal tax shelters out there, and the IRS uses its best people to track them down. Legal tax shelters include common things like your house and your retirement account, and also more sophisticated holdings like certain oil and gas investments and specialized techniques.

Measuring Gains and Losses

One part of tax planning is assessing where you stand on the gain/loss scale. If your investment losses exceed your gains, you can take small comfort in the fact that you've trimmed your tax bill. If you've scored a lot of gains throughout the year, though, you could get hit with a whopping tax bill—and that's where one key planning strategy comes into play.

October is the time to look at your holdings with an eye toward your tax bill. If you've been holding on to some losers, hoping they might turn around, you'll have a couple of months to sell them and at least reap a tax advantage. Every loss you incur helps offset the gains you've earned, and lower gains means a lower tax bill.

If you have racked up a large net loss, consider cashing in some investments that are currently showing large paper gains. The reason? Selling those investments now locks in the gains, and lets you keep more of that hard-earned profit. Your current existing losses will offset your gains, which allows you to realize those gains while legally avoiding the taxes you would otherwise have to pay.

ALERT

Is a foreign tax credit on your docket? You may be entitled to this lesser-known deduction if, for example, you own a mutual fund that invests in foreign securities. You can count foreign taxes as itemized deductions or as direct tax credits. The credit is usually worth more than the itemized deduction: deductions just reduce your taxable income, while credits reduce your actual tax liability, dollar for dollar.

That's great tax advice, but don't act impulsively. Keep in mind that tax consequences are like a side salad compared to the investments that comprise the meat and potatoes of your lifelong investment portfolio.

Know Your Holding Period

Your capital gains tax rate varies based on how long you've had the investment; that time period is officially known as your holding period. The rules are fairly straightforward. If you've held the investment for more than one year before selling, you've got a long-term capital gain (and, therefore, a lower tax rate). Investments held for one year or less are considered short term. So if you bought Stock XYZ on January 11, 2007, and sold it on January 11, 2008, you had a short-term capital gain. But if you waited the extra day and sold on January 12, 2008, you lowered the tax bill by transforming the trade into a long-term capital gains transaction.

How to Benefit from Deductions

Are investment-related expenses tax deductible? You bet. From phone calls to your broker to dividend redistribution plan charges, you can deduct in quite a few areas. In fact, many costs associated with helping you invest that produce taxable income are tax deductible (though expenses related to tax-free income, like the interest from municipal bonds, can't be deducted). Here are some expenses you may not have realized are deductible:

- Trading account maintenance fees
- Books, magazines, newsletters, and other materials you read to gain financial knowledge to apply to your trading
- Travel expenses when you meet with your financial advisor
- Any fees you pay to maintain your investments, like professional recordkeeping, IRA account setup, and custodial fees

Tips for Reducing Your Investment Tax Liability

Face it—no matter how much you'd like to try, you won't be able to get around paying taxes on your successful investments. If you're smart with your investing strategies, you can significantly minimize the taxes you'll have to pay, however. As a savvy investor, it's important that you be aware of the upsides and downsides of your investment plans as they relate to potential tax liability. The following sections provide some tips for how to go about investing wisely while keeping an eye on your taxes.

Stocks

You must keep purchase documents for every security you buy, especially if you've bought shares in the same company at different times. At sale time, you'll subtract the cost basis of your stock from your sale proceeds to determine the gain or loss. Your cost basis equals the amount you paid for the stock, plus commissions. Another key factor is the holding period, or length of time you owned the stock. That determines your tax rate, and the long-term holding rate is lower than the short-term tax bite.

Let's look at some numbers:

- You pick up 100 shares of XYZ, Inc., in January 2009 for $1,000 including commissions. Your basis is $10 per share.
- You buy another 100 shares in March 2009, this time for $2,000 including commissions; for those shares, the basis comes to $20 each.
- Finally, in January 2010 you add another 100 shares to your holdings, this time for a total (including commissions) of $3,000, for a per-share basis of $30.

In October 2010, the stock hit $50 per share, so you decide to sell off some of your holdings and take a profit. If you tell your broker to sell 100 shares, he'll follow the IRS guideline called first-in, first-out (or FIFO). That means he sells the shares you bought in 2009. However, you can tell him to sell particular shares when that will be more advantageous to you in terms of taxes. Regardless of which shares you sell, your proceeds will be $5,000. But your total gains—and the tax rate on them—depend on which stocks you've sold. With the January 2009 shares, you'll have a $4,000 long-term gain. The March 2009 shares bring a $3,000 long-term gain, and the 2010 shares net you a $2,000 short-term gain.

Which shares you choose to sell will depend on your overall tax picture at the time. If you have short-term losses to offset, you may want to shed the most recently purchased shares. If you have no other capital transactions, you may choose the 2009 shares for the smallest addition to your tax bill. In any case, the bottom line is that as long as you have your records, the impact on your taxes is up to you.

Mutual Funds

Mutual funds are treated a bit differently than stocks in that they are taxed in three distinct ways: dividend distributions, capital gains distributions, and gains or loss from selling shares. Just like a stock sale, when you sell your fund shares for more money than you've put into them, you'll be faced with a capital gains tax bill. The reverse is true as well: When you sell your mutual funds shares at a loss, you get to declare that loss on your taxes, reducing the rest of your income. The total amount you deduct from the sales price is called the basis, and it can be complicated to figure out—which is why most fund companies and brokers keep track of it for you.

If you invest in any mutual funds (except municipal bonds), you'll pay taxes on all the capital gains and dividends your shares earn. Dividend distributions come from the regular dividend and interest paid out on the underlying securities that make up the fund portfolio. As these earnings are periodically passed on to investors, they have to be reported by investors on their own personal tax returns. Likewise, capital gains distributions come from sales of securities held within the fund, and they get passed through to investors with the same tax-advantaged characteristics. Investors have to pay taxes on these distributions even if they are automatically reinvested in the fund.

Municipal Bonds

Just as interest earned on U.S. government securities doesn't generate state and local income taxes, interest on debt securities issued by states and municipalities don't get hit by the federal revenue squad. These debt securities are known as municipal bonds, or munis. They are exempt from federal income taxes (and often from state and local income taxes as well), and typically offer lower interest rates than bonds that are fully taxable. You can make up that earnings difference through their tax savings.

It would be handy if municipal bond investing were 100 percent tax free—but it isn't. Though the interest you earn on municipal bonds is federal income tax exempt, you still have the tax consequences from capital gains (or losses) that occur when you sell these bonds. If you sell a muni and get more than your basis, your profit counts as a fully taxable capital gain. On the other hand, if you sell it for a loss, you've got a deductible capital loss.

Life Insurance

Once a virtual afterthought at the Wall Street party during the late 1990s, life insurance is in big demand these days, thanks to recent changes by Congress that merge some elements of stocks and bonds into life insurance and boost its appeal. If you choose a policy that pairs your investments with some type of life insurance policy (for instance, whole life, universal life, or single-premium life), it will gain you tax-favored status.

Here's how it works: Instead of paying for insurance, a portion of your premiums go into investments that can build cash value. These investment earnings are protected from the IRS.

You don't have to die to get these tax benefits, either. You are allowed to borrow against your policy's cash value. They are very special loans because you don't have to pay them back, ever. Loans still outstanding at the time of death get deducted from the insurance proceeds due to your beneficiaries. Even though you will have to pay interest on that loan, policy earnings can counter it.

Annuities

A stronger investment-insurance hybrid, annuities also sport big tax advantages. With annuities, you know your heirs will inherit at least as much money as you have put into the annuity, even if it's lost some money. But the real allure of annuities is the tax-free earnings accumulation that goes on until you start withdrawing funds.

ALERT

If you cash out your annuity before you hit retirement age, beware. Most annuity contracts hit you with steep surrender charges if you withdraw funds during the first several years (the exception being immediate annuities). And if you're younger than the legal retirement age, 59½, you could be facing a 10 percent tax penalty.

An annuity contract prevents the taxman from taking your earnings, which differs from bank CDs and mutual funds. No taxes are due until you start taking funds out, which usually begins in retirement, which you can get either in steady periodic payments or in a single lump sum. Funds in an annuity have the same tax-deferred growth advantage as the money invested in an individual retirement account. But you aren't able to deduct amounts that are in an annuity, unlike an IRA.

Even aside from potential tax penalties, annuities don't come cheap. There are myriad fees associated with these instruments: surrender charges (usually very high fees—think 8 or 9 percent—for taking your money out before your contract allows); mortality and expense fees (charged based on customer risk characteristics); and administrative and management fees. Except for surrender charges, these are annual fees—and they typically run 0.50 to 0.75 percent higher than similar mutual fund fees.

Understanding (Legal) Tax Shelters

Everything you do to reduce your tax bill technically counts as a tax shelter. Essentially, you are sheltering your income from being eaten away by taxes. You can accomplish this two ways: defer the tax bill (such as when you put money into retirement accounts) or avoid it completely. Tax shelters include investments, special investment accounts, and planning strategies that either lower your current taxable income or offer favorable tax treatment to your income.

ALERT

The IRS always keeps an eagle eye on tax shelters. It looks for investments made solely for the purpose to evade taxes. And if they recharacterize your transaction, you could be hit not only with current taxes but also further taxes and penalties. Remember, it's okay to minimize your tax bills—even reduce them to zero—but tax evasion is illegal.

Real estate investment is one of the best tax shelters available. In fact, it's by far the most popular. That's largely due to the depreciation deduction you get on investment properties (especially rental properties). Depreciation is an on-paper expense, meaning you don't pay for it right now. The related tax deduction, though, puts real money in your pocket, or at least reduces the money you'll pay in taxes.

Novice investors don't use most other investment tax shelters. Oil and gas investments, for example, offer big deductions for drilling and developing costs. Investors typically take part in these investments through limited partnerships, usually found by their investment advisors. These investments do come with a downside, though: Your investment may not pay off if oil is not found, leaving you with deductions but no income to offset them with. Other tax-sheltered investments (again, usually purchased in the form of partnership shares through investment advisors) include equipment leasing and cattle breeding.

If you're looking for real life ways to shelter your investment earnings from taxes, there are a few very simple steps you can take. Whenever possible, hold on to investments longer than one year. Put as much money as you can into tax-sheltered accounts like IRAs and 401(k) plans and college savings accounts. Bump up your itemized deductions by remembering to take credit for all of your investment expenses. And work closely with your tax preparer, who can make sure you take advantage of every possible loophole available to you.

CHAPTER 19

Investing for Education

College costs are rising at an alarming pace. In order to make sure your kids will have the benefit of higher education, you need to start saving right now. Luckily, there are several investment options that can help you send your kids to college—without sacrificing your retirement. You can invest in state-sponsored plans, like a 529 plan, or you can set up your own plan, similar to an IRA. In fact, you can even do both. Whatever you decide, though, your best bet is to start right away.

Start Planning for College Tuition Now

If you take nothing else away from this chapter, remember this: Start saving now for your children's college tuition or a lot of choices could fall off the table. If you don't have children yet, start saving as soon as you begin thinking about having them. By starting earlier, you have more opportunity to let the power of compounding work for you, building your savings faster. Complete college costs today can run close to $14,000 a year for state schools and a whopping $41,000 and up for private schools.

Let's take a step back, though. How can you figure out how much to put away for a college education that won't begin for ten or twenty years? Quick and easy answer: online calculators. These can help you figure out the whole cost of college: tuition, books, room and board, even living expenses. Depending on your unique situation, you may also need to figure in transportation expenses if your child goes to school far from home.

One of the best websites for this calculation comes courtesy of Sallie Mae (*www.salliemae.com*). Their free planning tool, the Education Investment Planner (*www.salliemae.com/content/landing/planner/eip.html*), walks you through college costs and lets you compare costs among thousands of schools (both public and private). The site even helps parents look into the many different ways they can pay for college: savings, scholarships, grants, and student loans.

ALERT

Just because one college costs more than another doesn't necessarily mean you'll pay more out of pocket to send your child there. More expensive schools often offer more financial aid. That aid can translate into a lower cost than if you sent your child to a school with a lower tuition.

To use the Sallie Mae site for long-term planning, you'll be asked to fill in some basic information:

- The current cost of attending the college of choice
- The number of years left until your child will be starting college

- How much money you already have saved and earmarked for college costs
- The expected rate of return on your investments

Once you've come up with a projected bottom line, the site offers suggestions to help you create a savings plan to help you cope with the rising costs. Their first step: directing you toward all the potential sources of free money, in the form of scholarships.

Tax-Sheltered Education Savings Save the Day

Regular investments inevitably lead to tax bills, and that eats into your investment dollars. Until fairly recently, that was the only way to save money for college. Now, though, you have tax-advantaged choices, options that let your money grow tax-deferred, and (in some cases) let you use the money with no tax bill attached.

ESSENTIAL

The tax code offers breaks in the form of education tax credits and deductions. Ask your tax accountant if you're eligible to claim either the Hope credit of the Lifetime Learning credit. You may also be able to take advantage for special deductions for tuition and fees or student loan interest that you've paid.

Why is tax-deferred growth so important? It lets you keep more of your money working for you, and lets your nest egg grow faster than it would if you had to keep depleting it to pay taxes on your earnings. This works in the same way as retirement savings. The more taxes you can avoid, the better.

There are three kinds of tax advantages you can look for. First, the money you put away now isn't taxed or becomes temporarily tax-deductible. Second, the earnings aren't taxable now. Third, the money doesn't get taxed when you withdraw it to pay for college. Not all college investments offer this triple play; some of them don't offer any tax advantages at all. As you look for the savings vehicles that work best for your family situation, remember to consider the current and future impact that taxes will have on your hard-earned money.

All About 529 Plans

Qualified tuition plans, also known as 529 plans, have changed the college savings playing ground. These state-sponsored plans serve up big tax advantages, making it easier than ever to save for a college education. There are two main types of 529 plans: college savings plans (the type most people think of when they hear 529) and prepaid tuition plans.

ALERT

If you use the money from a college savings plan on expenses that don't qualify, you'll be subject to a hefty tax penalty on your earnings: an extra 10 percent on top of the normal taxes that will be due. For example, transportation to the school and dorm room decorating items do not qualify as education expenses.

College savings plans allow an account holder (usually a parent or grandparent) to set up an account for a future student (formally called the beneficiary). As the account holder, you make decisions about the account, which can include investment choices, though these may be limited depending on the state sponsoring the plan. When it's college time, you can use the funds in this 529 plan to pay for all "qualified higher education costs," which include fees, books, and computers along with tuition and room and board. And as long as you use the money for such qualified expenses, you won't have to pay federal income taxes; in most cases, the funds will be exempt from state income taxes, too. In fact, many states give their residents a current tax deduction for contributions to the home state 529 plan; some states even give you a deduction if you contribute to any state's plan.

Another huge advantage of these plans is the enormous contribution limit. You can get these tax-advantaged savings on contributions as large as $300,000 in some states. Plus, there are no income limitations, meaning you can't get phased out of the tax benefits on these plans. Of course, there's still a little tax catch (there always is): The contributions could be subject to federal (and possibly state) gift taxes. As of the date of this printing, gifts larger than $12,000 (or $24,000 from a couple) are typically subject to gift tax reporting. Luckily, there's a special exception that specifically addresses 529 plan contributions: a couple can put up to $100,000 into a qualified state tuition plan and it will count as $20,000 over five years, nullifying the whole gift tax issue. But they can't make any more gift-tax-free contributions until that five years is up.

It all sounds good, but there are some disadvantages. For example, you have limited control over where your money gets invested. Typically, the state invests the funds for you from a very limited menu. In some states, you may have as few as two investment choices, up to thirty in others. Plus, you can only change your choices once a year. Also, funds in a 529 plan account do reduce the amount of financial aid available to the student.

Coverdell Education Savings Accounts

A Coverdell Education Savings Account (ESA) is a tax-advantaged way to save for college with a unique, beneficial twist: The money can be used for any education expenses, including primary and secondary school. And while the contributions to the ESA are not tax-deductible, the earnings on the account are tax-free when you use them to pay for qualified education expenses.

ALERT

An ESA can severely limit (or even completely eliminate) the amount of financial aid your child would be otherwise eligible for. That's because the account is considered to be the child's asset, which is given extra weight when financial aid calculations are made.

To get started, you open an ESA at your bank (or other financial institution, like your brokerage firm) for each child who will benefit; three children would mean three separate ESAs. While each ESA can only be opened for one child, one child can have more than one ESA opened in his name.

Every year, you can contribute up to $2,000 into ESAs for a single beneficiary; if one child has more than one ESA, the total annual contribution among them is limited to $2,000. If more is contributed for a single child (even if the money comes from different taxpayers), the consequence is a tax penalty on the excess. You can, though, make multiple $2,000 contributions if you have more than one child. Contributions can only be made until the child turns 18, with one exception: you can contribute anything in the same year you use funds to pay for tuition.

As you probably expect by now, there are other hurdles to cross. Let's start with the income limitations; how much money you earn limits the amount of money you can put into the ESA. Single taxpayers earning less than $95,000 or joint taxpayers earning less than $190,000 can contribute the full amount. Earn more than that, though, and your maximum contribution drops until it's fully phased out when single earnings hit $110,000 and joint earnings hit $220,000. In addition, the funds have to be used by the time the beneficiary turns thirty.

FACT

These tax-advantaged college savings vehicles used to be called Education IRAs, until people realized they really had nothing at all to do with retirement. So in July 2001 these accounts were renamed Coverdell Education Savings Accounts, in order to honor late Georgia Senator Paul Coverdell.

Let's not overlook the very real advantages of the ESA, though. Unlike other college savings vehicles, you have complete control over the investments. You can invest the ESA funds in virtually anything: mutual funds, stocks, bonds, whatever you think will work. You can open the account wherever you want. And the ability to use these for any level of education makes them very flexible: You can send your child to private kindergarten with this money if you want to. Finally, you can contribute to both an ESA and a 529 (in most cases), allowing you more control of your child's future.

Should You Invest in a Prepaid Tuition Plan?

State-sponsored prepaid tuition plans fall under the 529 umbrella, but they are quite different than standard college savings plans. Though the details vary from state to state, the basic idea is standard. Parents pay money now to purchase future college tuition.

There are a lot of benefits here. To start, you pay today's tuition cost regardless of when your child will be attending. That payment secures you a guarantee that your child will be entitled to go to college in the future, no matter how much it costs then. Though most of these plans are designed for state schools, a lot of states include built-in flexibility that allows the funds to be used toward out-of-state or private colleges. If you don't end up using the account to send your child to college, you can transfer the account to another relative, hold on to it for grandchildren, or even get a full or partial refund. One big downside, though: These plans reduce your child's eligibility for financial aid dollar-for-dollar. So if your child wants to go to a private school and the prepaid plan doesn't cover the whole cost, you probably won't be able to turn to financial aid.

QUESTION

How will I know which plan to choose?
Each state's plan is different. But there's a single website that includes detailed information about all of them: the College Savings Plan Network (*www.collegesavings.org*). There you can find out individual plan characteristics and follow links to state websites to learn even more.

Exactly what the plan offers depends on the state sponsoring it. While all states offer full prepaid tuition for four-year colleges, many also let you prepay room and board costs. If you find a state plan that you like better than the one offered by your home state, you may be able to choose a different plan.

Now that you know the basics, it's time to answer the question: Does a prepaid tuition plan make sense for your family? This type of plan may be right for you if:

- You don't like risk and uncertainty
- You'll sleep better at night knowing that college tuition is guaranteed
- You don't expect to be eligible for financial aid
- The school your child wants to attend is covered by a prepaid plan

Remember, you've always got the option of investing in both a prepaid tuition plan and an ESA. So any costs not covered by the prepaid plan can be picked up by funds you've accumulated in the ESA, without affecting either's tax advantages.

Education Bonds and CDs

For the past ten years or so, anxious parents have had the option to invest in safe, guaranteed college investment vehicles—specifically education bonds and college CDs—and they've largely passed them by. After all, when the stock market was going higher every day, it was easy to ignore options that simply plodded along without bringing back super high returns. Now that the markets have seen big dips and the credit crunch has hit home, safe (but boring) investments suddenly have a lot more appeal.

They should, and not just because other investments have lost their allure. These college savings vehicles deserve a place in your college savings portfolio in every market. They serve as a safety net for your college savings, and they do provide returns—not exciting returns, but guaranteed steady returns. What you see is what you get.

Education Bonds

The U.S. Treasury wants your children to go to college, and to help you along they created an Education Bond Program, which is very similar to their plain old savings bond program. It's not just the name that sets these bonds apart, though; it's their tax treatment.

When you specifically buy an education savings bond (Series EE or Series I, as long as they were issued after 1989), your interest earnings will be at least partially (but usually completely) exempt from federal income tax. To be eligible for that favored tax treatment, which effectively ramps up your earnings, you have to jump through a few hoops.

- You have to pay for qualified education expenses with all of the bond proceeds (principal and interest) in the same year that you redeem the bonds.
- You have to be at least twenty-four years old when you buy the bond.

- You have to register the securities in your name if you plan to use them for yourself.
- You have to register them in your name or your spouse's name if you plan to use them for your children.
- If you're married, you have to file a joint tax return to get the tax break.
- You cannot list your child as a co-owner of the bond, only as a beneficiary.

On top of all that, the tax benefit is subject to income caps—if you make too much money, no tax-free interest. Your income is evaluated in the year you redeem the bonds, not the year you purchase them. For 2008, the tax break disappears for single taxpayers earning at least $82,100 and joint taxpayers earning at least $130,650. Only single taxpayers earning less than $67,100 and joint taxpayers earning less than $100,650 qualify for the full benefit. These income thresholds are adjusted every year, so the levels by the time you pay for college expenses will likely look substantially different.

College Certificates of Deposit

You already know about regular bank certificates of deposit, (CDs), but what you might not know is that there are special CDs whose sole purpose is education investing. More than ten years ago, the College Savings Bank created and introduced these targeted accounts called CollegeSure CDs. In some ways, they work just like regular CDs: For example, you deposit a lump of money for a specific long term and you can't take that money out early without paying a penalty. However, CollegeSure CDs have something you won't find in plain old bank CDs—a college-oriented interest rate.

FACT

Unlike other types of college investments, CollegeSure CDs are guaranteed in two ways. First, these CDs are covered by FDIC insurance, so your money won't disappear. Second, your rate of return is guaranteed, so you don't have to worry that your returns will decline or disappear.

Interest on CollegeSure CDs is based on the Independent College 500 Index (created by the College Board). The index, as its name implies, tracks the average cost of 500 private schools. And the CollegeSure interest rate equals the average cost increase in those colleges. In fact, the rate is guaranteed to be no lower than that average, but it can be higher.

Here's how college CDs work as a college-savings vehicle. The big lump you deposit is the amount you would need to pay to send your kid to college now. Each "unit" (these CDs are measured in units) equals one year of all-inclusive college costs. Of course, you don't have to deposit the full amount all in one shot—you can buy pieces of units. The minimum deposit to open a unit is $500, and you can add to it in increments of $250 or more ($100 increments if you use an automatic monthly savings plan). Then, thanks to the index-based interest rate, that deposit will grow at the same rate as college costs.

CHAPTER 20

Retirement Planning

Think you're too young to start thinking about your retirement? Think again. People are living longer, which means you'll likely have quite a few golden years to enjoy. Get the most out of them by planning your future goals now. Numerous investment options will help you attain your goals. You can invest in employer-based plans, like a 401(k), or you can set up your own plan, like an IRA. Don't plan to rely on Social Security as your sole source of income for retirement.

The Beauty of Tax-Deferred Investing

Taxable investments require that you pay taxes on annual interest or dividends and on any profit on investments you sell. For instance, if you have a savings account, you'll be taxed on the interest it earns. Tax-deferred investments, on the other hand, offer you a way to avoid paying taxes on your current earnings, at least until you reach a certain age or meet other qualifications. This chapter discusses the different types of tax-deferred investments and how you can best take advantage of them.

FACT

A tax-exempt (or tax-free) investment is one where current income earned on the investment is not taxed—for instance, most municipal bonds. Keep in mind that even tax-exempt investments aren't necessarily free of all taxes. Depending on the investment, you may be exempt only from certain taxes, like federal income tax or state and local taxes.

When you hold investments outside special tax-deferred accounts, you will likely be required to pay taxes on their earnings, both regular income (like interest and dividends) and capital gains. Virtually every type of investment is taxable on some level, from stocks to bonds to funds. Even real estate investments, businesses you own a piece of, and collectibles, basically, any investment you make where you can enjoy the profits (or suffer the losses) immediately (and not have to wait until some time in the future) can impact your current taxes.

If you have a tax-deferred investment and don't withdraw any money from the account, you don't pay taxes on it. Most of the time, the money you place into tax-deferred accounts will be at least partially, if not completely, tax deductible right now. Of course, some exceptions apply, like Roth IRA contributions or contributions whose deductibility gets phased out based on your income level. Keep in mind that these accounts are meant to be used for large and specific financial goals, like education or retirement. If you withdraw money from these accounts too soon, or use the money for other purposes, you can expect to pay some stiff penalties.

A big plus of tax-deferred investing is the ability to put pre-tax dollars into retirement accounts. For instance, with a 401(k) plan, your contribution to a tax-deferred retirement plan is deducted from your taxable income. This lets you invest money for the future that you would have otherwise paid to Uncle Sam. Let's say your income puts you in the 27 percent marginal income tax bracket, and your annual contribution to your tax-deferred retirement plan is $1,000. Your federal income taxes will drop by $270, or 27 percent of your retirement contribution. Your marginal tax rate (which is the rate you pay on your highest dollar of earnings) determines your savings. To find your marginal tax rate, visit the IRS website at *www.irs.gov.*

Advantages of Investing Early and Often

It's simple. The earlier you begin investing, the more money you'll have for retirement. That's because you're giving your money more time to grow. On top of that, you have more time to ride out market downturns. With more time on your side, your retirement savings will have more time to rebound if the markets take a dive.

Consider the story of two twenty-five-year-olds, Madison and Cooper. Madison invests $2,000 annually over ten years, stashing the money away in her company's 401(k) plan. Then she stops at age thirty-five, never adding another penny into her plan. Madison can expect an average 10 percent annual growth rate on her investments. Because she started early and gave her money time to grow before taking it out at retirement, she can cash out at age sixty-five with $556,197.

Starting at age thirty-four, Cooper socks $2,000 away in his 401(k) plan every year for the next thirty years. Cooper ends up putting away three times as much money as Madison. But his retirement stash—which has earned the same rate of return over the years—is just $328,988. That's much less— more than $225,000 less—than Madison's.

Both Madison and Cooper had the power of compound interest on their side. Madison harnessed it earlier and thus reaped higher gains. Here's the moral of the story: If you can afford to live without those tens or even hundreds of thousands of dollars in retirement, then by all means procrastinate. The easiest way to figure out the compounding effect on the money you're putting away is with an online retirement calculator (try the one at *www. finance.cch.com*).

The 401(k) Plan

For nearly twenty years, one of the most significant retirement investing tools has been the 401(k) plan. The 401(k) is set up by your employer and is designed to help you save (and build) money for retirement. The money you contribute to your 401(k) is pooled and invested in stocks, bonds, mutual funds, or other types of investments. You choose the type of investment from your company's list of options. Usually your contribution is deducted from your paycheck before taxes and goes directly into your 401(k) account.

If such a plan is offered where you work, there is no reason not to jump at the opportunity. Putting the money in a plan earmarks it for your retirement, and you don't have to pay taxes on it as the money grows. In addition, employers generally make a matching contribution, which can be as much as 10, 25, or even 50 percent of the amount you contribute.

ESSENTIAL

A 401(k) plan can be set up by an employer in a number of different manners, with some going into effect immediately and others kicking in after you've worked in the company for a certain length of time. As of 2008, you can contribute up to $15,500 of your salary to your 401(k) plan in a given year.

There is a big difference between investing in a 401(k) and in a mutual fund that you can buy or sell at will. The IRS will not tax your 401(k) earnings as long as they remain invested in your 401(k). As soon as the money starts coming out, you'll start paying taxes on it. And if you withdraw money before a set date (usually when you reach 59½ years of age), you may have to pay a penalty. With a current mutual fund investment, you'll pay taxes annually on the dividends and capital gains your fund earns, whether you take the money out or let it continue to work for you.

If your employer is making a matching contribution to your 401(k) of, say, 10 percent of what you put in, you are already seeing a 10 percent growth on your investment, plus whatever gains the total investment accrues over time. It is a simple solution to retirement planning that you do not have to set up yourself. You do, however, need to keep tabs on where your 401(k) money is being invested. Too many people just make a choice and let it ride.

If you work in a nonprofit organization, you may be able to choose a 403(b) plan, which works similarly to a 401(k). Such plans generally have fewer investment options, but they are also tax-deferred. Government workers may be offered a 457 plan, which is also similar in principle to a 401(k) or 403(b), with some additional restrictions.

Your 401(k) Investing Strategy

Since you are in a retirement plan for the long haul, you need not worry too much about the days, weeks, or even months when the stock market is down. In fact, drops in the market can be in your favor as you continue to put money into the plan through payroll deductions. This concept, called dollar-cost averaging (described in Chapter 9), enables you to buy more shares of a stock or mutual fund when the rate is lower. In the long term, of course, the market will go up, and all those inexpensive shares will increase in value.

Since a 401(k) plan is a long-term retirement vehicle, it's important that you remember your long-term goals and stick to them. Focus on the long term and, as you approach retirement, maintain a solid assessment of how much money you will have when you retire and what your income will be. Besides Social Security benefits, you may have a pension plan and other savings.

All in all, the 401(k) plan is an excellent opportunity to build for your retirement and do so at the level you feel most comfortable. As one financial analyst puts it, "No matter what I say or suggest, the bottom line is that the individual has to be able to sleep comfortably at night." It all goes back to risk tolerance. First, be proactive and don't just forget about the money in your retirement plan; second, determine what level of risk is okay for your 401(k).

Keeping Your 401(k) Through Job Changes

Regardless of when, why, or how often you change jobs, your 401(k) investment can retain its tax-deferred status. If your new employer offers a 401(k), you can have your existing investment directly transferred, or rolled over, to a new account.

In a rollover, the money in your 401(k) is never in your possession, and you can thus avoid paying taxes on it (at least for the time being). It goes from your old employer to your new one; in industry lingo, from direct trustee to direct trustee.

By law, employers have to allow you to roll over your 401(k). If you take possession of the money yourself, the company will issue you a check for your investment less 20 percent, the amount they're required to withhold and send to the IRS (where they treat it like an estimated tax payment) in case you don't roll the money over into another 401(k). You have to roll the money over within sixty days or you'll be hit with taxes and penalties, and you have to deposit the full amount of your rollover—including replacing the 20 percent your company withheld to avoid having that amount considered an early (and taxable) distribution. If you are not starting a new job or are joining a company that does not have a 401(k) plan, roll over the money into an IRA.

Taking Money out of a 401(k)

As soon as you hit age 59½, you're eligible to start taking money (called distributions) out of your 401(k), whether you're formally retired or not. Once you hit age 70½, you have to take out at least the minimum required distribution.

Sometimes people need to tap into their retirement funds early due to financial hardship, such as buying a primary residence, preventing foreclosure on your home, paying college tuition due in the next twelve months, and paying unreimbursed medical expenses. These withdrawals will cost you the full tax bill on the distribution plus a 10 percent penalty. You can escape the penalty under really extreme circumstances, but you'll always be stuck with the taxes. A better choice when you really need the money? A loan from your plan; many 401(k) plans allow loans, and there are no taxes or penalties at stake. The only caveat: The loan has to be repaid in full before you stop working for the employer who maintains the plan.

Individual Retirement Accounts (IRAs)

The most popular retirement plan of the last decade has certainly been the individual retirement account, or IRA. Now available in two varieties—

traditional and Roth—IRAs offer you a safe, tax-favored way for your money to grow for your retirement years. And now they're even safer: in April 2005, the U.S. Supreme Court unanimously ruled that IRAs are fully protected should you need to file for personal bankruptcy.

Traditional IRAs

You are allowed to contribute up to $5,000 per year to a traditional IRA (as of 2008). If you are married, you and your spouse may each contribute up to $4,000 into your own separate IRA accounts. If you are receiving alimony, you also qualify to contribute to an IRA. All or a portion of the contributions you make may be tax-deductible, but that depends on other factors like your adjusted gross income and other retirement contributions (if you participate in a qualified retirement plan through your job, for example). You'll have to look over the tax tables closely to determine the tax advantages a traditional IRA offers. For an easy-to-use online IRA advantage calculator, check out *www.finance.cch.com*. Go to the financial calculators section and choose "retirement."

FACT

Roth IRAs are named for its creator, the late Senator William Roth. Roth, a Republican from Delaware, sponsored legislation that would allow investors to pay taxes on their retirement savings up front and withdraw them without paying additional taxes. It was part of the Taxpayer Relief Act of 1997, which went into effect on January 1, 1998.

Once you are past 59½ years of age, you can withdraw the money; when you reach 70½, the government starts putting minimums on how much you need to withdraw annually. You pay income taxes on the investment earnings when making withdrawals, but the long period of tax-deferred income still outweighs this taxation. Also, it is very often the case that the income level for someone in her sixties, perhaps semiretired, is lower than it was in her forties, so she will fall into a lower tax bracket. Some experts feel that it makes sound financial sense to defer tax payment for another twenty years.

You can choose to start an IRA through a bank, brokerage house, or mutual fund. Traditionally, banks offer fewer options than brokerage houses, usually sticking with the safer options such as CDs. Brokerage houses offer a wider range of options should you choose to be more savvy with your IRA investment, or you can play it safe with a money market fund. Mutual funds are, by definition, supposed to be riskier than a CD or money market account. The long time frame of an IRA makes equities or equity funds more attractive for some investors. Like other investments, you can move your investments around within the IRA to suit your level of comfort in regard to risk.

Too many people put money into an IRA and don't do anything with it. There is often a feeling that because you cannot take it out until age 59½, you can't touch the money once it is in an IRA. That is not the case. There's nothing wrong with being proactive with the money you are investing within the IRA. In fact, you should be.

Roth IRAs

With this relatively new IRA, you are still limited to the same $5,000 annual investment ceiling. Your contributions to a Roth IRA are not tax deductible; you pay taxes on every dollar that goes into one of these retirement accounts. When it comes time to take money out of this account, however, you will not be subject to any more taxes—ever!

In fact, there are very few regulations when it comes to withdrawing the money from a Roth IRA. The money must be in the plan until you are at least 59½. However, you can withdraw up to $10,000 after five years, penalty-free, if you are using the money for qualifying first-time home-buying expenses, if you become disabled, or if the distribution is to a beneficiary upon the death of the original account owner.

Whereas the government eventually requires you to make minimum withdrawals from a traditional IRA, you can leave your money in a Roth IRA with no minimum distribution requirements. This can even allow for a large tax-free benefit to pass directly to your heirs, if you so choose.

Your income determines your eligibility to contribute to a Roth IRA. This income structuring is subject to change at any time, so ask about your eligibility. As of 2008, the Roth option is phased out as adjusted gross income reaches between $101,000 and $116,000 for single filers and between $159,000 and $16,000 for joint filers.

It is possible to roll money over from a traditional to a Roth IRA. The determination of whether to invest in or roll over your money is based on your own financial situation. For current contributions, if you can't deduct a traditional IRA but still want to put some money away, go for the Roth (if you're eligible). Also, if you think your retirement tax rate will be higher or that you may need some of the money before retirement, a Roth IRA could be a better choice. As for the future, many experts agree that taking the tax hit now, if you can afford it, is far better than taking it on the much larger sum later on. Right now, the tax hit is a known quantity: the amount of your rollover times your marginal tax rate. The future tax hit is a question mark, as both the tax rates and income are unknown factors; almost certainly, though, that future tax hit will be bigger.

ESSENTIAL

A Health Savings Account allows you to put money aside for medical expenses, tax free. You must have a special form of qualified health coverage called a high deductible health plan—basically emergency health insurance that comes with a very high minimum deductible. The higher the deductible of your HDHP, the more you're allowed to save. The money you put into your HSA and all of the compounded earnings are yours until you die.

If you choose to roll over an existing IRA, simply call the company that holds your account and tell them. They'll talk with you about your unique tax situation and send you all the required paperwork to make the switch. Your accountant will be able to provide you with the most accurate tax information, including the possible need to adjust your withholding taxes or make some estimated tax payments.

Which Is Better?

Assuming you are eligible for both traditional and Roth IRAs, the biggest determining factor is whether it is to your benefit to take a deduction now and pay taxes later when you withdraw the money, or to pay taxes on your contribution now and never worry about them again.

You must look at your own personal financial situation to determine which IRA is right for you. Nonetheless, websites have calculators and fancy ten-page sections devoted to figuring out the answer to this question. It shouldn't be all that complicated. And a good accountant should be able to help you figure it all out in less time than it takes to download and evaluate the calculation methods.

ALERT

In the late 1980s, the term "investment black holes" referred to the virtually complete disappearance of investment capital due to sudden heavy market losses. Since then, the market has seen the rise and fall of several of these market-shaking phenomena that rapidly cause enormous losses for investors. The 2008 markets saw similar shake-ups and threw millions of investors into a massive panic.

The bottom line is that no matter how much you calculate, you cannot know for sure what the next thirty years have in store in terms of taxes, the rate of inflation, the cost of living, your own health, and the stability of your job. While it is to your advantage to put money away for your retirement years, the decision to choose the traditional or the Roth IRA is not as tough as it is made out to be. Either way, you will have saved money for your retirement years. If you qualify for both plans, the simple equation is whether it's to your benefit to take tax deductions now or whether you can afford not to and have benefits later on. Figure out basic, approximate numbers with your accountant, consider other factors in your life, make an overall assessment of your future as you'd like it to be, and pick one. Since your future is not a certainty, go with your best assumption.

Stay Focused

There's no rule that says you can't invest in both a 401(k) plan and an IRA. The most important point is to take advantage of all the tax-deferred investment opportunities you can. Start as early as you can and keep filling them up with money, come rain or shine.

The future of Social Security looks uncertain at best—the shrinking number of younger workers means fewer workers are supporting each Social Security retiree. Compare the numbers: In 1950, sixteen workers were supporting each retiree, as opposed to three workers per retiree in 2000. The number continues to decrease. If you instead focus on tax-deferred investing, you'll be taking a crucial step toward building a safe, secure, and sustainable financial future.

APPENDIX A

Online and Discount Brokers

These are just some of the most popular, easily accessible online and discount brokers in the United States. While all of these brokerages allow for DIY investing, many also provide investing advice and guidance for those who want these services. Discount brokers that offer walk-in, face-to-face assistance in addition to their automated trading services are noted.

Bank of America

www.baisidirect.com

800-926-1111

Easy trading for self-directed investors, both online and through their Intellibroker touchtone service. Also offers full-service investing.

Charles Schwab

www.schwab.com

800-435-4500

High volume and low prices from one of the biggest of the brokerage houses. Local branches located throughout the United States.

E*TRADE Financial

www.etrade.com

800-786-2575

High volume, very popular site with low prices. Walk-in branches in several states.

Fidelity

www.fidelity.com

800-544-6666

Recently rated best online broker by Kiplinger's. Many investor centers located throughout the United States.

Marquette De Bary Company

www.debary.com

800-221-3305

Oldest discount broker in New York City. Offices in New York City.

Regal Discount Securities
www.regaldiscount.com
800-786-9000
Offices in the Chicago area.

Scottrade
www.scottrade.com
800-906-7268
Has more than 400 walk-in branches throughout the United States.

Sharebuilder
www.sharebuilder.com
866-590 -7629
A service of ING Direct.

TD Ameritrade
www.tdameritrade.com
800-669-3900
More than 100 local branch offices nationwide.

Tradex Brokerage Service
800-231-6455
No online trading thus far. Offices in the Houston area.

USAA Brokerage Services
www.usaa.com
800-531-8343
Services are offered to current and former military personnel and their families.

Vanguard Brokerage Services
www.vanguard.com
800-992-8327

Zecco
www.zecco.com
877-700-7862 (only during standard business hours)
Offers only online trading at this time.

Investment Publications

There are dozens of publications that can be very helpful to investors. These financially oriented newspapers, magazines, and newsletters offer valuable insights about the markets, including stock tips, mutual fund rankings, and in-depth articles with a more educational angle. Publications can be a good place to get investing ideas, but you must still do your own research and analysis and make sure an investment fits well in your portfolio before you make any purchase decision.

Subscription prices listed are those posted on the publications' websites as of April 2009 and may represent special or limited-time offers. To help you decide which publications are the most useful to you before you shell out the money for a long-term subscription, visit your local library. Among other resources, you can gain valuable insight about investing from the following:

The *Wall Street Journal*

Published by Dow Jones and Company, the *Wall Street Journal* is a leading global newspaper with a focus on business. Founded in 1889, the newspaper has grown to a worldwide daily circulation of more than 2 million readers. In 1994, Dow Jones introduced the *Wall Street Journal Special Editions*, special sections written in local languages that are featured in more than thirty leading national newspapers worldwide. The *Wall Street Journal Americas*, published in Spanish and Portuguese, is included in approximately twenty leading Latin American newspapers. The *Wall Street Journal* offers one-year print-only subscriptions for $119, one-year online subscriptions for $104, and a combination one-year print and online subscription for $140.

800-568-7625
www.wallstreetjournal.com

Barron's

Barron's is also known as the *Dow Jones Business and Financial Weekly.* With its first edition published in 1921, *Barron's* offers its readers news reports and analyses on financial markets worldwide. Investors will also find a wealth of tips regarding investment techniques. One-year print-only subscriptions are $99, a one-year print plus online subscription runs $149, and a one-year online-only subscription costs $79.

800-975-8620
www.barrons.com

Investor's Business Daily

Founded in 1984, Investor's Business Daily is a newspaper focusing on business, financial, economic, and national news. The publication places a strong emphasis on offering its readers timely information on stock market and stock market–related issues. The front page of each issue provides a brief overview of the most important business news of the day. It's published five days a week, Monday through Friday, and you can get a one-year subscription for $295, which includes full access to its website. The strictly online edition, called eIBD, offers annual subscriptions for $235 or monthly subscriptions for $28.95 per month. A one-year subscription to the daily print edition and eIBD is $365.

800-459-6706
www.investors.com

Forbes

Forbes magazine is a biweekly business magazine for "those who run business today—or aspire to." Each issue contains stories on companies, management strategies, global trends, technology, taxes, law, capital markets, and investments. A one-year subscription, or twenty-six issues, is $59.95, and that comes with complete access to it's real-time website.

800-888-9896
www.forbesmagazine.com

Money

Money is a monthly personal finance magazine from Time-Warner publications, covering such topics as family finances, investment careers, taxes, and insurance. Each issue includes tips, advice, and strategies for smart investing. The magazine also features other related matters like finding cheap flights, buying a home, and preparing for tax season. It also offers a substantive annual mutual fund guide. A one-year subscription, or thirteen issues, is $14.95.

800-633-9970
http://money.cnn.com

BusinessWeek

This weekly publication comes jam-packed with comprehensive coverage of both the U.S. and global business scene. From the economy to politics to how both impact stock prices, *BusinessWeek* provides in-depth market analysis and incisive investigative reporting. A twelve-week subscription costs $12 and a fifty-week subscription is $46, including online access.

888-878-5151

www.businessweek.com

Fortune

Every month, *Fortune* magazine, a Time-Warner publication, offers analysis of the business marketplace. The publication's annual ranking of the top 500 American companies is one of its most widely read features. *Fortune* has been covering business and business-related topics since its origins in 1930. A one-year subscription, or twenty-five issues, is $19.99.

800-621-8000

www.fortune.com

Smart Money

Smart Money, a monthly personal finance magazine, offers readers ideas for investing, spending, and saving. The publication also covers automotive, technology, and lifestyle subjects, including upscale travel, footwear, fine wine, and music. One-year subscriptions are $11, and two-year subscriptions cost $18.

800-444-4204

www.smartmoney.com

Kiplinger's Personal Finance

One of the most respected names in financial publications, *Kiplinger's* offers investing ideas, updates on companies, insider interviews with top financial experts and fund managers, and very detailed listings of the best-performing mutual funds in a wide range of categories. One-year subscriptions cost $12 for either the print or digital edition.

800-544-0155

www.kiplingers.com

ValueLine Investment Survey

A weekly publication available at most libraries and through subscription, it offers ratings, reports, opinions, and analysis on about 130 stocks in seven or eight industries on a weekly basis. Approximately 1,700 stocks in about ninety-four industries are covered every thirteen weeks. CD-ROM subscribers can also purchase an expanded version containing reviews of 5,000 stocks. A thirteen-week trial subscription, which includes full online access, costs $75; a one-year subscription costs $598.

800-634-3583

www.valueline.com

APPENDIX C

Investment Websites

The Internet has made an unparalleled impact on the world of investing. The web has significantly affected the manner in which business is conducted worldwide. It has taken the information once found buried in the business sections of newspapers and made it easily accessible to investors at all levels. Add to that a vast array of software, as well as investment websites designed for the investment professional, and you have a whole new world of investing, literally at your fingertips.

A majority of the major financial institutions and nearly all of the major brokerage houses offer their own websites. The most comprehensive of the many websites offered by major investment firms include the following:

www.invescoaim.com
www.americancentury.com
www.fidelity.com
www.franklintempleton.com
www.iShares.com
www.invescopowershares.com
www.prudential.com
www.wellsfargoadvantagefunds.com
www.vanguard.com

Historical information, fund holdings, performance updates, fund profiles, information on fund managers, libraries of articles and general information, and even glossaries and investor tips can be found on various websites. Needless to say, the investor tips and how-to information can lean in favor of the funds offered by a fund family. You usually won't find the virtues of REITs or advantages of muni bond funds discussed by a fund family that doesn't handle them. Nevertheless, you will get a lot of overall information at the websites of financial institutions.

Hone in on the specific areas that you are looking for, such as tax-free investments, socially responsible investing (try *http://coopamerica.org*), or information on particular funds. This will narrow down your search and reduce your time spent online, since some websites are loaded with promotional material and hype or are simply confusing with numerous bells and whistles.

There are dozens of sites on the Internet devoted to investing and investment advice. Some will give you an overall picture of investing as a whole, and others will focus on a particular area. The list on the following page includes just a sampling of the many investment-related websites available:

Bloomberg

www.bloomberg.com

Bloomberg's online financial news and information site, with real-time streaming quotes.

Bondtrac Financial Information

www.bondtrac.com

If you're looking for bond information and the latest in bond offerings, this site should be of help.

CCH Financial Planning Toolkit

www.finance.cch.com

This website offers expert advice on financial planning and investing, including free planning tools and financial calculators.

CNN Money

www.money.com

The CNN Financial News Network offers a site with an extensive amount of information about U.S. and global markets.

Co-Op America

http://coopamerica.org

Describes how to integrate social investing into your financial plan and portfolio.

Dogs of the Dow

www.dogsofthedow.com

Gives you the lowdown on the stocks in the Dow Jones, from historical information to the latest quotes, plus news and updates.

Dow Jones Business Directory

www.dowjones.com

Offers you a comprehensive listing of all sorts of financial sites on the web, even reviewing many of them.

The Green Money Journal

www.greenmoneyjournal.com

Advice and information especially for green investors.

The Global Investor Directory

www.global-investor.com

As the name indicates, this site provides access to a plethora of international investing information, including performance information on worldwide alternative and emerging markets.

Hoovers Online

www.hoovers.com

Gives you the scoop on more than 32 million companies, from IPOs to industry profiles.

Investopedia

www.investopedia.com

This website is jam-packed with articles, tutorials, and investment calculators, all designed to help you become an even better investor.

Investor Guide

www.investorguide.com

Offers a long list of subjects, with plenty of information and tons of links.

U.S. Government Investment and Tax Information

www.treasury.gov

The government's website for government investments and tax information, plus news on the U.S. and world financial markets.

MarketWatch

www.marketwatch.com

This financial site has information on stocks, bonds, mutual funds, the economy, and more, plus charts and commentary.

The Mutual Fund Investor's Center

www.mfea.com

Helps you pull together all the information you need to select the right mutual funds.

Moody's

www.moodys.com

The place to go for bond ratings, including a downgrade watchlist, authoritative reports on credit trends and corporate finance.

Morningstar

www.morningstar.com

One of the most comprehensive investing websites on the Internet, you'll find information about mutual funds, ETFs, bonds, stocks, and options; a veritable wealth of information.

The Motley Fool

www.fool.com

Provides a wide variety of information, including a lot of investing basics, in plain clear language.

Investing in Bonds

www.investinginbonds.com

Legislative and statistical information, research, prices, and more, all tailored for bond investors.

Quote.com

www.quote.com

Up-to-the-minute quotes from numerous markets, along with analysis and commentary.

Reuters

www.reuters.com

Offers all the latest financial news you need, from one of the most trusted sources in the world.

U.S. Securities and Exchange Commission

www.sec.gov

Information on corporations, brokerage houses, SEC policies, and news, as well as a place for individual investors to learn about current fraud investigations and personal fraud protection (including reporting suspected instances of investment fraud).

Treasury Direct

www.easysaver.gov

The U.S. Treasury Department's site designed to help you invest in government bonds, even by using direct deposit, to make saving and investing very easy.

Yahoo Finance

www.finance.yahoo.com

From personal financial tutorials to streaming real-time quotes, this site offers lots of advice to novice investors.

Zack's Investment Research

www.zacks.com

A research site with market commentary and information.

APPENDIX D

Glossary of Terms

Investing has a language all its own, but it doesn't have to be intimidating. The average investor only needs to know the basics, so if you have an understanding of the terms in this glossary, you're off to a good start.

annuity

A contractual financial agreement between you and an issuing company. You give the issuing company a certain amount of money, and in turn the company promises to invest your money and repay you according to the option or payment method that you choose.

arbitrage

The practice of taking advantage of the difference in price of the same security traded on two different markets. For instance, if Nortel Networks were trading at $100 (U.S.) on the Toronto exchange and $99 on the NYSE, an arbitrageur would buy shares on the NYSE and sell them on the Toronto exchange.

asset

Anything you own that has monetary value, including cash, stocks, bonds, mutual funds, cars, real estate, and other items.

asset allocation

The specific distribution of funds among a number of different asset classes within an investment portfolio. Investment funds may be split among a number of different asset classes, such as stocks, bonds, and cash funds, each of which has unique risk and return characteristics. Determining just how to allocate funds depends on the financial plans of the individual investor.

average daily volume

The average number of shares traded per day over a specified period.

bankruptcy

A legal process where a party acknowledges that he is unable to pay his debts, and makes arrangements for those debts to be legally (if not financially) settled. The party declaring bankruptcy either allows his assets to be sold to repay creditors to the extent possible (liquidation bankruptcy), or works with the court to set up a plan to pay all or some of his debt over a period of several years (reorganization bankruptcy).

bear

Someone who believes that the securities market(s) or a specific security will decline in value.

bear market

A market in which a group of assets (normally securities) falls in price or loses value over a period of time. A prolonged bear market may result in a decrease of 20 percent or more in market prices. A bear market in stocks may be due to investors' expectations of economic trends; in bonds, a bear market results from rising interest rates.

beneficiary

A person (or other entity, like a charitable foundation) who is named in a legal document (like a will or a trust agreement) to receive specific assets or to have the right to use specific assets.

beta

A statistical calculation that compares a security's volatility to a benchmark, usually the S&P 500 Index for stocks, for example. A beta greater than 1 means the security is more volatile than the index. For instance, a beta of 1.5 means the security is historically 50 percent more volatile than the index.

bid price

The price a prospective buyer is ready to pay for a security. The term is commonly used by traders who stand ready to buy or sell security units at publicly quoted prices.

blue chip

A term used to describe companies that have established themselves as reliably successful over time, often by demonstrating sound management and creating quality products and services. Such companies have shown the capability to function in both good and bad economic times, and usually pay dividends to investors even during lean years. Most blue chips are large cap, Fortune 500-type stocks like IBM or General Electric.

bonds

Loans from investors to corporations and governments given in exchange for interest payments and timely repayment of the debt. Interest rates are usually fixed.

bottom-up analysis

The search for outstanding performance of individual stocks before considering the impact of economic trends. Such companies may be identified from research reports, stock screens, or personal knowledge of the products and services.

budget

A detailed listing of income and expenses by category, usually prepared with an eye toward the future. Used by households and businesses alike to gain a tighter control over incoming and outgoing cash.

bull

Someone who believes that the securities market(s) or a particular security will increase in value.

bull market

An extended period of rising securities prices. Bull markets generally involve heavy trading, and are marked by a general upward trend in the market, independent of daily fluctuations.

capital gain

The appreciation in the value of an asset that occurs when its selling price is greater than the original price for which the asset was bought. The tax rate on capital gains depends on how long the asset was held, and is often lower than the rate on ordinary income.

capital gain distributions

Payments to the shareholders of a mutual fund based on profits earned from selling securities in the fund's portfolio. Capital gain distributions are usually paid once a year.

certificate of deposit (CD)

Money deposited with banks for a fixed period of time, usually between one month and five years, in exchange for compound interest, usually at a fixed rate. At the end of this term, on the maturity date, the principal may either be repaid to the depositor or rolled over into another CD. Any money deposited into a CD is insured by the bank (up to FDIC limits), making these very low-risk investments. Most banks set heavy penalties for early withdrawal of monies from a CD.

closed-end fund

A mutual fund where investors trade shares on an exchange, rather than buying shares from and redeeming them with the fund itself. Share price is determined by supply and demand for fund shares (as opposed to net asset value for regular mutual funds, also called open-end funds).

commission

A fee charged by a stockbroker (and, in some cases, a financial advisor) who executes securities trade transactions for an investor. This fee is generally a percentage based on either the number of shares bought or sold or the value of the shares bought or sold.

compound interest

Interest earned on the original investment (or deposit) amount plus any previously earned interest; effectively new interest is paid on already-earned interest. This helps the investment grow more quickly than it would with simple interest, which is applied only to the original investment amount.

cost basis

The total original purchase price of an asset, which may include items other than just the asset price, such as sales tax, commissions, and delivery and installation fees. This total amount is subtracted from the sale price of the asset to compute the capital gain or loss when that asset is eventually sold.

creditor

Any person (or entity) to whom you owe money.

credit risk

The risk that the principal you've invested through debt securities (like bonds) will not be repaid at all or on time. If the issuer of a debt security fails to repay the principal, the issuer is deemed to be in default.

default

To fail to repay principal or make timely payments on a bond or other debt investment security as promised. More likely to happen with high-yield corporate bonds (a.k.a. junk bonds) than other types of bonds.

defined-contribution retirement plan

A retirement plan offered by employers that allows employees to contribute to the plan but does not guarantee a predetermined benefit at retirement. Rather, the amount of the contribution is predetermined by the employee, typically as a percentage of pay. Examples of such plans include 401(k), 403(b), 457, and profit-sharing plans.

discount broker

Brokerage firms that offer cut-rate fees for buying and selling securities, usually online or over an automated tele-service, although some also offer fax trade order options. Among the most prominent are Charles Schwab and TD Ameritrade.

diversification

The process of optimizing an investment portfolio by allocating funds to a number of different assets. Diversification minimizes risks while maximizing returns by spreading out risk across a number of investments. Different types of assets, such as stocks, bonds, and cash funds, carry different types of risk. For an optimal portfolio, it is important to diversify among assets with dissimilar risk levels. Investing in a number of assets allows for unexpected negative performances to balance out with or be superseded by positive performances.

dividend

A payment made by a corporation to its shareholders that represents a portion of the profits of the company. The amount to be paid is determined by the board of directors, and dividends may be paid even during a time when the company is not performing profitably. Dividends are paid on a set schedule, such as quarterly, semiannually, or annually. Dividends may be paid directly to the investor or reinvested into more shares of the company's stock. Even if dividends are reinvested, the individual is responsible for paying taxes on the dividends earned. Mutual funds also pay dividends, from the income earned on the underlying investments of the fund portfolio. Dividends usually are not guaranteed (except with certain types of preferred stock) and may vary each time they are paid.

dividend yield

The current or estimated annual dividend divided by the market price per share of a security. Used to compare dividend-paying shares of different corporations.

Dow Jones Industrial Average

An index to which the performance of individual stocks or mutual funds can be compared; it is a means of measuring the change in stock prices. This index is a composite of 30 blue-chip companies ranging from AT&T and Hewlett Packard to Kodak and Johnson & Johnson. These 30 companies represent not just the United States; rather, they are involved with commerce on a global scale. The DJIA is computed by adding the prices of these 30 stocks and dividing by an adjusted number that takes into account stock splits and other divisions that would interfere with the average. Stocks represented on the Dow Jones Industrial Average make up between 15 percent and 20 percent of the total market.

dividend reinvestment plan (DRIP)

A plan allowing investors to automatically reinvest their dividends in the company's stock rather than receive them in cash. Many companies waive the sales charges for stock purchased under the DRIP.

due diligence

An in-depth examination of a company's business prospects. Used by investors to analyze prospective investments.

earnings growth

A pattern of increasing rate of growth in earnings per share from one period to another, which usually causes a stock's price to rise.

equity

Equity is the total ownership or partial ownership of an asset minus any debts that are owed in relation to that asset (like a home with a mortgage). Equity also refers to the amount of interest shareholders hold in a company as a part of their rights of partial ownership. Equity is considered synonymous with ownership, a share of ownership, or the rights of ownership.

escrow

Money or other assets held by an agent until the terms of a contract or agreement are fulfilled. For example, many mortgage companies require borrowers to pay prorated property taxes monthly along with their mortgage payments; these funds are held in an escrow account until payment is due to the local government.

exchange-traded fund (ETF)

An investment pool, similar to a mutual fund, whose shares trade over an exchange much like shares of stock. Most ETFs mirror a benchmark index, holding the securities tracked by that index.

financial advisor

A financial planning professional (typically licensed and accredited) who helps people manage their wealth. Functions may include preparing a retirement savings plan, devising tax strategies, and preparing an estate planning strategy, among other financial services.

fiscal year

Any 12-month period designated by a business as its accounting year. Once declared, a company's fiscal year does not change, unless it makes a formal change approved by the IRS.

foreclosure

A legal process that terminates an owner's right to a property, usually because the borrower defaults on payments. Home foreclosures usually result in a forced sale of the property to pay off the mortgage.

forex

Foreign currency exchange markets.

fundamental analysis

An analysis of a company's current and past balance sheets and income statements used to forecast its future stock price movements. Fundamental analysts consider past records of assets, earnings, sales, products, management, and markets in predicting future trends of a company's success or failure. By appraising a company's prospects, these analysts assess whether a particular stock or group of stocks is undervalued or overvalued at its current market price.

going public

When a company that has previously been wholly privately owned offers its stock to the general public for the first time.

good for the day

Buy or sell limit order that will expire at close of trading if not executed.

good until cancelled

Buy or sell limit order that remains active until cancelled.

growth investing

An investment style that emphasizes companies with strong earnings growth, which typically leads to stock price increases. Growth investing is generally considered more aggressive than "value" investing.

hedge

Hedging is a strategy of reducing risk by offsetting investments with investments of opposite risks. Risks must be negatively correlated in order to hedge each other—for example, pairing an investment with high inflation risk and low immediate returns with investments with low inflation risk and high immediate returns. Long hedges protect against a short-term position, and short hedges protect against a long-term position. Hedging is not the same as diversification; it aims to protect against risk by counterbalancing that specific area of risk.

inflation

A general increase in prices coinciding with a fall in the real value of money, as measured by the Consumer Price Index.

inflation risk

The risk that rising prices of goods and services over time will decrease the value of the return on investments. Inflation risk is also known as purchasing-power risk because it refers to increased prices of goods and services and a decreased value of cash.

intrinsic value

A term favored by value-oriented fundamental analysts to express the actual value of a corporation, as opposed to the current value based on the stock price. It is usually calculated by adding the current value of estimated future earnings to the book value.

individual retirement account (IRA)

A retirement account that anyone who has earned income can contribute to. Amounts contributed to traditional IRAs are usually tax-deferred. Amounts contributed to Roth IRAs are not currently deductible but taxes are never levied on the earnings.

junk bond

A high-yield bond that comes with a high risk of default. Junk bonds are generally low-rated bonds and are usually bought on speculation. Investors hope for the yield rather than the default. An investor with high risk-tolerance may choose to invest in junk bonds.

liability

An amount owed to creditors or others. Common personal liabilities include mortgage, car payments, student loans, and credit card debt.

liquidity

The ease with which an asset can be converted to cash at its present market value. High liquidity is associated with a high number of buyers and sellers trading investments at a high volume.

load

A sales charge or commission paid to a broker or other third-party when mutual funds are bought or sold. Front-end loads are incurred when an investor purchases the shares and back-end loads are incurred when investors sell the shares.

market capitalization

The current market price of a company's shares multiplied by the number of shares outstanding, commonly referred to as "market cap." Large-cap corporations generally have over $10 billion in market capitalization, mid-cap companies between $2 billion and $10 billion, and small-cap companies less than $2 billion. These capitalization figures may vary depending upon the index being used or the guidelines used by the portfolio manager.

market risk

The risk that investments will lose money based on the daily fluctuations of the overall market. Bond market risk results from fluctuations in prevailing interest rates. Stock market risk is influenced by a wide range of factors, such as the state of the economy, political news, and events of national importance. Though time is a stabilizing element in the markets, as returns tend to outweigh risks over long periods of time, market risk cannot be systematically diversified away.

market value

The value of an asset if it were to be immediately sold, or the current price of a security being sold on the market.

mutual fund

An investment that allows thousands of investors to pool their money to collectively invest in stocks, bonds, or other types of assets, depending on the objectives of the fund. Mutual funds are convenient, particularly for small investors, because they diversify an individual's portfolio among a large number of investments, more different securities than an individual could normally purchase on her own. Investors share in the profits of a mutual fund, and mutual fund shares can be sold back to the company on any business day at the net asset value price.

National Association of Securities Dealers Automated Quotation (NASDAQ)

A global automated computer system that provides up-to-the-minute information on approximately 5,500 over-the-counter stocks. Whereas on the New York Stock Exchange (NYSE) securities are bought and sold on the trading floor, securities on the NASDAQ are traded via computer.

net worth

The value of all of a person's assets (anything owned that has a monetary value) minus all of the person's liabilities (amounts owed to others).

New York Stock Exchange (NYSE)
The largest securities exchange in the United States, where securities are traded by brokers and dealers for customers on the trading floor at 11 Wall Street in New York City.

price-to-earnings (P/E) ratio
A measure of how much buyers are willing to pay for each dollar of a company's earnings, calculated by dividing the current share price by the stock's earnings per share. This ratio is a useful way of comparing the value of stocks and helps to indicate expectations for the company's growth in earnings, most useful when comparing companies within similar industries. The P/E ratio is sometimes also called the "multiple."

price-to-book ratio
Current market price of a stock divided by its book value, or net asset value. Sometimes used to assess companies with a high proportion of fixed assets or heavy equipment.

quotation
The current price of a security, be it either the highest bid price for that security or the lowest ask price. Sometimes also called a "quote."

real rate of return
The annual return on an investment after being adjusted for inflation and taxes.

reinvestment

The use of capital gains, interest, and dividends to buy more of the same investment. For example, the dividends received from stock shares may be reinvested by buying more shares of the same stock.

return on equity

The amount, expressed as a percentage, earned on a company's common stock investment for a given period. This tells common shareholders how effectively their money is being employed.

risk tolerance

An investor's ability to tolerate fluctuations (including sharp downturns) in the value of an investment in the expectation of receiving a higher return.

rollover

Immediate reinvestment of a distribution from a qualified retirement plan into an IRA or another qualified plan in order to retain its tax-deferred status and avoid taxes and penalties for early withdrawal.

Standard & Poor's (S&P) 500 Index

A market index of five hundred of the top-performing U.S. corporations. This index, a more comprehensive measure of the domestic market than the Dow Jones Industrial Average, indicates broad market changes.

Securities and Exchange Commission (SEC)

A federal government agency that was established to protect individual investors from fraud and malpractice in the marketplace. The commission oversees and regulates the activities of registered investment advisors, stock and bond markets, broker/dealers, and mutual funds.

security

Any investment purchased with the expectation of making a profit. Securities include total or partial ownership of an asset, rights to ownership of an asset, and certificates of debt from an institution. Examples of securities include stocks, bonds, certificates of deposit, and options.

socially responsible investing

Investing in companies that meet an ethical standard, by using a carefully employed screening process before purchasing any securities.

split

When a corporation increases its number of shares outstanding. The total shareholders' equity does not change; instead, the number of shares increases while the value of each share decreases proportionally. For example, in a 2-for-1 split, a shareholder with 100 shares prior to the split would now own 200 shares. The price of the shares, however, would be cut in half; shares that cost $40 before the split would be worth $20 after the split.

stock

An ownership share in a corporation, entitling the investor to a pro rata share of the corporation's earnings and assets.

technical analysis

The use of charts and statistics to predict movements in securities prices. Technical analysis uses manual charts and computer programs to identify and project price trends in a market, security, mutual fund, or futures contract.

ticker

An information stream appearing on a movable tape or as a scrolling electronic display on a screen. The symbols and numbers shown on the ticker indicate the security being traded, the latest sale price of the security, and the volume of the most recent transaction.

top-down approach

An investment-selection method in which an investor first looks at trends in the general economy, then selects attractive industries and, finally, companies that should benefit from those trends.

total return

The change in value of an investment over a specific time period, typically expressed as a percentage. Total return calculations assume all earnings are reinvested in additional shares of the investment.

underwriter

A person (or company) who distributes securities as an intermediary between the issuer and the buyer of the securities. For example, an underwriter may be the agent selling insurance policies or the person distributing shares of a mutual fund to broker/dealers or investors. Generally, the underwriter agrees to purchase the remaining units of the security, such as remaining shares of stocks or bonds, from the issuer if the public does not buy all specified units. An underwriter may also be a company that backs the issue of a contract by agreeing to accept responsibility for fulfilling the contract in return for a premium.

value investing

An investment approach that focuses on companies that may be temporarily out of favor despite strong success potential or whose earnings or assets are not fully reflected in their stock prices. Value stocks will tend to have a lower price-to-earnings ratio than growth stocks, and are considered to be currently under-valued, making them good investment 'deals.'

volatility

An indicator of expected risk, categorized by the range of price movement of a security. It demonstrates the degree to which the market price of an asset, rate, or index fluctuates from its average. Volatility is calculated by finding the standard deviation from the mean, or average, return.

yield

The return, or earnings, on an investment. Yield refers to the interest earned on a bond, or the dividend earnings on an equity investment. Yield does not include capital gains.

Index

A

Advantages of a company, 58
Annual report, 55-56, 114-15
Annuities, 221-22
Appraisal, 3
Asset allocation, 23-25
    fund, 123-24
    methods, 25
    and time, 24-25
Assets, 3

B

Balanced funds, 123-24
Baruch, Bernard, 63
Behavioral finance, 63-64
Bonds, 81-93, 94-102
    buying and selling, 92-93
    calls, 100
    choosing, 103
    corporate, 99-101
    defined, 82-83
    green, 156-57
    high-yield, 101-2
    interest, 82
    maturity, 82-83
    mortgage-backed securities,
        102-3
    municipal, 96-99
    mutual funds, 125-29
    pricing, 91-92
    ratings, 87-88
    risks, 83-84, 85-87
    sinking-fund provision,
        100-1
    types of, 94-102

versus stock, 83
    U.S Treasury securities, 96
    yields, 89-91
    zero-coupon, 99
Broker. *See* Stockbroker
Budget, 4-7
    expenses, 5
    guidelines, 6
    income, 5
    net cash flow, 6
    savings, 5
Buffett, Warren, 59
Business
    inventories, 34
    model, 58
Buttonwood Agreement, 43
Buy-and-hold investing, 27-
    28

C

Capital gains, 215, 217
Certified financial planner
    (CFP), 197
Chartered life underwriter
    (CLU), 197-98
Chartered financial consultant
    (ChFC), 198
Commodities, 182-84
Consumer
    confidence, 33
    price index (CPI), 32-33
Corporate bond funds, 127-
    28
Coverdell Education Savings
    Account (ESA), 228-29

Credit card, 5
    statements, 8
Cubes, 149
Currency trading, 185-87
    differences from other
        investments, 186
    rates drive returns, 187

D

Debt, 10
Derivatives, 187-88
Developments by a company,
    58
Diamond, 149
Diversification, 22-23, 107-8
    to minimize risk 133
Dividend, 60, 61
    reinvestment plans (DRIPs),
        71-72
    taxes, 214-15
Do-it-yourself (DYI) investing,
    203-12
    online investing, 203-12
Dollar-cost averaging, 116-17
Dow Jones Industrial Average
    (DJIA), 36-37

E

Earnings per share (EPS),
    60
Economic indicators, 31-35
    business inventories, 34
    consumer confidence, 33

consumer price index (CPI), 32-33

gross domestic product (GDP), 32

housing starts, 34

job growth, 33

producer price index (PPI), 35

unemployment index, 33-34

Economy, importance of, 30

Education investing, 224-33

college certificates of deposit (CDs), 232-33

Coverdell Education Savings Account (ESA), 228-29

education bonds, 231-32

529 plans, 227-28

pre-paid tuition plan, 229-31

tax-sheltered, 226

tuition planning, 225-26

Employee stock options, 190

Exchange-traded funds (ETFs), 144-52

buying and selling, 151-52

choosing, 150-51

cubes, 149

defined, 145

Diamond, 149

iShares, 149

versus mutual funds, 146-47

Standard & Poor's

Depository Receipts (SPDRs), 148

tracking, 152

types, 147-48

VIPERs, 149

and your portfolio, 149-50

Expenses, 5

F

Filing, 7-9

credit card and bank statements, 8

financial software, 9

investment information, 8

medical bills, 8

personal documents, 9

real estate records, 9

tax returns, 8

Financial

inventory, 2-4

planner, 78

software, 9

Financial advisor, 193-201

certified financial planner (CFP), 197

chartered life underwriter (CLU), 197-98

chartered financial consultant (ChFC), 198

commissions, 199-100

fees, 200

finding, 201

percent of assets, 200

personal financial specialist

(PFS), 198-99

shopping for, 196-97

type of advice you need, 193-94

what to expect from, 194-96

529 plans, 227-28

401(k) plan, 237-39

investing strategy, 238

and job changes, 238-39

taking money out of, 239

Futures, 190-91

G

Global

funds, 122-23

impact on stocks, 38

Green investing, 49, 50, 153-62

alternative energy funds, 158

bonds, 156-57

building a profitable green portfolio, 161-62

defined, 154-55

eco-friendly funds, 157

funds, 157-60

greenwashing 160-61

scams, 160-61

socially responsible, 129-30, 159-60

stocks, 155-56

sustainable resource funds, 158-59

Greenwashing, 160-61
Gross domestic product
    (GDP), 32
Growth
    funds, 120-21
    investing, 54

H
Health Savings Account, 242
Housing starts, 34

I
Income, 5
    funds, 120, 121
Indexes, 36-38
    Dow Jones Industrial
        Average (DJIA), 36-37
    Russell 2000, 37
    Standard & Poor's 500 Index
        (S&P 500), 37
    Value Line Index, 38
Index funds, 119-20
Individual retirement accounts
    (IRAs), 239-43
    comparing, 242-43
    Roth, 241-42
    traditional, 240-42
Industry, 35
Initial Public Offerings (IPOs),
    180-82
    getting in on, 181
Interest, taxable, 215
Interest rates

and Fed, 31
    impact of, 30-31
International funds, 122-23
Investment
    choices, 15
    club, 79-80
    goals, 11-13
    strategy, lifelong, 26, 65-
        66
    tracking, 74-75
Investor profile, 26-28
IShares, 149

J
Job growth, 33

K
Kelley Blue Book, 3

L
Leading economic indicators
    (LEI), 34
Liabilities, 3
Life insurance, 220
Limit order, 69-70
    buy, 69
    sell, 69-70
Liquid assets, 4
Long-term equity anticipation
    securities (LEAPS), 188,
    189

M
Management of company, 58
Margin buying, 179-80
Market
    order, 68
    share, 58
    timing, 28
Mortgage-backed securities,
    102-3
Municipal bonds, 97-99
    floating and variable-rate,
        98
    funds, 126
    general obligation, 98
    moral obligation, 98
    private activity, 98
    put, 98
    revenue, 98
    taxable, 98
Mutual funds, 104-17, 118-30,
    131-43
    administrative fees, 113
    alternative energy, 158
    asset allocation, 12-24
    balanced, 123-24
    benefits of investing in, 119
    bond, 125-29
    capital, 124-25
    combination growth and
        income funds, 120, 121
    defined, 105
    diversification, 107-8
    diversification to minimize
        risk, 133-34
    dollar-cost averaging,
        116-17
    eco-friendly, 157

families and styles, 110-11
fees, expenses and
    operating costs, 112-13
fund managers, 109-10
global, 122
green, 157-60
growth funds, 120-21
history of, 105-7
income funds, 120, 121
index funds, 119-20
international, 122-23
investment strategies,
    138-40
large-cap, 124-25
load vs. no-load, 111
management fees, 113
mega, 125
mid-cap, 124-25
past performance, 136-38
prospectus, 134-36
reducing taxes on, 219-20
reports, 114-15
risk tolerance, 132
sector, 122
selling, 143
service fees, 113
small-cap, 124-25
socially responsible, 129-30,
    159-60
sustainable resource,
    158-59
tracking performance,
    140-42
trading, 115-16
12b-1 fee, 113
types of, 118-30
value, 122

N
NASDAQ, 41-42
Net
    cash flow, 6
    worth, 3-4
NYSE, 40-41

O
Online investing, 203-12
    advantages of, 205-6
    best investment websites,
        211-12
    internet scams, 208-9
    knowing your orders, 205
    network crashes, 206-7
    risks, 206-8
    what to look for in an
        investment website, 210
Option, 188-90
    call, 188
    employee stock, 190
    long-term equity
        anticipation securities
        (LEAPS), 188, 189
    put, 188
    stock, 189
    strike price, 188

P
Personal financial specialist
    (PFS), 198-99
Precious metals, 182-83,
    184-85

Price/earnings ratio (P/E), 60
Price volatility, 61
Producer price index (PPI), 35
Prospectus, 134-36
    financial history, 136
    fund's objective, 134-35
    investment breakdown,
        135-36
    investment risks, 135

R
Real estate, 163-76
    choosing profitable, 171-
        72
    flipping, 165-68
    investing basics, 164
    investment trusts (REIT),
        172-76
    investment trusts,
        comparing, 174-75
    investment trusts, tracking,
        175-76
    leverage, 164-65
    rental properties, 168-71
    speculators, 165
Rental properties, 168-71
    managing, 170-71
    questions to ask, 169
Research, 52-66
Retirement
    accounts, 4
    needs, 12
Retirement planning, 234-44
    advantages of investing for
        retirement, 236-37

Retirement planning—*cont.*
  401(k) plan, 237-39
  individual retirement
    accounts (IRAs), 239-
    43
  tax-deferred, 235-36
Risk, 15-21
  bonds, 85-87
  credit, 17, 85-86
  currency, 17-18
  and diversification, 22-23,
    133-34
  economic, 18
  income, 87
  inflation rate, 16-17
  interest rate, 18, 86-87
  market, 17
  online investing, 206-7
  of passivity, 16-17
  stock specific, 16
  tolerance, 36, 132-
Risky investment strategies,
  178-80
  margin buying, 179-80
  short selling, 178-79
Roth, William, 240
Russell 2000, 37

S

Sector, 122
  funds, 122
Securities Exchange Act, 42
Short selling, 178-79
Socially responsible investing,
  49

Spending reduction, 11
Standard & Poor's
  Depository Receipts
    (SPDRs), 148
  500 Index (S&P 500), 37
Stock, 39-51
  analysis, 56-57
  bargain, 72-73
  blue-chip, 46
  book value, 61
  capitalization of, 46
  common, 45
  cyclical, 48-49
  defensive, 49
  defined, 44-45
  dividend reinvestment plans
    (DRIPs), 71-72
  dividends, 60, 61
  earnings per share (EPS),
    60
  exchanges, 40-42
  fundamental analysis, 56-
    57
  future outlook, 57-58
  green 155-56
  growth, 46-47
  income, 47, 49-50
  large-cap, 46, 48
  limit order, 69-70
  market order, 68-69
  math basics, 59-62
  mid-cap, 46, 48
  penny, 50-51
  preferred, 45, 47-48
  price/earnings ratio (P/E),
    60
  price volatility, 61

reducing taxes on, 218-19
  risk, 16
  Securities Exchange Act, 42
  selling, 64-65
  shares outstanding, 61-
    62
  small-cap, 46, 48
  speculative, 50
  stop order, 70
  symbols, 73-74
  tables, 74-75
  technical analysis, 56-57
  total return, 62
  trades, 68-71
  types, 45-51
  U.S. Securities and
    Exchange Commission
    (SEC), 42-43
  value, 49
Stockbroker, 75-78
  discount broker, 75-76
  financial planners, 78
  full-service broker, 76-77
  monitoring brokers, 77-78
Stop order, 70-71
  buy, 70
  sell, 71

T

Taxes, 213-23
  annuities, 221-22
  on capital gains, 215, 217
  charitable deductions, 10
  deductible investment
    interest, 215-16

deductions, benefiting from, 218
on dividends, 214-15
gains and losses, 216-17
holding period, 217
impact on portfolio, 213
on interest, 215
life insurance, 220-21
on municipal bonds, 220
on mutual funds, 219-20
reducing tax liability, 218-22
returns, 8
on stocks, 218-19
strategy for investments, 216-18
tax shelters, 222-23
types of investment taxes, 214-16
Time, 21-22
Total return, 62

V
Value
funds, 122
investing, 54
Line Index, 38
VIPERs, 149

Y
Yield, 89-91
current, 89
curve, 90-91
interest rates, 90
to maturity, 90

U
Unemployment index, 33-34
U.S.
government bond funds, 126-27
Securities and Exchange Commission (SEC), 42-43
Treasury securities, 96

THE EVERYTHING SERIES!

BUSINESS & PERSONAL FINANCE

Everything® Accounting Book
Everything® Budgeting Book, 2nd Ed.
Everything® Business Planning Book
Everything® Coaching and Mentoring Book, 2nd Ed.
Everything® Fundraising Book
Everything® Get Out of Debt Book
Everything® Grant Writing Book, 2nd Ed.
Everything® Guide to Buying Foreclosures
Everything® Guide to Fundraising, $15.95
Everything® Guide to Mortgages
Everything® Guide to Personal Finance for Single Mothers
Everything® Home-Based Business Book, 2nd Ed.
Everything® Homebuying Book, 3rd Ed., $15.95
Everything® Homeselling Book, 2nd Ed.
Everything® Human Resource Management Book
Everything® Improve Your Credit Book
Everything® Investing Book, 2nd Ed.
Everything® Landlording Book
Everything® Leadership Book, 2nd Ed.
Everything® Managing People Book, 2nd Ed.
Everything® Negotiating Book
Everything® Online Auctions Book
Everything® Online Business Book
Everything® Personal Finance Book
Everything® Personal Finance in Your 20s & 30s Book, 2nd Ed.
Everything® Personal Finance in Your 40s & 50s Book, $15.95
Everything® Project Management Book, 2nd Ed.
Everything® Real Estate Investing Book
Everything® Retirement Planning Book
Everything® Robert's Rules Book, $7.95
Everything® Selling Book
Everything® Start Your Own Business Book, 2nd Ed.
Everything® Wills & Estate Planning Book

COOKING

Everything® Barbecue Cookbook
Everything® Bartender's Book, 2nd Ed., $9.95
Everything® Calorie Counting Cookbook
Everything® Cheese Book
Everything® Chinese Cookbook
Everything® Classic Recipes Book
Everything® Cocktail Parties & Drinks Book
Everything® College Cookbook
Everything® Cooking for Baby and Toddler Book
Everything® Diabetes Cookbook
Everything® Easy Gourmet Cookbook
Everything® Fondue Cookbook
Everything® Food Allergy Cookbook, $15.95
Everything® Fondue Party Book
Everything® Gluten-Free Cookbook
Everything® Glycemic Index Cookbook
Everything® Grilling Cookbook
Everything® Healthy Cooking for Parties Book, $15.95
Everything® Holiday Cookbook
Everything® Indian Cookbook
Everything® Lactose-Free Cookbook
Everything® Low-Cholesterol Cookbook

Everything® Low-Fat High-Flavor Cookbook, 2nd Ed., $15.95
Everything® Low-Salt Cookbook
Everything® Meals for a Month Cookbook
Everything® Meals on a Budget Cookbook
Everything® Mediterranean Cookbook
Everything® Mexican Cookbook
Everything® No Trans Fat Cookbook
Everything® One-Pot Cookbook, 2nd Ed., $15.95
Everything® Organic Cooking for Baby & Toddler Book, $15.95
Everything® Pizza Cookbook
Everything® Quick Meals Cookbook, 2nd Ed., $15.95
Everything® Slow Cooker Cookbook
Everything® Slow Cooking for a Crowd Cookbook
Everything® Soup Cookbook
Everything® Stir-Fry Cookbook
Everything® Sugar-Free Cookbook
Everything® Tapas and Small Plates Cookbook
Everything® Tex-Mex Cookbook
Everything® Thai Cookbook
Everything® Vegetarian Cookbook
Everything® Whole-Grain, High-Fiber Cookbook
Everything® Wild Game Cookbook
Everything® Wine Book, 2nd Ed.

GAMES

Everything® 15-Minute Sudoku Book, $9.95
Everything® 30-Minute Sudoku Book, $9.95
Everything® Bible Crosswords Book, $9.95
Everything® Blackjack Strategy Book
Everything® Brain Strain Book, $9.95
Everything® Bridge Book
Everything® Card Games Book
Everything® Card Tricks Book, $9.95
Everything® Casino Gambling Book, 2nd Ed.
Everything® Chess Basics Book
Everything® Christmas Crosswords Book, $9.95
Everything® Craps Strategy Book
Everything® Crossword and Puzzle Book
Everything® Crosswords and Puzzles for Quote Lovers Book, $9.95
Everything® Crossword Challenge Book
Everything® Crosswords for the Beach Book, $9.95
Everything® Cryptic Crosswords Book, $9.95
Everything® Cryptograms Book, $9.95
Everything® Easy Crosswords Book
Everything® Easy Kakuro Book, $9.95
Everything® Easy Large-Print Crosswords Book
Everything® Games Book, 2nd Ed.
Everything® Giant Book of Crosswords
Everything® Giant Sudoku Book, $9.95
Everything® Giant Word Search Book
Everything® Kakuro Challenge Book, $9.95
Everything® Large-Print Crossword Challenge Book
Everything® Large-Print Crosswords Book
Everything® Large-Print Travel Crosswords Book
Everything® Lateral Thinking Puzzles Book, $9.95
Everything® Literary Crosswords Book, $9.95
Everything® Mazes Book
Everything® Memory Booster Puzzles Book, $9.95

Everything® Movie Crosswords Book, $9.95
Everything® Music Crosswords Book, $9.95
Everything® Online Poker Book
Everything® Pencil Puzzles Book, $9.95
Everything® Poker Strategy Book
Everything® Pool & Billiards Book
Everything® Puzzles for Commuters Book, $9.95
Everything® Puzzles for Dog Lovers Book, $9.95
Everything® Sports Crosswords Book, $9.95
Everything® Test Your IQ Book, $9.95
Everything® Texas Hold 'Em Book, $9.95
Everything® Travel Crosswords Book, $9.95
Everything® Travel Mazes Book, $9.95
Everything® Travel Word Search Book, $9.95
Everything® TV Crosswords Book, $9.95
Everything® Word Games Challenge Book
Everything® Word Scramble Book
Everything® Word Search Book

HEALTH

Everything® Alzheimer's Book
Everything® Diabetes Book
Everything® First Aid Book, $9.95
Everything® Green Living Book
Everything® Health Guide to Addiction and Recovery
Everything® Health Guide to Adult Bipolar Disorder
Everything® Health Guide to Arthritis
Everything® Health Guide to Controlling Anxiety
Everything® Health Guide to Depression
Everything® Health Guide to Diabetes, 2nd Ed.
Everything® Health Guide to Fibromyalgia
Everything® Health Guide to Menopause, 2nd Ed.
Everything® Health Guide to Migraines
Everything® Health Guide to Multiple Sclerosis
Everything® Health Guide to OCD
Everything® Health Guide to PMS
Everything® Health Guide to Postpartum Care
Everything® Health Guide to Thyroid Disease
Everything® Hypnosis Book
Everything® Low Cholesterol Book
Everything® Menopause Book
Everything® Nutrition Book
Everything® Reflexology Book
Everything® Stress Management Book
Everything® Superfoods Book, $15.95

HISTORY

Everything® American Government Book
Everything® American History Book, 2nd Ed.
Everything® American Revolution Book, $15.95
Everything® Civil War Book
Everything® Freemasons Book
Everything® Irish History & Heritage Book
Everything® World War II Book, 2nd Ed.

HOBBIES

Everything® Candlemaking Book
Everything® Cartooning Book
Everything® Coin Collecting Book
Everything® Digital Photography Book, 2nd Ed.

Everything® Drawing Book
Everything® Family Tree Book, 2nd Ed.
Everything® Guide to Online Genealogy, $15.95
Everything® Knitting Book
Everything® Knots Book
Everything® Photography Book
Everything® Quilting Book
Everything® Sewing Book
Everything® Soapmaking Book, 2nd Ed.
Everything® Woodworking Book

HOME IMPROVEMENT

Everything® Feng Shui Book
Everything® Feng Shui Decluttering Book, $9.95
Everything® Fix-It Book
Everything® Green Living Book
Everything® Home Decorating Book
Everything® Home Storage Solutions Book
Everything® Homebuilding Book
Everything® Organize Your Home Book, 2nd Ed.

KIDS' BOOKS

All titles are $7.95
Everything® Fairy Tales Book, $14.95
Everything® Kids' Animal Puzzle & Activity Book
Everything® Kids' Astronomy Book
Everything® Kids' Baseball Book, 5th Ed.
Everything® Kids' Bible Trivia Book
Everything® Kids' Bugs Book
Everything® Kids' Cars and Trucks Puzzle and Activity Book
Everything® Kids' Christmas Puzzle & Activity Book
Everything® Kids' Connect the Dots
    Puzzle and Activity Book
Everything® Kids' Cookbook, 2nd Ed.
Everything® Kids' Crazy Puzzles Book
Everything® Kids' Dinosaurs Book
Everything® Kids' Dragons Puzzle and Activity Book
Everything® Kids' Environment Book $7.95
Everything® Kids' Fairies Puzzle and Activity Book
Everything® Kids' First Spanish Puzzle and Activity Book
Everything® Kids' Football Book
Everything® Kids' Geography Book
Everything® Kids' Gross Cookbook
Everything® Kids' Gross Hidden Pictures Book
Everything® Kids' Gross Jokes Book
Everything® Kids' Gross Mazes Book
Everything® Kids' Gross Puzzle & Activity Book
Everything® Kids' Halloween Puzzle & Activity Book
Everything® Kids' Hanukkah Puzzle and Activity Book
Everything® Kids' Hidden Pictures Book
Everything® Kids' Horses Book
Everything® Kids' Joke Book
Everything® Kids' Knock Knock Book
Everything® Kids' Learning French Book
Everything® Kids' Learning Spanish Book
Everything® Kids' Magical Science Experiments Book
Everything® Kids' Math Puzzles Book
Everything® Kids' Mazes Book
Everything® Kids' Money Book, 2nd Ed.
Everything® Kids' Mummies, Pharaoh's, and Pyramids
    Puzzle and Activity Book
Everything® Kids' Nature Book
Everything® Kids' Pirates Puzzle and Activity Book
Everything® Kids' Presidents Book
Everything® Kids' Princess Puzzle and Activity Book
Everything® Kids' Puzzle Book

Everything® Kids' Racecars Puzzle and Activity Book
Everything® Kids' Riddles & Brain Teasers Book
Everything® Kids' Science Experiments Book
Everything® Kids' Sharks Book
Everything® Kids' Soccer Book
Everything® Kids' Spelling Book
Everything® Kids' Spies Puzzle and Activity Book
Everything® Kids' States Book
Everything® Kids' Travel Activity Book
Everything® Kids' Word Search Puzzle and Activity Book

LANGUAGE

Everything® Conversational Japanese Book with CD, $19.95
Everything® French Grammar Book
Everything® French Phrase Book, $9.95
Everything® French Verb Book, $9.95
Everything® German Phrase Book, $9.95
Everything® German Practice Book with CD, $19.95
Everything® Inglés Book
Everything® Intermediate Spanish Book with CD, $19.95
Everything® Italian Phrase Book, $9.95
Everything® Italian Practice Book with CD, $19.95
Everything® Learning Brazilian Portuguese Book with CD, $19.95
Everything® Learning French Book with CD, 2nd Ed., $19.95
Everything® Learning German Book
Everything® Learning Italian Book
Everything® Learning Latin Book
Everything® Learning Russian Book with CD, $19.95
Everything® Learning Spanish Book
Everything® Learning Spanish Book with CD, 2nd Ed., $19.95
Everything® Russian Practice Book with CD, $19.95
Everything® Sign Language Book, $15.95
Everything® Spanish Grammar Book
Everything® Spanish Phrase Book, $9.95
Everything® Spanish Practice Book with CD, $19.95
Everything® Spanish Verb Book, $9.95
Everything® Speaking Mandarin Chinese Book with CD, $19.95

MUSIC

Everything® Bass Guitar Book with CD, $19.95
Everything® Drums Book with CD, $19.95
Everything® Guitar Book with CD, 2nd Ed., $19.95
Everything® Guitar Chords Book with CD, $19.95
Everything® Guitar Scales Book with CD, $19.95
Everything® Harmonica Book with CD, $15.95
Everything® Home Recording Book
Everything® Music Theory Book with CD, $19.95
Everything® Reading Music Book with CD, $19.95
Everything® Rock & Blues Guitar Book with CD, $19.95
Everything® Rock & Blues Piano Book with CD, $19.95
Everything® Rock Drums Book with CD, $19.95
Everything® Singing Book with CD, $19.95
Everything® Songwriting Book

NEW AGE

Everything® Astrology Book, 2nd Ed.
Everything® Birthday Personology Book
Everything® Celtic Wisdom Book, $15.95
Everything® Dreams Book, 2nd Ed.
Everything® Law of Attraction Book, $15.95
Everything® Love Signs Book, $9.95
Everything® Love Spells Book, $9.95
Everything® Palmistry Book
Everything® Psychic Book
Everything® Reiki Book

Everything® Sex Signs Book, $9.95
Everything® Spells & Charms Book, 2nd Ed.
Everything® Tarot Book, 2nd Ed.
Everything® Toltec Wisdom Book
Everything® Wicca & Witchcraft Book, 2nd Ed.

PARENTING

Everything® Baby Names Book, 2nd Ed.
Everything® Baby Shower Book, 2nd Ed.
Everything® Baby Sign Language Book with DVD
Everything® Baby's First Year Book
Everything® Birthing Book
Everything® Breastfeeding Book
Everything® Father-to-Be Book
Everything® Father's First Year Book
Everything® Get Ready for Baby Book, 2nd Ed.
Everything® Get Your Baby to Sleep Book, $9.95
Everything® Getting Pregnant Book
Everything® Guide to Pregnancy Over 35
Everything® Guide to Raising a One-Year-Old
Everything® Guide to Raising a Two-Year-Old
Everything® Guide to Raising Adolescent Boys
Everything® Guide to Raising Adolescent Girls
Everything® Mother's First Year Book
Everything® Parent's Guide to Childhood Illnesses
Everything® Parent's Guide to Children and Divorce
Everything® Parent's Guide to Children with ADD/ADHD
Everything® Parent's Guide to Children with Asperger's
    Syndrome
Everything® Parent's Guide to Children with Anxiety
Everything® Parent's Guide to Children with Asthma
Everything® Parent's Guide to Children with Autism
Everything® Parent's Guide to Children with Bipolar Disorder
Everything® Parent's Guide to Children with Depression
Everything® Parent's Guide to Children with Dyslexia
Everything® Parent's Guide to Children with Juvenile Diabetes
Everything® Parent's Guide to Children with OCD
Everything® Parent's Guide to Positive Discipline
Everything® Parent's Guide to Raising Boys
Everything® Parent's Guide to Raising Girls
Everything® Parent's Guide to Raising Siblings
Everything® Parent's Guide to Raising Your
    Adopted Child
Everything® Parent's Guide to Sensory Integration Disorder
Everything® Parent's Guide to Tantrums
Everything® Parent's Guide to the Strong-Willed Child
Everything® Parenting a Teenager Book
Everything® Potty Training Book, $9.95
Everything® Pregnancy Book, 3rd Ed.
Everything® Pregnancy Fitness Book
Everything® Pregnancy Nutrition Book
Everything® Pregnancy Organizer, 2nd Ed., $16.95
Everything® Toddler Activities Book
Everything® Toddler Book
Everything® Tween Book
Everything® Twins, Triplets, and More Book

PETS

Everything® Aquarium Book
Everything® Boxer Book
Everything® Cat Book, 2nd Ed.
Everything® Chihuahua Book
Everything® Cooking for Dogs Book
Everything® Dachshund Book
Everything® Dog Book, 2nd Ed.
Everything® Dog Grooming Book

Everything® Dog Obedience Book
Everything® Dog Owner's Organizer, $16.95
Everything® Dog Training and Tricks Book
Everything® German Shepherd Book
Everything® Golden Retriever Book
Everything® Horse Book, 2nd Ed., $15.95
Everything® Horse Care Book
Everything® Horseback Riding Book
Everything® Labrador Retriever Book
Everything® Poodle Book
Everything® Pug Book
Everything® Puppy Book
Everything® Small Dogs Book
Everything® Tropical Fish Book
Everything® Yorkshire Terrier Book

REFERENCE

Everything® American Presidents Book
Everything® Blogging Book
Everything® Build Your Vocabulary Book, $9.95
Everything® Car Care Book
Everything® Classical Mythology Book
Everything® Da Vinci Book
Everything® Einstein Book
Everything® Enneagram Book
Everything® Etiquette Book, 2nd Ed.
Everything® Family Christmas Book, $15.95
Everything® Guide to C. S. Lewis & Narnia
Everything® Guide to Divorce, 2nd Ed., $15.95
Everything® Guide to Edgar Allan Poe
Everything® Guide to Understanding Philosophy
Everything® Inventions and Patents Book
Everything® Jacqueline Kennedy Onassis Book
Everything® John F. Kennedy Book
Everything® Mafia Book
Everything® Martin Luther King Jr. Book
Everything® Pirates Book
Everything® Private Investigation Book
Everything® Psychology Book
Everything® Public Speaking Book, $9.95
Everything® Shakespeare Book, 2nd Ed.

RELIGION

Everything® Angels Book
Everything® Bible Book
Everything® Bible Study Book with CD, $19.95
Everything® Buddhism Book
Everything® Catholicism Book
Everything® Christianity Book
Everything® Gnostic Gospels Book
Everything® Hinduism Book, $15.95
Everything® History of the Bible Book
Everything® Jesus Book
Everything® Jewish History & Heritage Book
Everything® Judaism Book
Everything® Kabbalah Book
Everything® Koran Book
Everything® Mary Book
Everything® Mary Magdalene Book
Everything® Prayer Book

Everything® Saints Book, 2nd Ed.
Everything® Torah Book
Everything® Understanding Islam Book
Everything® Women of the Bible Book
Everything® World's Religions Book

SCHOOL & CAREERS

Everything® Career Tests Book
Everything® College Major Test Book
Everything® College Survival Book, 2nd Ed.
Everything® Cover Letter Book, 2nd Ed.
Everything® Filmmaking Book
Everything® Get-a-Job Book, 2nd Ed.
Everything® Guide to Being a Paralegal
Everything® Guide to Being a Personal Trainer
Everything® Guide to Being a Real Estate Agent
Everything® Guide to Being a Sales Rep
Everything® Guide to Being an Event Planner
Everything® Guide to Careers in Health Care
Everything® Guide to Careers in Law Enforcement
Everything® Guide to Government Jobs
Everything® Guide to Starting and Running a Catering
    Business
Everything® Guide to Starting and Running a Restaurant
**Everything® Guide to Starting and Running
    a Retail Store**
Everything® Job Interview Book, 2nd Ed.
Everything® New Nurse Book
Everything® New Teacher Book
Everything® Paying for College Book
Everything® Practice Interview Book
Everything® Resume Book, 3rd Ed.
Everything® Study Book

SELF-HELP

Everything® Body Language Book
Everything® Dating Book, 2nd Ed.
Everything® Great Sex Book
**Everything® Guide to Caring for Aging Parents,
    $15.95**
Everything® Self-Esteem Book
Everything® Self-Hypnosis Book, $9.95
Everything® Tantric Sex Book

SPORTS & FITNESS

Everything® Easy Fitness Book
Everything® Fishing Book
Everything® Guide to Weight Training, $15.95
Everything® Krav Maga for Fitness Book
Everything® Running Book, 2nd Ed.
Everything® Triathlon Training Book, $15.95

TRAVEL

Everything® Family Guide to Coastal Florida
Everything® Family Guide to Cruise Vacations
Everything® Family Guide to Hawaii
Everything® Family Guide to Las Vegas, 2nd Ed.
Everything® Family Guide to Mexico
Everything® Family Guide to New England, 2nd Ed.

Everything® Family Guide to New York City, 3rd Ed.
**Everything® Family Guide to Northern California
    and Lake Tahoe**
Everything® Family Guide to RV Travel & Campgrounds
Everything® Family Guide to the Caribbean
Everything® Family Guide to the Disneyland® Resort, California
    Adventure®, Universal Studios®, and the Anaheim
    Area, 2nd Ed.
Everything® Family Guide to the Walt Disney World Resort®,
    Universal Studios®, and Greater Orlando, 5th Ed.
Everything® Family Guide to Timeshares
Everything® Family Guide to Washington D.C., 2nd Ed.

WEDDINGS

Everything® Bachelorette Party Book, $9.95
Everything® Bridesmaid Book, $9.95
Everything® Destination Wedding Book
Everything® Father of the Bride Book, $9.95
Everything® Green Wedding Book, $15.95
Everything® Groom Book, $9.95
Everything® Jewish Wedding Book, 2nd Ed., $15.95
Everything® Mother of the Bride Book, $9.95
Everything® Outdoor Wedding Book
Everything® Wedding Book, 3rd Ed.
Everything® Wedding Checklist, $9.95
Everything® Wedding Etiquette Book, $9.95
Everything® Wedding Organizer, 2nd Ed., $16.95
Everything® Wedding Shower Book, $9.95
Everything® Wedding Vows Book, 3rd Ed., $9.95
Everything® Wedding Workout Book
Everything® Weddings on a Budget Book, 2nd Ed., $9.95

WRITING

Everything® Creative Writing Book
Everything® Get Published Book, 2nd Ed.
Everything® Grammar and Style Book, 2nd Ed.
Everything® Guide to Magazine Writing
Everything® Guide to Writing a Book Proposal
Everything® Guide to Writing a Novel
Everything® Guide to Writing Children's Books
Everything® Guide to Writing Copy
Everything® Guide to Writing Graphic Novels
Everything® Guide to Writing Research Papers
Everything® Guide to Writing a Romance Novel, $15.95
Everything® Improve Your Writing Book, 2nd Ed.
Everything® Writing Poetry Book